Reading the Body

Regendering the Past

Cheryl Claassen, Series Editor

A complete list of books in the series
is available from the publisher.

Reading the Body

Representations and Remains in
the Archaeological Record

Edited by Alison E. Rautman

PENN

University of Pennsylvania Press

Philadelphia

10 9 8 7 6 5 4 3 2 1

Published by
University of Pennsylvania Press
Philadelphia, Pennsylvania 19104-4011

Library of Congress Cataloging-in-Publication Data
Reading the body : representations and remains in the archaeological
    record / edited by Alison E. Rautman.
        p.   cm. — (Regendering the past)
    Includes bibliographical references and index.
    ISBN 0-8122-3521-5 (acid-free paper). —
ISBN 0-8122-1709-8 (pbk. : acid-free paper)
    1. Social archaeology.   2. Women, Prehistoric.   3. Sex role —
History.   4. Sex differences — History.   5. Human remains
(Archaeology).   6. Body, Human — Symbolic aspects.   I. Rautman,
Alison E.   II. Series.
    CC72.4.R444   1999   2000
    930.1′028′5 — dc21   99-33513
                                                              CIP

Contents

Figures

Tables

Chapter 1
Introduction
Diverse Approaches to the
Study of Gender in Archaeology

Alison E. Rautman and Lauren E. Talalay

Classical archaeologists and anthropologists share many of the same interests and confront many of the same problems in studying now-extinct cultures. Despite differences in background and training, scholars in these disciplines are engaged in analyzing and interpreting the material remains that constitute the archaeological record. Traditionally, however, there have been few opportunities for Classical and anthropological archaeologists to meet, exchange information, and discuss recent advances in method and theory.

The study of gender in past societies offers promising possibilities for bridging this long-standing disciplinary divide. As one of the main axes of social differentiation, gender is equally relevant to archaeologists and anthropologists studying small egalitarian societies in the Americas or Eurasia, ancient empires of the Maya or the Romans, or Classical *poleis* of the Greek world.

The Fourth Gender and Archaeology Conference, therefore, convened around the topic of "Diverse Approaches to the Study of Gender in Antiquity" in order to provide an opportunity for Classical and anthropological archaeologists to report on recent research in their respective fields and to contemplate fresh perspectives from which to view their data.[1] The original conference papers covered a range of topics, including gender and technology (Dunham 1996; Hayter 1996), gender and the construction and use of space (Frink et al. 1996; Price 1996; Tobey 1996), and the cultural construction, negotiation, and transmission of gender ideologies (Chester 1996; Cohodas 1996; Nobles 1996; Schoenholz 1996). At least half of the presenters, however, explored the concept of the Body; their chapters form the integrating focus of this volume.

As defined here, the Body encompasses two distinct but related aspects of the human form. On the one hand, it refers literally to the body—all the physical or skeletal components that define the human species. On the other hand, it designates any representation or depiction of a human image (e.g., a clay or stone figurine, painting, or rock carving). In the former instance, the body is seen as a record of ancient diet, health, life span, and physical activities, as well as of cultural ideas regarding the treatment of the dead. In the latter instance, images of the Body are construed as "the scene of display" or forum where cultural ideas of maleness and femaleness, masculinity and femininity, are played out (Meskell, this volume).

Reflecting these dual concepts of the Body, the papers in this volume are divided into two sections. The authors in Part I concentrate on the interpretation of the body's physical remains and/or its mortuary treatment; those in Part II focus on the interpretation of anthropomorphic images in a variety of media, including seals, sealings, stone relief, and painting on pottery. Tying these chapters together are four interrelated issues pertinent to the interpretation of the Body: (1) the cultural meanings of gendered images and gender ambiguity in anthropomorphic images; (2) gender differences and gender roles, particularly in relationship to labor and social status; (3) gender ideology as seen in the treatment and representation of the body, both in life and in death; and (4) the interconnections among cultural constructions of gender, politics, and religion.[2]

Gendered Images and Gender Ambiguity

Recently, anthropologists and archaeologists have become increasingly sensitive to the ambiguities involved in the construction of gender and sex in different societies. Ambiguous gender ascriptions, whether found in images, belief systems, burial materials, or behavioral expectations suggest that not every society was (or is) organized exclusively around a bipolar model of male/female or man/woman. Societies can employ multiple or fluid gender categories, including male, female, neuter, third-gender persons, or even a dynamic classification that moves in and out of sexual/gender identities (Shore 1981; Roscoe 1991; Epstein and Straub 1991; Bolin 1992; Sampson 1993; Bailey 1994; Hamilton 1994; Herdt 1994; Ajootian 1997; Hamilton in press). Some archaeologists argue that an awareness of gender ambiguity can affect not only sex assignment of burials,[3] but also the interpretation of human images recovered from archaeological excavations (Cullen and Talalay 1994; Arnold 1996; Weglian 1996; Pollock and Bernbeck, this volume; Hays-Gilpin, this volume; Talalay in press b). Depictions of apparently "sexless" or "intersexed" representations (i.e., figures that incorporate both male and female sexes in a single image) are now known from contexts spanning from the Greek Neolithic to the American Southwest.

Such sexless, sexually indeterminate, and dual-sexed images raise important questions regarding ancient constructions of gender and sexuality. Can we assume, for example, that sexless images were viewed as truly "neuter," possibly embodying gender-free concepts? Or were they seen as subsuming male and female (and possibly other) categories, capable of moving along this spectrum of possible gender identities depending on their uses? The dual-sexed images pose similar kinds of queries: were they conceived as truly "hermaphroditic," as individuals of a third gender category (see Hollimon, this volume), or again, as a kind of either/or proposition that fluctuated with the images' functions?

Some scholars have argued that modern Western notions of gender duality have constrained our thinking, exerting a hegemonic force in research that has limited investigations of different gender configurations within our own and other cultures (Ortner and Whitehead 1981:6–7; see also Meskell 1994 and in press). As the authors in this volume demonstrate, it is more productive to consider sexual/gender categories as gradational and, in some cases, context-dependent. Multiple genders and sexual ambiguity may have played a special role in the dominant social order of past societies. In some cultures, for example, official iconography suggests that certain female attributes were purposely "grafted" onto predominantly male figures (or vice versa) as a way of empowering the image by subsuming both sexes (see Hitchcock in press for a discussion of Minoan iconography; see also Joyce 1992, 1993, and Hamann 1997 for similar interpretations of ancient Mayan images).

Meskell's chapter in this volume provides an important perspective on the issue by teasing out some of the historical underpinnings of Western assumptions regarding gender categories. She also notes that, with the recent elevation of the Body to a kind of theoretical space or "site of mapped and inscribed social relations," scholars have lost sight of the *individual* within this social context. The multiple genders found in figurines, seals, and paintings may have also played a role in the construction of the self and individual identity. Meskell exhorts us to look more closely at the relationships between these images and *persons*, not just *categories* (see also Knapp and Meskell 1997).

These recent explorations into gender ambiguity have reshaped current discourse and raised profoundly significant questions about the definition and meaning of gender and gender categories in every society, including our own. As the following chapters suggest, simplistic assumptions that early societies adhered to a masculine-feminine dyad can no longer be accepted.

Gender Differences and Gender Roles

Recent research on gender has also centered on the issues of gender definition and differentiation, especially women's roles and status in antiquity (e.g., Brumfiel 1991; Gero 1991; Wright 1991; Archer 1994; Fischler 1994; King 1994; Koloski-Ostrow and Lyons 1997) and to a lesser extent on masculinist scholarship (e.g., Cornwall and Lindisfarne 1994). Anthropological and Classical archaeologists who venture into this area of research face similar basic methodological questions. First, how does one identify the roles of men versus the roles of women from the archaeological record? Second, how does one differentiate among those material attributes that may be associated with male as opposed to female roles and activities without adopting an essentialist model (e.g., claiming that all weapons and flaked tools are made and used by males, or that all spindle whorls represent female activities)? Finally, how are the relationships between men and women established, negotiated, and reinterpreted over time? Given the lack of writing or relevant texts in many ancient societies, both Classical and anthropological archaeologists have frequently turned to evidence from burials, household assemblages, and figurative imagery, and in some cases from analogies with traditions that are known from the ethnographic record (e.g., Frink et al. 1996).

Burials in particular have provided fruitful information regarding gender roles and status (e.g., Hodder 1984; Whelan 1991; Arnold 1991; Hollimon 1992). Evidence from funerary contexts has allowed archaeologists to analyze survival profiles, variation in nutritional patterns, positioning of individuals or groups within a cemetery or settlement, and the distribution, quantity, and quality of associated grave goods. Some of these markers of gender differences, however, may not necessarily correlate with a given person's life experiences. Indeed, status in life may be inverted or altered in the mortuary ritual (Huntington and Metcalf 1979: 122; Hodder 1982: 197–201). Moreover, the strong symbolic nature of burial patterns argues against any simplistic correlation between burial treatment and the lived experience of the individual.

Savage's chapter on predynastic Egypt presents a good example of the challenges confronting archaeologists who attempt to interpret mortuary data. The Egyptian data reveals that female burials appear to include a broad range of artifact types as grave goods. Savage reads this typological variety as indicating that women had some freedom to occupy multiple roles in life. What is not clear, however, is that such flexibility represents a freedom born of higher status, with true social and political equality with men, or alternatively, the comparative social freedom of a lower-status individual who has little to lose.

Figurative images also provide valuable sources of information for gender differentiation but, like burials, are problematic. It is often difficult, for example, to distinguish which images represent daily activities (as Shaffer et al. argue for the Southwestern Mimbres, this volume), and which images are intended to convey ideas we might more correctly label mythic, religious, or metaphoric (e.g., Hays-Gilpin, this volume). Similarly, identifying which depictions represent deities or idealized heroes rather than mere mortals engaged in sacred activity is not at all straightforward. Nor can we assume that anthropomorphic images in the realm of religion or myth were ever seen as having a particular sex. Even when the sex of such figures can be determined, it is difficult to know whether that ascription was deemed a significant, or even a constant, attribute.

Those problems notwithstanding, several of the authors in this volume attempt to identify the roles and status of women and deities using various types of archaeological evidence. Shaffer, Gardner, and Powell consider the time depth of historic patterns of labor organization among the Southwestern Pueblo from painted images on pottery; Savage and Hollimon utilize a range of mortuary data, and Peterson evaluates sexual labor patterns in the southern Levant using evidence from the skeletal body itself. Investigations into the roles and meanings of gendered deities depicted in painted images are examined by Hays-Gilpin for the American Southwest and by Roth for ancient Egypt.

Gender and Representations of the Body

For the past two decades the subject of representations of the Body has emerged as a powerful component of gender study (Blacking 1977; Feher 1989; Butler 1990a; Bynum 1995). While discussions have ranged from the biological and philosophical to the artistic, the topics of nudity, costuming, and depiction of body parts have been particularly emphasized (for recent archaeological discussions see Yates 1993; Brumfiel 1996a; Kampen 1996; Rehak 1996a, 1996b; Cohen 1997; Wilfong and Jones in press; Talalay in press a and b).

In depicting the human body, the artist or craftsperson can choose to suppress, enhance, adorn, or alter any aspect of the form. In the process, the body becomes a kind of encoding device for ideas and behaviors (Wright 1996:14). Viewed as a kind of symbolic vocabulary, images of the Body can prove to be extremely informative when considering questions of gender and its links to social relations, status, and ideologies.

Brumfiel's recent reconsideration of Aztec figurines (1996a) offers an instructive case study in deciphering symbolic encoding. Comparing popular images of female figures manufactured in the Aztec hinterlands to officially sanctioned depictions produced in the Aztec capital, Brumfiel finds two quite distinct vocabularies. Popular images emphasize fertility while official depictions represent mutilated and androgynous women or stress their role as producers of cloth and food. Brumfiel reads these differences as expressions of opposing gender ideologies among separate female collectives in Aztec society. Moreover, the existence of a distinctive image of women in popular culture suggests that the elite was unsuccessful in imposing a dominant ideology in the hinterlands (Wright 1996:10; Brumfiel 1996a).

Several authors in this volume also attempt to decode the symbolic vocabulary and underlying ideologies signaled by depictions of male and female bodies. Using evidence from the prehistoric Aegean and Classical Greece, Mireille Lee argues that clothing is a particularly appropriate medium for communicating social constructions of gender since the messages broadcast by dress might be inappropriate for articulation in verbal language. Senta German also looks at bodily depictions in the Mediterranean, focusing on the Late Bronze Age Aegean. She shows how images of the human form (in figurines) are sexualized and eroticized by both the depiction of clothing and also its absence. She suggests that this emphasis on gender and sexuality was used to define and empower gender constructions during a time of political consolidation in Minoan society.

Gender, Politics, and Religion

The fourth major cross-cutting theme in this volume concerns the relationship of gendered images to political and religious systems, especially in terms of who is creating and using the art and images of a given society. Feminist scholars and art historians in particular have recently attempted to understand the visual mechanisms that regulate gendered behavior by questioning, for example, who the intended audience of certain images might have been (see, for example, various essays in Koloski-Ostrow and Lyons 1997); whether ancient representations (and texts) were articulated from a male or female perspective (e.g., Cohodas 1996, Koloski-Ostrow 1997; Foxhall 1997); under what circumstances artifacts created by females might have been appropriated by males for social or political ends such as status negotiation, or conversely, used by women to resist a predominantly male political order (e.g., Ruscheinsky 1996); and finally, how scholars can employ the ancient visual record to recover the often muted voices of populations such as children, gay, or lesbian people (e.g., Moore and Scott 1997; Younger 1997).

Systematic investigations of these complex topics have embraced a wide range of media and types of images, including frescoes, seals, vase paintings, stone reliefs, statues, and figurines. Studies have focused on an equally broad range of variables, encompassing such features as color conventions, body morphology, hairstyles, costumes, jewelry, and scale, position, and pose in figurative compositions (e.g., Rehak 1995, 1996b; Younger 1992).

While several authors in this volume grapple with various aspects of these concerns, the chapter by Susan Pollock and Reinhart Bernbeck deals most directly with the topic of gendered representations and the iconography of power. Focusing on seals and sealings from ancient Mesopotamia, they are able to identify what appear to be clearly delineated areas of power that break along gender lines.

Contributions to This Volume

All of the contributions to this volume engage in one way or another with the themes discussed above. In Part I, four of the authors focus on interpretations of gender-specific activities, health, and status primarily using the body itself (the skeleton and its characteristics) as evidence. In addition, two chapters specifically examine mortuary ritual, including the positioning of the body and the associated artifactual assemblages.

Sandra Hollimon compares ethnohistoric information on the Arikara of the North American Plains with the skeletal record of men's and women's health. Differences between females and males in the frequencies of activity-induced pathologies such as degenerative joint diseases, dental pathologies, and trauma indicate the health consequences of gender roles in this society.

More detailed information regarding habitual activity patterns can be obtained through analysis of musculoskeletal stress markers, the markings on cortical bone at the sites of muscle and ligament attachments. Jane Peterson shows the relevance of this kind of analysis for reconstructing sexual labor patterns by using data from the Levant of southwest Asia during the transition from foraging to the farming of domesticated plants. This evidence helps identify shifts in sex roles during this time of transition as well as the nature and pace of change in labor organization at the household level.

Marshall Becker explores an unusual phenomenon: the dental pontic, or decorative false tooth, which he views as an expression of women's social status in the Etruscan world. Highlighting cultural differences within the world of Classical antiquity, Becker reminds us of the wide range of variation in gender roles that may be present even within what we might normally think of as one "culture."

Burial evidence reveals not only health and activities of the individual during life, but also provides information regarding gender ideology and gender symbolism in the individual's culture. Barbara Crass's discussion of mortuary belief and burial ritual among the Inuit hunters in the Arctic is a compelling example of how conceptions of gender may differ considerably from the traditional Euro-American model. Her contribution emphasizes that, in some cultures, a person's biological sex may be a contributing, but not necessarily defining factor affecting his or her adult gender role. In this study, Inuit mortuary practices are shown to make sense in terms of Inuit conceptions of gender roles in life and after death.

Stephen Savage considers gender role and social status in a state society, using data provided by mortuary objects and burial practices in Egypt. He argues that the range of roles occupied by women may result from relative gender equity in the territorial Egyptian state — a situation that contrasts with evidence of gender status in contemporaneous segmentary states in Mesopotamia.

Part II of this volume contains case studies concerning the interpretation of anthropomorphic images. The authors consider what these images can tell us about male, female, and possibly gender-neutral activities, the definition of "men," "women," and "third gender" persons as cultural categories, the social status and roles associated with these definitions, and their cultural justification, presentation, standardization, and perpetuation.

The first chapter in this section, by Senta German, examines representations of the human form on seals and sealings in the Late Bronze Age Aegean. Images contemporary with the emergence of complex "palatial" centers on Crete emphasize the physical aspects of gender and sexuality. German suggests that these overt symbols simultaneously defined and empowered one cultural construction of gender in this increasingly complex society. The chapter by Mireille Lee further evaluates the social significance of dress and its role as a reflection and means of maintaining social definitions of gender in Minoan society. She argues that clothing not only communicates gender constructions to the viewer, but also has a physical and psychological effect on the wearer, reinforcing those social expectations.

Timothy McNiven similarly focuses on how social constructions of gender are maintained, emphasizing the importance of gender as a cultural system. He considers how the definition of women and women's roles also helped delineate male identity and men's roles. Focusing on Classical Greece, McNiven explains how the Greek concept of "manliness" was largely defined in contrast to "womanly" behavior (and the behavior of other part-human creatures such as satyrs). These distinctions, he argues, arose from the overriding Athenian concern with maintaining separations between the privileged minority of freeborn male citizens and "everyone else," a category that of course included women.

Alice Kehoe examines a very different type of symbolic vocabulary in her reinterpretation of two well-known objects from the Mississippian center of Cahokia (Missouri). She proposes that the female Keller figurine may have represented a weaver at work. Moreover, she posits that women's activities such as weaving may have formed an integrating metaphor in Mississippian society, evoking multiple metaphors of matriarchs weaving their clans together. Kehoe also proposes that the companion Birger figurine may represent a woman scraping a hide, an identification that again involves symbolic evocations of the importance of women's activities, both economically and metaphorically, in Mississippian society.

Brian Shaffer, Karen Gardner, and Joseph Powell mine information from painted ceramic vessels from the Mimbres region of the American Southwest. Gender-specific activities represented on the vessels are used to argue for the presence of very specific gendered divisions of labor relating to subsistence activities, technology, domestic behavior, and ceremonial performances.

The final chapters consider, among other things, the depiction and cultural significance of gendered deities. Susan Pollock and Reinhard Bernbeck examine male, female, and gender-neutral figures found on seals and sealings of ancient Mesopotamia. They suggest that female power was exalted in its divine form but that, in contrast, human power was depicted exclusively as male. The gender ideology recorded in these media therefore appear to disparage the actual economic and political contributions made by women. Kelly Hays-Gilpin investigates Native American rock art in the Southwest in order to evaluate the time depth of the popular modern figures of Mother Earth and Father Sky. Her research uncovers diversity and temporal changes in these images that express a far richer and more complex gender ideology than the one indicated by the popularized versions of the figures. As an interesting contrast, Ann Macy Roth examines ancient Egyptian beliefs about Father Earth and Mother Sky. She suggests that, contrary to most interpretations, the ancient Egyptians located the source of creative fertility in the male, not in the female. Finally, in the last chapter of this volume, Margaret Beck steps back from the many analyses of Upper Paleolithic European "Venus" figurines to examine how selective sampling and researcher bias have affected interpretation of these figurines.

Conclusion

The analyses included here, while differing in terms of research objectives and methodology, conceive of gender as culturally constructed and hence variable in its definition, function, and importance in any given situation. The authors agree that gender and gender categories are not unchanging, but are subject to diverse interpretations and also "negotiation" — a process that encompasses the term's dual meanings of debate (as to negotiate a deal) and lived individual experience or struggle (as to negotiate a river) (Ginsburg and Tsing 1990:2).

This perspective poses gender as one possible dimension of individual as well as group identity and difference; other differences might include age, rank, ethnicity, class, sexual preference, sexual practice, and religion (Ginsburg and Tsing 1990:5; see also Kulick 1997 for a recent ethnographic example). According to this view, the archaeology of gender cannot assume a priori that gender is "about" labor or power or sexuality; it can be and sometimes is about all these topics and more. Biological sex (that is, the appearance of external sexual organs as opposed to the internal organs or even chromosomal sex) is one possible axis of differentiation that can be elaborated to greater or lesser extent in a given culture. For example, deities can be assigned to biological categories, or alternatively, remain sexless or be considered to be beyond sexual characterization. In some cultures, males can be thought to be primarily responsible for fertility; in others, females are deemed the essential individuals; in still others, they are considered to have complementary roles. The cultural construction of gender and gender roles for both men and women may begin with biology (as among the Inuit discussed above), but depends also on continual cultural negotiation and re-production of gendered individuals (see Joyce and Claassen 1997:3). As archaeologists, one of our interests should be the ways in which gender is actively negotiated and the ways in which negotiated cultural gender categories are translated into individual lives.

The Classical and anthropological archaeologists represented in this volume generally agree that culturally constructed gender can be employed in various aspects of society, for example, to assign responsibility for fertility, to obtain certain political roles, or to organize economic or ritual duties. But the question "why is there gender?" (or gender differences? or gender categories?) may not lead further than the less-than-satisfying answer of "because that's the way many (if not all) societies are organized." A more helpful way of posing this question therefore might be: "In what contexts or situations is gender a significant cultural variable?" This question leads to a number of specific problems, including how definitions of gender and gender roles are constructed, how they differ in various societies, how we evaluate "significance," and for whom this significance is important. By contextualizing variance in gender roles and ideologies, we will be better equipped to consider how these differences correlate with other cultural variables such as economic organization or religious ideology, and how gender categories are created, elaborated, challenged, and sustained.

In fact, these concerns derive from, and also rejuvenate, some basic questions in the study of culture in anthropology and, more generally, in social science. Several of these studies, for example, ask about the relationship of the individual and individual experience to a person's culture and question the definition of "culture" itself. Is culture to be identified as the jural rules reported by members of a society, and if so, which members? How do these rules relate to people's actual behavior? To what extent is any individual autonomous, and to what extent is human behavior patterned, structured, constrained, and expressed by culture? How are such cultural ideas created, legitimized, and perpetuated in material remains? Conversely, to what extent can cultural ideas, rules, or norms be seen as the unintended aggregate consequence of individual actions, or be attributable to the unique history of the given society (e.g., Johnson 1989)?

As the contributors to this volume demonstrate, discussions of gender in past societies inevitably confront such basic queries about culture and individuals. The aim of the conference was not to provide an overarching framework or universal theory about gender and culture. Rather, the intention was to share data and ideas across the disciplinary divides between art history, Classics, and anthropology as archaeologists in all these fields wrestled with these complex relationships among sex, gender, and the larger social and cultural matrices in which they are embedded. It was not surprising to us that the individuals who convened found a great deal of common ground. We hope that this volume will encourage greater interaction among archaeologists from divergent backgrounds and that future dialogues will provide new insights to help us better understand the past — insights that may help us understand our own society as well.

Notes

Many thanks are due to a number of people who made possible the Fourth Gender and Archaeology Conference and this resulting volume. Alison Rautman organized the conference at Michigan State University with invaluable institutional support from Lynne Goldstein, chair of the department of anthropology. Many students in the department helped the conference run smoothly, and many members of the interdisciplinary Consortium for Archaeological Research at MSU generously took the time to attend the conference, read various papers, and discuss them. Peg Holman was particularly helpful in defining a coherent volume from the many excellent papers that were submitted for consideration, but which could not all be accommodated in a single volume. Various chapters in the final volume also benefited from comments by Elizabeth Brumfiel and two anonymous reviewers. The volume editor particularly thanks Cheryl Claassen for the opportunity to host the conference at MSU and for her advice and encouragement throughout the process of organizing the conference and editing this volume.

1. The first three Gender and Archaeology Conferences were organized by Cheryl Claassen and held every other year at Appalachian State University in Boone, N.C. The fourth conference was held at Michigan State University in October 1996, marking its maturation into a mobile format.

2. This chapter is structured around the organization of Talalay's paper surveying the state of gender studies in Aegean prehistory and incorporates many of her general observations (Talalay 1996).

3. Even the bipolar model of biological maleness and femaleness has recently been challenged (Fausto-Sterling 1992, 1993).

Chapter 2
Writing the Body in Archaeology

Lynn M. Meskell

In the past few decades the body has become the critical nexus for theorizing society and self and has similarly resulted in an outpouring of literature in anthropological archaeology. It is axiomatic that a significant dimension of the individual, personhood, and identity is located in the body itself: at times a somatic grounding for the self and at other times merely a linked entity. Sociological debates revolving around the self and the individual are fundamentally connected with the recent emergence of a sociology of the body (Turner 1996:190). This domain is one which archaeology has eagerly seized upon, given its wealth of related data—whether textual, iconographic, or material—and the project has met with varied success. Some have deemed it easier to uncover cultural concepts of the body than to identify individuals in the past. Previously, the body has been cast as an object, a thing, a metaphor for society, or a product of semantics (Jackson 1989:123). Such isomorphic relationships might be compelling, but these reductive elisions cannot be epistemologically sustained. Following Grosz (1995:104), the body is a concrete, material, animate organization of flesh, organs, nerves, skeletal structure and substances, which are given a unity and cohesiveness through psychical and social inscription of the body's surface. The *body* is not tantamount to embodiment. I have previously argued (Meskell 1996, 1997b, 1998a) that embodied individuals constitute the site of intersection for a host of social factors and determinants. An embodied body represents, and is, a lived experience where the interplay of natural, social, cultural, and psychical phenomena are brought to fruition through each individual's resolution of external structure, embodied experience, and choice (Berthelot 1991:395–398).

Sex, Gender, and Sexuality

Clearly, archaeology has been remiss in recognizing the relationship between sex and gender, resulting in significant terminological confusion

(Butler 1990a, 1990b, 1993; Moore 1994). Few scholars specifically define their terms of reference, and thus we cannot assume consensus on even such basic designations. The terms "sex," "gender," and "sexuality" are used in a number of quite distinct and different ways by different scholars. Hence these terms can never refer to pure concepts (see Knapp and Meskell 1997 for a fuller discussion). There is, moreover, a burgeoning field of literature devoted to the concept of sexual difference, which seeks to incorporate concepts of biological, sociocultural, psychical, and sexual embodiment (Gatens 1996). These conceptualizations reveal the inadequacies of our current sex/gender terminologies and categories.

In fact, archaeology has been slow to acknowledge that the fundamental concepts of sex and gender may in fact be similarly constituted, if not one and the same. But the problem of disembedding sex and gender remains. Thomas Laqueur's impressive study (1990) has shown that sex is also a contextual issue, and that the notion of two distinct sexes depends very much on the site of knowledge production. Prior to the Enlightenment, a one-sex model held prominence, influenced largely by Classical authors such as Plato, Aristotle, and Galen, who proposed that female biology was merely a variation on the male (see Meskell 1996:3). Thus, sex before the seventeenth century was still a sociological and not an ontological category. Whatever the setting, the particular construction and understanding of sex cannot be isolated from its discursive milieu (Foucault 1972:52, 157).

Judith Butler, perhaps the most renowned queer theorist of the 1990s, also argues that there is no distinction at all between sex and gender (Butler 1993). She asserts that it is no longer tenable to advocate the existence of prediscursive sex that acts as the stable referent on top of which the cultural construction of gender proceeds. The whole question of sexuality has forced the once normative categories of sex and gender to be refigured. Both are constructed categories and neither are intransigent; both are inextricably linked to the individual's experience of being-in-the-body. This idea is clearly illustrated by a look beyond Western culture to other social constructions of sex (Knapp and Meskell 1997). We might be able to argue the sex:gender scenario in our culture, yet can we legitimately project this model across temporal and cultural boundaries?

Corporeal Philosophies

Other dualities which pervade the body literature—nature/culture, mind/body, reason/emotion—can be traced directly to Descartes and his essential separation of mind and body, along with the elevation of mind over body (Grosz 1994, 1995; Strathern 1996). The roots of Descartes's reasoning, however, were firmly established in Classical antiquity, as is witnessed in the works of Aristotle. This Cartesian bifurcation of mind and body does not represent a neutral division, but is ranked in a hierarchical scheme, thus privileging one term and suppressing and subordinating the other (Hekman 1990). In essence, Cartesian dualism establishes an unbridgeable gulf between mind and matter (Grosz 1994). This false dichotomy has serious implications for our reconstruction of individuals in an archaeological past and, more specifically, for feminist scholars who are attempting to challenge the inherently androcentric modes of thinking within Western intellectualism. Recent developments in corporeal philosophy are also guilty of perpetuating many philosophical assumptions regarding the role of the body in social, political, cultural, psychical, and sexual life. In confronting corporeality, many feminist philosophers, particularly from the French school, depict women as being more embodied than men, reaffirming the tacit link between *woman* and *the body*. Feminists like Cixous see a direct connection between feminine writing and the body; Cixous claims that women must bring themselves into the text (Hekman 1990:45). In short, women must "write the body" and since "woman is body more than man is . . . more body, hence more writing" (Cixous and Clement 1986:94–95). The female sex is restricted to its body while the male, fully disavowed, becomes the incorporeal instrument of freedom and philosophical formulation (Butler 1990a:12). Many feminist voices thus seem to be echoing elements of the misogyny that characterizes Western reason.

Recently, archaeology has engaged with corporeal philosophy, producing two distinct trends. One might be described as a consideration of the body as the scene of display, a perspective that can be seen in Mediterranean, Near Eastern, and Egyptian archaeologies. These analyses follow from the work of social constructionists such as Michel Foucault. Many of these studies employ engendered analyses, largely construed as the identification of women, ancient sexualities, and the feminization of specific groups (Meskell 1998a). In archaeology, the data employed are generally visually evocative, namely wall paintings, iconography, motifs, jewelry, and ornamentation (Marcus 1993; Winter 1996; Wright 1996). In these examples, as in some of the chapters in this volume, scholars are preoccupied with posture, gesture, costume, sexuality, and representation, sometimes in preference to the construction of individual identities, bodily experience, or "lived bodies" in any corporeal sense. While such interests are valid enterprises, those engaging in this discourse should be aware of the intellectual inheritance and its implications.

What underlies the body project, quite insidiously, is the antique belief that women are well situated within a flesh zone as designated by men. What is doubly disconcerting is that some feminists are actively pursuing and claiming this site as their own forum of expertise without recognizing this undesirable heritage. Reclamation of *individual* bodies, rather than generalized collectives, may be a way out of the dilemma. For example, Grosz (1994:22) argues that if corporeality can no longer be linked with one sex, then women can no longer take on the function of being *the body* for men, who are thereby left free to soar the heights of theoretical reflection and cultural production. In a similar manner, people of color, indigenous people, or slaves can no longer fulfill the role of the *working body* for white elites, who are thereby freed to create values, morality, and knowledge.

In view of this assertion, the central dilemma for gender studies within archaeology is that Western elite males have claimed the body as their own area of specialty and positioned themselves as privileged in these discourses. However, in retrospect, if while claiming or reclaiming the Body, we have failed to produce any radical perspectives or alternatives, then we have simply adhered to the dichotomous structures already established by elite Western males since the time of Descartes.

The second point of contact for archaeology and the body exists primarily in the literature of British and European prehistory: a predilection for the body as artifact (Barrett 1994, Shanks and Tilley 1982, Thomas 1993, Yates 1993). This social body is described in relationship to its landscape or as spatially experiencing the phenomenon of monuments, again without any reference to corporeal, lived, or individual identity. The physical body is the object that describes the monument, not as an embodied individual in his/her own right. Influenced largely by the Giddensian model of structuralism, sets of bodies are described as social actors, normative representatives of larger social entities fulfilling their negotiated roles, circumscribed by powerful social forces. As Merleau-Ponty (1980:73) forcefully argues, the body cannot be reduced to the status of an object, since objects are involved only in "external and mechanical relationships." He continues: "[one is conscious of one's] body via the world, that it is the unperceived term in the centre of the world towards which all objects turn their face, it is true for the same reason that my body is the pivot of the world" (1980:82).

But archaeologies of the body, while borrowing heavily from developments in social theory over the past few decades, have turned not to the phenomenological approaches of Merleau-Ponty, but rather to the power-based narratives of Michel Foucault. Few would deny that archaeology has been seduced by Foucault — long after his death (Meskell 1996: 8–9). Yet there are fundamental problems with his more extreme formulations of power, his depersonalized, uninhabited histories, and his general failure to address individuals and levels of difference. A Foucauldian archaeology posits that control and power relations are mapped on the body as a surface which can be analyzed as a forum for display. It has been said that late in Foucault's career "power" was endowed with enough theoretical elasticity to serve as a descriptive gloss for many qualities within social relations (Anderson 1995).

Foucault's conceptualizations of the body or power changed significantly throughout his work, yet it is his more evocative tales of the prison, the madhouse, and the clinic that have fired the imagination (Foucault 1977, 1989a, 1989b). Generally, Foucault's notion of power is inscribed on bodies through a discursive potentiality that undervalues the active corporeality of the body, thus reducing it simply to a product of representations. The contributions of real bodies to their own experience within the milieu of power, and consequently to their own production, remains an undeveloped theme. Indeed, most of this theorizing has served only to mystify or render mute the materiality of the body.

It is difficult to apprehend the massive influence of Foucault's oeuvre in archaeology (see Meskell 1996, 1998a; Knapp and Meskell 1997). And it is perhaps more pressing that students of historical disciplines become engaged in this discourse, given Foucault's writings on ancient cultures— despite the numerous criticisms concerning his historical knowledge (Cohen and Saller 1994; Goldhill 1995). Additionally, his work has met with criticism from feminist quarters (Diamond and Quinby 1988; Nicholson 1990; Sawicki 1991; McNay 1992). Feminist Classicists, for example, have charged him with ignoring the female subject and the voices of children, slaves, and other class groups (duBois 1988:96; Richlin 1998) though he has kept us from reifying and essentializing the category *woman*. Although many scholars find fault with the fine details of Foucault's thesis, most appreciate the overall contribution that *The History of Sexuality* has made to fields as diverse as history, Classics, feminist theory, and the social sciences, and both feminist and queer theory have benefited greatly from his controversial insights.

It is impossible to summarize adequately this three-volume magnum opus. The first volume is perhaps the most influential, and perhaps the most definitive work. Here Foucault demolishes the repressive hypothesis and argues that the construction of sexuality is a relatively recent development. In fact, he attempts to take the sex out of sexuality, focusing instead on the operation of discourses in the construction or "technologies" of the self. From this perspective, he was in fact writing a *pre*history of sexuality. Some see this development as a reaction against Freud's work on sexuality, although Freud centered on the emotions and personality, whereas Foucault denied these factors completely.

The second volume, *The Uses of Pleasure*, attempts to show a shift in the sexual interests of the self-fashioning subject in Imperial Rome, from boy love to reciprocal marriage (Larmour et al. 1998:27). The third volume, *The Care of the Self*, focuses on the control of the body and knowledges of bodily practices from pagan to Christian times, where ideology constructs and shapes sexuality. It presents a history of the way the self has been constituted in its own self-relation as the subject of desire, rather than a history of moral codes (Larmour et al. 1998:32). These were studies in self-construction, care of the self, and embodied ethics which eventually led to *scientia sexualis*, or the modern mode of sexual/scientific knowledge (Black 1998:54). In these later works, Foucault was more concerned with a hermeneutics of the self, rather than with sex per se — which, he famously said, was actually boring. Although the fourth volume, *Les aveux de la chair*, was not completed before his death, Foucault's work impacted ancient world studies irreversibly. Although there are problems with the earlier works, as noted above, these volumes on sexuality offer real possibilities for refiguring the body, particularly the sexed body, in antiquity.

Embodied Individuals

But there are other techniques by which archaeologists can reveal the body in antiquity. For many archaeologists, it should be possible to explore the social construction of the individual as a constellation of factors such as the interplay of difference. I am arguing for an idiographic focus rather than the traditional nomothetic one. Thus, we might view the body as a social being, that is, the articulation of agency and structure, causality and meaning, rationality and imagination, physical determinations and symbolic resonances (Berthelot 1991; Frank 1991). However, accessing the individual in antiquity obviously presents major challenges, given that the concept itself is a loaded, historically situated term that assumes various meanings cross-culturally. Historic contexts such as ancient Egypt are particularly informative and suggest that archaeologists might apprehend ancient constructions of selfhood and embodiments.

For example, in New Kingdom Egypt, the human being was viewed as a complex composite of many parts, each essential to individual existence. The loss of one meant the loss of all. Some of these elements were thought to exist during life, while others were activated only after death. In the eighteenth Dynasty Theban tomb of Amenemhet (TT82), some of these constituents are mentioned: his fate, his corpse, his lifetime/character, and all his manifestations. They are each presented as divinities that can receive offerings and confer blessings, yet they are still integral elements of the individual. Another constituent often mentioned was the heart, which was the seat of reason, memory, consciousness, desire, and emotion. It was also the center of free will and had a personality of its own. An individual's name similarly had its own identity: to destroy the name meant the total destruction of the individual. Thus, defacement of the name of the deceased was seen as a negation of a person's existence and his or her opportunity to attain the afterlife. Conversely, the continued use of the name perpetuated the personality: you do not *have* a name, you *are* a name just as you *are* a body (Milde 1988). The name was not an abstract entity since it belonged to the physical world. In fact, it resembled the Egyptian conception of the human shadow, in that it was able to carry and transfer power (Hornung 1992:179). These various components of the self entail multiple aspects: an individual's vitality, capacity for movement and effectiveness, physical appearance, personality, and the mysterious shadow, as well as the individual's intellectual, emotional, and moral dimensions (Lloyd 1989:120).

Egyptians believed that individual selves persisted after death and were in fact multiply constituted. Five essential components of the individual could survive after death: one's name, shadow, personal magic, the double self (*ka*), and the individual's character (*ba*) (Zandee 1960:20; Pinch 1993:147). None of these elements, however, translates exactly as a *soul*. For example, the *ba* depended on the physical body for existence; even after death it had need of material sustenance such as bread and beer (Hornung 1992:181). This entity was usually depicted as a human-headed bird that journeyed into the underworld and was at risk of dying a second and final death. After surviving various trials, however, the deceased could attain the status of a transfigured and effective spirit (Pinch 1994).

Thus, within this scheme the various elements of the individual remained, although a person could ultimately adopt various trajectories through time, benevolent or otherwise. An individual could thus be multiply constituted within his or her own body. Textual evidence of this order obviously substantiates the mortuary data. It also serves to embody Egyptian individuals in the manner specific to their own culture and imbues our interpretations with some measure of legitimacy (see Meskell 1999).

In the last decade, post-processual archaeology has in theory placed great emphasis on the individual and his or her intentions — although in practice we still omit real people. The attempt to locate individuals involves two quite different projects. The first is what Johnson (1989:190) refers to as a practical concern with "specifically existing moments, present particularly in historical archaeology where one can identify 'real people' and relate them to traces in the archaeological record."

The second project, and one which is more generally attainable in archaeology, is a search for the construction of identity or self. My own preliminary investigations into the villagers of Deir el Medina, a site in New Kingdom Egypt, suggests it is possible to see reflections of individual selves in all their variability (Meskell 1994, 1996, 1997, 1998b, 1999). This view does not discount constituting factors of age, status, class, sex, ethnicity, or marital status, yet it does not prioritize these categories as opposed to individual or family choices. I am not advocating access to individual self consciousness — anthropology has clearly illustrated the problematic nature of this position — rather, the formulation of identity. In the Egyptian context, single burials of children, couples, family groups, often named individuals with written histories, may show how notions of identity or constructions of self were embodied. Individual selves were also presented to other members of the community during life (through individual houses, decoration, and material culture) and to other individuals, family, and members of the afterworld (by means of burials, tombs, chapels, and monuments).

Summing Up

Finally, I would like to address another bifurcation — that of society and self. Archaeology has tended to ignore the relationship of the individual to society in favor of treating individuals simply as micro-versions of larger social entities. This is achieved by extrapolating from the supposedly representative sample of *society* to the assumption that subjects are the normative constituents that aggregate to make the whole. Western social science proceeds from the top downward, from society to the individual, deriving individuals from the social structures to which they belong: class, nationality, state, sex, religion, generation, and so on (Cohen 1994:6). This view from the top does not easily facilitate an archaeology of *différance*, or individuality, or allow for an analysis of the construction of self. Generally, we focus on collective structures and categories, leaving the individual sadly under-theorized. The corollary is that we have simply created fictions that need serious revision. Archaeology's concern has always been with representativeness, aiming for generalizing practices and behaviors rather than individual responses, the latter being portrayed as an insurmountable task. Archaeology has too readily succumbed to Foucauldian concepts, theories of structuration (Giddens 1984, 1991), or habitus (Bourdieu 1977, 1998). Even habitus, which seemingly directs attention toward individual behavior, nonetheless renders moot the question of agency and consciousness. According to Strathern (1996:28), even Bourdieu attributes the strongest role in determining action to the habitus, leaving little room for individuals to maneuver. There has been a general failure to see society as created by selves, which similarly fails to accord them their creative input.

In conclusion, I impute that most archaeological studies on the body leave their bodies uninhabited and without materiality. The way out of this dilemma may be significantly impeded if emphasis is placed upon the body in an uncritical, untheorized milieu at the expense of a more rounded, holistic notion of individuality. Subjective bodily experience is mitigated by factors such as social constraints, practicality, contingency, and free will; this dialectical position potentially circumvents the determinism associated with extreme social constructionism, Cartesianism, and essentialism (Frank 1991:48–49).

Prioritizing and elevating the body as a central project for an engendered archaeology is also problematic if we are claiming political awareness coupled with a desire to change the trajectory of the discipline. If we give primacy to sexed difference, we are excluding other significant forms of difference such as the discourses of race, class, ethnicity, religion, sexuality and so forth. We are then returning to the same binary modes of thinking and the same dogmatic structure we seek to critique. All these major axes of difference intersect with sex in ways which proffer a multiplicity of subject positions that need to be examined in context.

Finally, the body represents the particular site of interface between several different irreducible domains: the biological and the social, the collective and the individual, structure and agent, cause and meaning, constraint and free will. We are now in a position to build on synchronic developments in anthropology and sociology that go beyond the body in a generic sense to explore the construction of identity and self, thus offering new avenues to culturally specific concepts of embodiment and to accessing individuals in the past.

Acknowledgments

This chapter has benefited from my discussions with a variety of people during my time at Cambridge and Oxford. I would like to thank Ian Hodder, Dominic Montserrat, Richard Parkinson, Bernard Knapp, and Sarah Tarlow for their ongoing support and constructive comments. My current research is funded by New College, Oxford University. An earlier version of this chapter appeared in 1996 in the *Norwegian Archaeological Review*.

Part I
Reading the Body from Mortuary Remains

Chapter 3
Sex, Health, and Gender Roles Among the Arikara of the Northern Plains

Sandra E. Hollimon

The use of osteological remains holds promise for testing archaeologically and historically derived hypotheses. For example, in the Great Plains of North America, such analyses have addressed questions of the effects of Euro-American contact and exploration on demography and population health, tribal interactions and warfare, subsistence, and mortuary practices (Owsley and Jantz 1994:4). By including sex and gender as explicit analytical categories, the differential effects on women, men, alternative gender persons, and children in these past societies can be evaluated. Perhaps the examination of osteological data holds the greatest promise in identifying alternative genders in the archaeological record, through the analysis of patterns of activity-induced pathology, such as degenerative joint disease and musculoskeletal stress markers (see Peterson, this volume).

The Arikara of the Northern Plains have been the focus of numerous anthropological studies that have examined changes in Arikara society as reflected in material culture and the adoption of European trade goods (Orser 1984; Orser and Zimmerman 1984; Rogers 1990); mortuary practices (Orser 1980; O'Shea 1984; Ubelaker and Willey 1978); and the skeletal biology of pre- and protohistoric populations (Owsley and Jantz 1994). With few exceptions, the Arikara gender system has not been an explicit research focus in these examinations.

This study contributes to an understanding of these people during late prehistory and the protohistoric period by focusing specifically on sex differences in health. By examining patterns of mortality, disease, and trauma in females and males, it is possible to address the health consequences of gender roles in Arikara society. Employing gender as an explicit research variable provides a perspective on Arikara culture that has been less than fully utilized in previous analyses.

Arikara Society

The Arikara lived in settled earth-lodge villages on the Upper Missouri River. During the Historic period, these people had a mixed subsistence economy, in which the women were primarily responsible for the growing of corn, beans, squash, and sunflowers, while the men were primarily hunters of buffalo (Holder 1970; Will and Hyde 1964). Reconstructions of the precontact Arikara diet also shows this emphasis on horticultural produce and bison meat (Hurt 1969; Parmalee 1979; Ramenofsky 1987).

Arikara villages were under the control of local hereditary chiefs (Curtis 1970). The society was organized into several classes, consisting of elites, those who had gained war honors, doctors, priests, and the general populace (Gilmore 1928; Rogers 1990). The Arikara were generally matrilineal (Tabeau 1939:181–182) with matrilocal postmarital residence (Curtis 1970:63).

Ethnographic Sources

Prior to the late 1860s, the Arikara came in contact primarily with Euro-American traders; additionally, some explorers, naturalists, and painters visited Arikara territory (Rogers 1990:62). While the traders were driven by a profit motive, the other observers generally were not, and the different nature of these interactions probably accounts for conflicting depictions of the Arikara in ethnohistoric sources. Rogers (1990:67) notes that accounts of the Arikara by painters, naturalists, and explorers are generally more positive than those by fur traders.

In the twentieth century, anthropologically trained observers collected ethnographic information about the Arikara. Data concerning social organization, cosmology, rituals, and division of labor were recorded. These ethnographic and ethnohistoric sources provide information concerning Arikara genders and roles, particularly with regard to the division of labor.

It should be noted that the majority of ethnohistoric sources refer to Arikara society during the nineteenth century, while most of the skeletal samples discussed here date to the eighteenth century. Undoubtedly, significant changes took place between these periods, and caution should be exercised in the interpretation of archaeological data using historic documentation (Rogers, personal communication).

Of particular concern are the sources of and types of bias in the ethnohistoric record. The inability of European and Euro-American observers to shed their world view when writing about Native Americans is particularly apparent in their treatment of Arikara customs regarding sex, gender systems, and the division of labor. The European model of male-dominated economic, religious, and political life was also a poor fit for the people of the Upper Missouri. For example, this lack of fit between European models and Arikara behavior may be a factor in the relatively frequent descriptions of female drudgery and male laziness in the ethnohistoric documents. Clearly, the Arikara division of labor violated Europeans' idealized division of labor in their own society, a society based on an agricultural or pastoral economy.

The Gender-Based Division of Labor

There are many references to the Arikara division of labor in the ethnohistoric literature, and apparently, gender was an important organizing principle. Later ethnographic information confirms this idea, in the form of myths that describe the Arikara gender-based division of labor (Dorsey 1904:47) and the rituals for disposal of a newborn's umbilical cord (Gilmore 1930:74–75). These rituals describe ideal behaviors associated with Arikara gender roles. Fathers buried their sons' umbilical cords on hilltops, praying for the boys to grow up to be strong, brave, and courageous. Mothers buried their daughters' umbilical cords in cornfields, praying that the girls would grow up to be quiet, kind, helpful to others, virtuous, and hospitable (Gilmore 1930:75).

With the exception of bows and arrows, Arikara women were said to manufacture virtually all household implements, such as pottery, baskets, mats, wooden mortars and bowls, and spoons made of buffalo horn (De Land 1918:308–309). Many references indicate that these women led extremely difficult lives, filled with hardship, privation, and backbreaking labor. Sources state that working in the cornfields, carrying heavy loads, procuring and preparing food, and caring for children made Arikara women old beyond their years (Boller 1959; De Land 1918:308; de Trobriand 1941:309–310; Denig 1961:61; Miller 1968; Perrin du Lac 1817; Sunder 1965:197). In contrast, men are depicted as loafers who smoked, gambled, and indirectly caused famine among their people because of their distaste for physical labor (Tabeau 1939:148; de Trobriand 1941:224, 247). These accounts contribute to the stereotypes of male and female roles in Plains societies (see Kehoe 1983 and Weist 1983 for discussions of the drudge stereotype among Plains women).

Arikara Genders and Gender Roles

Ethnographic information and several Arikara oral traditions mention that the principal component of a man's status revolved around being a warrior, as was the case in many Plains societies (Denig 1961:62; Gilmore 1926a). However, warfare was an intermittent pursuit, and one observer went so far as to say that the lack of war-related activities was the cause of extramarital sex (the "idle hands" explanation) (Denig 1961:62).

When they were not describing Arikara women as beasts of burden (de Trobriand 1941:224; Tabeau 1939:148), observers commented on the sexual behavior of these women. If some of the ethnohistoric sources are to be believed, Arikara women were among the most sexually accessible of the groups living along the Missouri River (Brackenridge 1904; Coues 1893:157; Maximilian 1906:354).

Rogers (1990:57) provides an economic motive for what was perceived as the licentious behavior of Arikara women. Arikara men may have provided their wives, sisters, and daughters as sex partners for Euro-American men in order to gain symbolic power and material goods. The transfer of power from a Euro-American man to an Arikara man could be accomplished through sexual intercourse with an Arikara woman (Rogers 1990:57; see also Kehoe 1970). For example, Tabeau observed: "A savage regards the infidelity of his wife in favor of a white man less of a sin, in that she is won by the allurement of gain and he does not dream that his rival presumes to think that he is preferred to himself" (Tabeau 1939:180).

As in many Native American societies, the Arikara gender system was not limited to "men" and "women." Alternative gender roles existed among the Arikara: "Dr. Best, of Fort Berthold, Dakota, informs me that among his Indians, Gros Ventres, Mandans and Rees [Arikara], [there are] 'a few bucks who have the dress and manner of the squaws and who cohabit with other bucks,' but in what manner or for what purpose is unable to say" (Holder 1889:623; see also Meyer 1977:75). Additional possible evidence of alternative gender roles is inferred from the Wolf Dance stories, in which a very handsome young man disdains young women as well as the warpath, and is taunted by other young men for his lack of interest in male pursuits (Dorsey 1904:101–107).

The presence of individuals actually belonging to this possible third gender category can also be inferred from the journal of Peter Garrioch, who lived with fur traders at Fort Clark. In commenting on the "prostitution" of Arikara women at the fort, he suggests that some of the "women" were female in appearance only: "If the [sexual] object . . . bore the semblance of a woman it was enough, the reality was taken on chance to be discovered in the secret chamber" (Athearn 1967:29).

Although such individuals no doubt existed among the Arikara, it was extremely difficult to identify them by their skeletal remains in this study. I did not examine burial accompaniments or other data that might provide tentative identification of such graves (see Hollimon 1997 for a discussion of possible indicators of analogous third-gender burials among the Chumash). As this analysis was limited to skeletal remains, it was not possible to address the question of whether some of the skeletal remains were from individuals of this third gender category (see Hollimon 1996).

Skeletal Analyses

In order to address the relative health of Arikara women, men, third-gender persons, and children, I analyzed a total of 632 skeletons from the following archaeological sites in South Dakota: Black Widow Ridge (39ST203), Buffalo Pasture (39ST216), Cheyenne River (39ST1), Four Bear (39DW2), Indian Creek (39ST15), Larson (39WW2), Leavenworth (39CO9), Leavitt (39ST215), Mobridge (39WW1), Sully (39SL4), and Swan Creek (39WW7). These sites range in age from A.D. 1600 to 1832, with the majority of the burials dating to the seventeenth and eighteenth centuries (Owsley 1992:77; Rogers 1990:124). These sites span the Extended and Postcontact variants of the Coalescent Tradition of the Middle Missouri subarea (Lehmer 1971; Rogers 1990).

Individuals were aged using dental development standards established by Moorrees and others (1963a; 1963b), and pubic symphysis morphology as described by McKern and Stewart (1957) and by Gilbert and McKern (1973). Sex determination was based on pelvic and cranial morphology (Bass et al. 1971; Ubelaker 1989).

Demography

Demographic analyses of Arikara skeletal populations have underscored the devastating impact of Euro-American contact on native peoples. Staggering population losses were experienced by many groups of the Northern Plains following the introduction and diffusion of infectious diseases (Lehmer 1971, 1977; Owsley 1992; Ramenofsky 1987; Trimble 1979, 1989). As the predominant group along the Missouri River, the Arikara appear to have suffered tremendous depopulation during the eighteenth century (Owsley 1992:75).

While Owsley's study (1992) highlighted the importance of subadult mortality in declining population size, his analysis did not separate the sample by sex. Using some of the sites employed in his study, I have examined mortality patterns with regard to differences between females and males.

The present demographic analysis reiterates the very high subadult mortality presented in previous studies of Arikara populations (Bass et al. 1971; Jantz and Owsley 1984; Owsley 1992; Owsley and Bass 1979; Owsley and Bradtmiller 1983; Palkovich 1981). Roughly half of the population was comprised of subadult individuals (less than 20 years old). Of this

Table 3.1 Abridged Life Table Values for Prehistoric and Protohistoric Arikara
         Populations

Age	N	%	Survivors	Probability of Death in the Next Age Range
Age (x)	Dx	dx	lx	qx
0–4	218	38.51	100.00	.3851
5–9	36	6.36	61.49	.1034
10–14	29	5.12	55.13	.0928
15–19	31	5.47	50.01	.1093
20–29	92	16.25	44.54	.3648
30–39	56	9.89	28.29	.3495
40–49	70	12.36	18.40	.6717
50+	34	6.04	6.04	1.000

group, the vast majority of individuals were less than five years old, with the largest age cohort consisting of infants less than one year old (Table 3.1).

Patterns of female and male mortality differ in a few aspects. The mean age at death for females was between twenty-five and twenty-nine years, while the mean age at death for males was between thirty and thirty-four years. The greatest number of female deaths occurred between the ages of twenty and twenty-four years, while the corresponding peak for male deaths occurred between the ages of forty and forty-four years. Five females and sixteen males survived to old age (older than fifty-five years).

Very high subadult mortality rates most likely reflect a combination of several factors, including childbirth complications and the synergistic effects of poor nutrition and infectious diseases (Owsley and Bass 1979: 151–152). In the case of perinatal infants, difficulties with childbirth would appear to be the most likely explanation. Although they may not be directly identifiable in human skeletal remains, immediate postpartum experiences such as maternal hemorrhage and puerperal sepsis could easily account for high mortality among young females and perinatal infants (Owsley and Bradtmiller 1983:335–336). While these hazards were apparently uncommon among the Arikara (Gilmore 1930:76–77), treatments for postpartum hemorrhage were reported by an Arikara midwife (Gilmore 1930:74). This explanation for high perinatal infant mortality is supported by demographic data from the Larson site, where the peak of female mortality was between the ages of 15 and 19 years (Owsley and Bass 1979). The pattern of multiple burials at Larson, in which females of childbearing age were buried with perinatal infants, suggests that maternal death was associated with infant death, either directly or indirectly (Owsley and Bass 1979:151).

In the case of older children, stable isotope data indicate that Arikara women weaned their infants around the age of one year (Tuross and Fogel 1994:287). These data also indicate that between the ages of two and five years, Arikara children at the Sully site ate more plant foods and less meat than their elders (Tuross and Fogel 1994:287). The relative lack of protein in the diet of children and the possibility of diarrheal disease associated with weaning (Mata et al. 1980; Walker 1986) could account for the high mortality among children, in spite of the general nutritional adequacy of the Arikara diet (see below).

It has been suggested that the interaction between poor nutrition and infectious disease differentially affected subadults among Northern Plains populations (Owsley 1992). While increasing sedentism and its concomitant sanitation problems undoubtedly account for some of the observed mortality (Owsley and Bass 1979: see also Brackenridge 1904: 114; Denig 1961:54; Stearn and Stearn 1945:47), it is also probable that acute crowd infections, such as smallpox and tuberculosis, were responsible for a large percentage of the subadult deaths (Owsley 1992). Skeletal lesions consistent with tuberculosis have been documented among Arikara skeletal series; before the introduction of antibiotics, this disease primarily affected infants and older adults (Heffron 1939; Kelley et al. 1994; Palkovich 1981).

Degenerative Joint Disease

The emphasis on physical labor in ethnohistoric accounts of Arikara women lends the impression that men did very little work. This implies that female and male skeletons should display markedly different patterns in the location and severity of arthritic joints.

In contrast to this expectation, female and male skeletons show comparable patterns of degeneration (Table 3.2). Greater numbers of males displayed degenerative joint disease (DJD), but the average severity and location of the arthritic joints are comparable between males and females. The older age of the males in the sample may have contributed to the higher incidence of DJD among males. Had the females lived as long as the males, they may have surpassed the rate of DJD exhibited in the male population.

This finding differs from the results of a study of Omaha skeletons from Northeast Nebraska (Reinhard et al. 1994). The contact-period females (c. A.D. 1780 to 1820) showed greater rates of spinal DJD than did males; this was attributed to their increased work load associated with the fur trade (Reinhard et al. 1994:63–64).

Biomechanical (Ruff 1994) and size and shape (Cole 1994) analyses of

Table 3.2 Average Severity of Degenerative Joint Disease

	Female		Male	
	Severity Index[a]	N	Severity Index[a]	N
Upper Spine	1.33	26	1.50	62
Middle Spine	1.13	19	1.44	54
Lower Spine	1.48	32	1.63	64
Hip	1.09	22	1.09	58
Shoulder	0.82	19	0.81	59
Arm	0.50	21	0.67	70
Leg	0.46	17	0.62	51

[a] Severity score: 0=absent, 1=mild, 2=moderate, 3=severe, 4=ankylosis.
Severity scores were calculated by adding individual scores for each bone comprising the upper spine, hip, and so on, then dividing by the number of total number of bones. (Ex. "leg" = distal femur + proximal and distal tibiae and fibulae divided by 5.) The more severe side (right or left) was used for this calculation (see Walker and Hollimon 1989).

femora from Northern Plains populations suggest that Arikara females and males may have incurred similar mechanical stresses by virtue of their gender-based subsistence activities. Ruff (1994:244) contends that the adoption of the horse for bison hunting could have reduced the mechanical force exerted on male legs by reducing the amount of long-distance travel by foot. Over time, male leg bones would begin to resemble (presumably) more sedentary female lower limbs in this aspect (Ruff 1994:242).

Similarly, Cole's (1994) analysis of the size and shape of lower leg bones among Northern Plains groups suggests that a combination of factors may explain the relative comparability between males and females. A continued emphasis on bison hunting, and perhaps the contribution of male labor to horticultural activities, could account for the observed pattern in which male femora and tibiae began to resemble those of females over time (Cole 1994:230–231).

Arikara male and female skeletons did not display significant differences in the location or severity of arthritic joints. This result precludes the use of DJD patterns to identify alternative-gender burials. The association between degenerative changes in the skeleton and habitual movements allows the reconstruction of some activity patterns (Merbs 1983). It could be argued that men or alternative-gender persons who engaged in the same habitual activities as women might display similar patterns of DJD. This approach was used successfully in tentative identification of Chumash alternative-gender burials (Hollimon 1996). However, Arikara skeletons do not show characteristic male and female DJD patterns, limiting the applicability of this method in the present study.

Nutritional Status

Evidence of nutritional stress was inferred from the presence of hypoplastic defects in the tooth enamel, cribra orbitalia, porotic hyperostosis, and periosteal lesions. Several studies have suggested that these are osseous indicators of the synergistic effects of malnutrition and infectious diseases (Hengen 1971; Lallo et al. 1977; Mensforth et al. 1978).

Sixty-four individuals displayed hypoplastic defects and/or cribra orbitalia (Table 3.3). There were no instances of porotic hyperostosis. Of these, twenty could be identified as female and twenty-four as male. The number of individuals was evenly divided between adult (over the age of twenty) and subadult ages. Subadult individuals numbered thirty-four of sixty-three, while thirty adults were represented. This finding does not support the contention that nutritionally stressed persons would be more likely to die at younger ages (cf. Palkovich 1981:76).

Only thirty-one individuals (5 percent) displayed evidence of periostitis. There were thirteen females and fourteen males (Table 3.4). The relatively small number of individuals displaying these lesions may be due to the fact that the protohistoric Arikara suffered greater mortality from epidemic diseases such as smallpox that leave few, if any, lesions on bone (Ortner and Putschar 1985:227; Owsley and Jantz 1985; Rogers 1990).

The presence of periosteal lesions, usually attributed to staphylococcal and streptococcal infections, is associated with poor sanitary conditions, high population density, and nutritional stress among affected individuals (Ortner and Putschar 1985:106). It is probable that the population density of Arikara villages was not as high as that evidenced in other areas of North America (Owsley and Jantz 1994). For example, the prehistoric people of the Santa Barbara Channel area lived in densely populated

Table 3.3 Incidence of Nutritional/Disease Stress

Age	Total	Females	Males
0–4 years	5[a]	0	0
5–9	9[a]	0	0
10–14	9[a]	0	2
15–19	11[a]	6	2
20–24	13	7	6
25–29	6	2	4
30–34	5	2	3
35–39	1	0	1
40–44	3	2	1
45–49	2	1	1
Total	64	20	20

[a]The sex of most juveniles could not be accurately determined.

Table 3.4 Incidence of Periosteal Lesions

Age	Total	Female	Male
5–9	2[b]	0	0
15–19	6	5	1
20–24	6	3	3
25–29	3	1	2
30–34	1	0	1
35–39	5	2	3
40–44	4	2	2
45–49	1	0	1
60+	1	0	1
Total[a]	29[b]	13	14

[a]Two females that could not be accurately aged are excluded from this sample.
[b]The sex of the two juveniles could not be determined.

coastal villages. As a result, they displayed much higher rates of periosteal lesions than did the Arikara (Hollimon 1992:85; Walker and Lambert 1989).

The relative scarcity of indicators of nutritional stress may reflect the general adequacy of the Arikara diet. Stable isotope analysis of human remains from the Sully site indicates a dietary reliance on bison meat, with contributions from maize, pumpkin, and other plants. Faunal remains exhibited deer, antelope, bison, dog, jackrabbit, and other mammals and fish (Tuross and Fogel 1994). A study of skeletal size through time among Northern Plains populations also suggests the high nutritional quality of the Arikara diet (Cole 1994:230).

In addition, several authors have noted that Arikara crop surpluses allowed them to trade with other groups (Blakeslee 1975; Ewers 1968; Gilmore 1926b; Rogers 1990; Wood 1980; Zimmerman 1985). This ethnohistoric and ethnographic evidence supports archaeological and osteological data indicating the relative adequacy of the Arikara diet (Cole 1994; Jantz and Owsley 1984; Lehmer and Jones 1968). It appears that episodes of severe nutritional stress were limited to the period after A.D. 1780 (Owsley 1992). Ethnohistoric data suggest that the Arikara experienced periodic poor nutrition, as well as episodes of starvation during this time (La Verendrye 1914:332; Tabeau 1939:72).

Dental Pathologies

Evidence of carious lesions and alveolar abscesses were observed in 197 individuals (31 percent of the total population). Of these individuals, 74 were female (52 percent of the entire female population) and 106 were male (60 percent of the entire male population). Most individuals had fewer than five carious lesions, and the average number of abscesses for both females and males was seven.

The slightly higher rate of dental decay among males suggests that they may have eaten more cariogenic foods than did females. An alternative explanation is that the older average age of males provided a few extra years of opportunity for dental decay. The latter explanation seems likely in the case of antemortem tooth loss as well. The majority of individuals who lost five or more teeth were males over the age of fifty years (fifteen of nineteen individuals). The remaining four individuals were females who were also older than fifty. The preponderance of males in this group may be attributed to the fact that they lived, on average, longer than females, allowing more time for the ravages of dental decay to proceed.

Evidence of Trauma

The overwhelming majority of cranial and postcranial fractures were incurred by males. Of thirty individuals displaying traumatic injuries, twenty-two were male and six were female (Table 3.5). Two individuals were too young for accurate sex determinations. The largest number of males with fractures were between the ages of forty-five and forty-nine years when they died.

Two individuals had projectile points embedded in bone. Both these individuals were males; one was aged thirty-five to thirty-nine years, and the other was between forty-five and forty-nine years of age at death.

The age and sex distribution of traumatic injuries may be explained by the role of Arikara males in warfare. Ethnographic and ethnohistoric information suggest that this pursuit was primarily the domain of men (Denig 1961; Gilmore 1926a; Robarchek 1994). Demographic analysis of scalped Arikara crania also supports this explanation of traumatic injuries among Arikara males (Owsley 1994:341). The largest group of males displaying these injuries were aged between twenty and thirty-four years when they died, suggesting that they were warriors who may have been killed during raids or village defense (Owsley 1994:341). While male and female crania were scalped in roughly equal numbers, the age distribution of females spans all ranges, unlike the concentration found among young males. This suggests that the risk of violence for females was fairly even over the entire lifespan, while the greatest risk for males occurred during young adulthood (Owsley 1994:341).

Although there are few references describing the role of Arikara women in organized warfare (Chardon 1932:193; Ewers 1994), they were not immune to the effects of raids. Some explorers noted that the women were sometimes raided while tending their gardens away from the village.

Table 3.5 Incidence of Traumatic Injuries

Age	Total	Female	Male
Unknown	4	1	3
20–24	3	2	1
25–29	0	0	0
30–34	2	0	2
35–39	3	0	3
40–44	2	0	2
45–49	8	1	7
50–54	3	1	2
55–59	1	0	1
60+	2	1	1
Total	28	6	22

This raiding may have included shooting and scalping (Taylor 1897:60). Arikara women may have been particularly susceptible to violence inflicted by the Sioux. For example, Tabeau (1939:131) noted that the Sioux would steal horses from the Arikara and beat their women. Chardon (1932:188) suggests that native women in general were specific targets of violence when he noted that the Hidatsas would kidnap and kill Arikara women in retaliation for the death of Hidatsa women at the hands of the Arikara.

Osteological evidence of warfare, including scalping and perimortem mutilation, has been documented among several Arikara skeletal series (Olsen and Shipman 1994; Owsley 1994:335). These include Crow Creek (39BF11), the site of a massacre (Willey 1982, 1990), Larson (Olsen and Shipman 1994:385; Owsley et al. 1977), Leavenworth (Olsen and Shipman 1994:384), Mobridge (Owsley 1994), and Sully (Hollimon and Owsley 1994).

Conclusion

Despite ethnographic information suggesting that Arikara women suffered poorer health than their male contemporaries, osteological data indicate that it was Arikara men who experienced greater health risks during their lives. With the exception of a shorter life expectancy for females, the skeletal data demonstrate that males were more apt to have decayed or missing teeth, and to have suffered traumatic injuries. Males and females displayed roughly comparable rates of degenerative joint disease, indicators of nutritional stress, and evidence of infectious disease.

This analysis has been an example of the use of gender as an explicit research variable. In addition, it should serve as a cautionary example in the use of ethnohistoric and ethnographic information in the interpretation of archaeological data. These sources from the eighteenth and nineteenth centuries suggest a gender-based division of labor among the Arikara in which women performed far more laborious and physically strenuous tasks than did men. However, osteological evidence from the protohistoric period suggests otherwise. The lack of a gendered difference in the overall work load may be due to a number of factors. First, significant changes may have occurred in Arikara labor organization through time. Second, European and Euro-American observers may have exaggerated the differences in Arikara male and female roles and work loads as a result of their own ethnocentric perspective. Third, it is also possible that, with death occurring at relatively young ages for this protohistoric Arikara population, the skeletal indicators of age-dependent conditions such as degenerative joint disease are simply not observable in this sample. These possibilities should be taken into consideration when archaeologists and physical anthropologists use ethnohistoric and ethnographic information to interpret osteological material.

The approach used here may be among the most productive for investigating not only gender in the archaeological record but also for shedding new light on commonly held conceptions about divisions of labor in past societies (Claassen 1992). While it may be tempting to conclude that some ethnohistoric sources are so biased as to be of little use in understanding the archaeological record, it should be noted that this study is not an argument for abandoning such data. Rather, this examination of osteological patterns of health and disease among the Arikara benefits from the historical record of epidemic diseases on the Upper Missouri River. Without this information, one might conclude that the protohistoric Arikara people died young, but in a state of relatively good health. The evidence provided by the historical record is of great value in belying such an assumption.

Acknowledgments

This research was supported in part by a postdoctoral fellowship at the Smithsonian Institution, National Museum of Natural History.

Chapter 4
Labor Patterns in the Southern Levant in the Early Bronze Age

Jane D. Peterson

Interest in gender issues has taken root in a variety of archaeological fields. This chapter concerns gender relations and household organization during the development of domestication economies in the Near East. During the transition to production-based economies, dramatic social changes were undoubtedly taking place. The success of early farming depended on a group's ability to meet new organizational demands, including a restructuring of sexual labor patterns.

Current findings confirm that sexual labor patterns undergo transformations with the advent of domestication economies. However no single developmental trajectory can be identified from either ethnographic (Burton et al. 1977; Burton and White 1984; Ember 1983; Guyer 1988, 1991; Leacock 1981; Martin and Voorhies 1975; Murdock and Provost 1973) or archaeological investigations (Bridges 1991; Larsen and Ruff 1991; Molleson 1994; Smith et al. 1984). Rather, a number of distinctive labor arrangements appear feasible.

An engendered perspective on this aspect of Levantine prehistory is valuable from a critical angle because it affords the opportunity to expose some particularly unreflective scholarship that continues to be perpetuated in models of the origins of agriculture and the Levant (for critiques see Crabtree 1991; Peterson 1994). Beyond remedial efforts, the engendered perspective has proven productive as part of the larger, agent-centered paradigm that considers culture process in terms of its participants (Brumfiel 1992; Cowgill 1975; Wylie 1991a, 1991b). Despite the recognized importance of social organizational variables during the rise of agriculture (Bender 1978, 1985; Flannery 1973; Redman 1978; Smith 1976; Stark 1986), archaeologists have made few efforts to incorporate household changes into Levantine models. Several notable exceptions rely on architectural or human skeletal data sets (Banning and Byrd 1987, 1989; Byrd 1994; Flannery 1972; Molleson 1989, 1994; Rathbun 1984; Smith et al. 1984). The vast majority of studies, however, continue to focus on systems-level analyses that examine the ecological genetics of domestication (Blumler and Byrne 1990; Rindos 1980); propose refinements of climatic and radiocarbon chronologies (Harris 1986; McCorriston and Hole 1991); question the reality of the "broad spectrum revolution" (Edwards 1989); and elaborate extant multicausal models (Layton et al. 1991; MacNeish 1992; Redding 1989).

In contrast, the agent-centered perspective on the transition to domestication economies asks some distinctive questions. For example, what organizational solutions were devised by households in the face of sedentary agricultural life? How did households cope with the demands of new subsistence pursuits and increased sedentism? These are crucial issues that I will address here, in the context of changing patterns of labor and its gendered organization (Peterson 1994, 1997).

But where does one start? How can we begin to reconstruct systems of sexual task differentiation for prehistoric contexts dating back 10,000 years (*sensu* Conkey and Spector 1984; Spector 1982)? For the time periods in question, there are no clues from documentary sources about the sexual division of labor. Neither are there preserved graphic illustrations on ceramics or textiles. We might use ethnographic parallels based on the observed continuities from prehistoric to historic periods in the Levant (Charles 1984; Hillman 1984; Jacobs 1979; Kamp 1987; Kramer 1979, 1982; Watson 1978, 1979a, 1979b). These continuities are particularly evident, for example, in the vernacular architecture and in the economic system of extensive agro-pastoralism.

However, extending this analogy back to prehistoric sexual labor systems fails to recognize several essential factors. First, as any student of Near Eastern cultures can attest, there are no monolithic or static gender divisions in these cultures (Beck 1978; Cosar 1978; Peters 1978; Tapper 1978; Tavakalian 1984; Watson 1979a). Furthermore, the strength of modern Islam as an ideological system, a system defining traditional roles for men and women, cannot be overlooked. The ideal position for women, codified jointly as religion and law in the Koran, is one of economic dependency, not active participation (White 1978). Thus, the use of ethnographic parallels requires accepting a good deal of ideological baggage that may be quite inappropriate for prehistoric contexts. However, one way in which archaeologists can examine the sexual division of labor in the prehistoric period (Spector 1982) is to investigate evidence of task differentiation through the study of occupational stress markers on human bone.

Occupational Stress Markers

There are many kinds of activity-induced occupational stress markers on the human skeleton, including patterns of trauma, joint degeneration from osteoarthritis, and dental attrition (Barrett 1977; Farquharson-Roberts and Fulford 1980; Larsen 1985; Levy 1968; Merbs 1983; Tainter 1980). Here, I discuss a subset of these markers called enthesopathies. Enthesopathies are the distinct skeletal marks that occur where a muscle, tendon, or ligament attaches to bone. The term musculoskeletal stress marker (MSM) has recently been used as a synonym for "enthesopathy" (Hawkey and Merbs 1995).

Very briefly, bone is covered by fibrous membrane, the periosteum, that is well supplied with blood vessels (Weineck 1986). When regular minor stress occurs, such as the "pull" of a muscle, the number of capillaries that supply the periosteum increases (Wirhed 1984). This increased blood flow stimulates osteon remodeling, or the local build-up of bone (Hawkey and Merbs 1995; Little 1973). The result is enlargement, or hypertrophy, of the bone at the muscle attachment site (Kennedy 1989; Weineck 1986). Rough patches and surface irregularities, sometimes referred to as tuberosities, are formed. Thus the continual stress of a muscle in daily, repetitive tasks creates a skeletal record of an individual's habitual activity patterns.

Efforts to measure and interpret MSM have increased dramatically over the past few years, and these studies benefit those archaeologists who are interested in reconstructing prehistoric sexual labor patterns. A number of criteria have been established that have proven beneficial, and perhaps necessary, for conducting a study of MSM patterning. Many were first outlined by Merbs (1983) in his comprehensive skeletal study of activity-induced skeletal alterations. The criteria include the following:

1. There must be good skeletal preservation and recovery. In situations where the outer surface of the bone has been eroded by chemical actions of the soils or modified by overly rigorous excavation and cleaning, MSM cannot be satisfactorily identified.
2. Sample size must be adequate (see the discussion in Stirland [1991] specifically).
3. Reliable age and sex data must be available.
4. Record of trauma or pathology for each individual is needed. Many studies exclude those individuals with pronounced pathological or traumatic injuries that would have disrupted normal activity patterns (Hawkey 1988; Peterson 1994).
5. Because the genetic factors affecting MSM development and ex-

pression are not fully understood at this point, a situation of genetic isolation is preferable.

6. Using skeletal remains from a relatively narrow time span mitigates, to some degree, the possible effects of diachronic cultural/techno-logical change.

7. A limited number of specialized, but known, habitual activities that might lead to MSM development will be more readily detected in skeletal remains than many generalized activities, or activities per-formed only episodically. This prerequisite is, perhaps, the most limiting for archaeological applications.

Methods of Musculoskeletal Stress Marker Analysis

As can be expected with any methodology which is, in many ways, still emerging, the techniques for identifying and measuring MSM are contin-uously being reexamined and refined. This flux, which should be con-sidered healthy, can be simultaneously exciting and exasperating. The excitement comes as refinements reinforce our assumptions that the degree and type of markers are directly related to the amount and dura-tion of habitual stress placed on a specific muscle (Berget and Churchill 1994; Hawkey and Merbs 1995; Peterson 1997). The exasperation comes when one's results are rather quickly in need of reassessment based on methodological improvements.

The historical background for activity-induced skeletal changes was comprehensively synthesized by Kennedy (1989). By the late nineteenth century, a number of anatomists and surgeons became aware of an array of morphological and size irregularities in the human skeleton that could be related to life habits (Kennedy 1989; Meiklejohn 1957). Practition-ers of industrial medicine examined patients from the working classes, whose bodies had been shaped by years of heavy physical labor (Kennedy 1989:130). These doctors described a number of specific, trade-related skeletal modifications, and the value of these clinical descriptions was recognized by physical anthropologists (Kennedy 1989:131). More re-cently, the fields of industrial, athletic, and forensic medicine have pro-vided additional clinical diagnoses that refine the connections between muscle use and the skeletal manifestations of that use (Hawkey and Merbs 1995).

Research using MSM involves selecting a set of muscle attachment sites and scoring them with respect to their robusticity. One widely used scor-ing technique involves assigning ordinal scores, which reflect the surface extent, degree of roughening, amount of bony build-up, and so on, per muscle site. Visual and descriptive systems for these categories have been

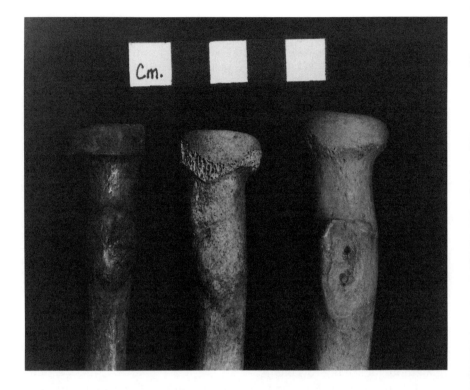

Figure 4.1. Varying robusticity scores on the proximal radius. Robusticity scores for the biceps brachii insertion site (L to R): 1.5, 2.5, and 3.0 (photo by the author).

described by a number of researchers and are becoming increasingly standardized (Benjamin 1993; Hawkey 1988; Peterson 1994; Robb 1994). This is a significant accomplishment because the sites are morphologically complex, and each one is unique (Figs. 4.1 and 4.2).

Beyond robusticity, a second characteristic of MSM with implications for discerning activity level has been suggested. It is described in the literature as stress lesioning (Hawkey 1988; Hawkey and Merbs 1995). The precise etiology is still poorly understood, but it appears that under certain conditions of continual microtrauma (overuse of the muscle) bone may respond by resorption. Thus bone is removed more quickly than it is laid down (Hawkey 1988; Kennedy 1989). The results of the bone resorption are furrows produced into the bone cortex (Fig. 4.3).

Progress has also been made in selecting which muscle, tendon, and ligament attachment sites are more straightforward to "read." The fact is, that from the analyst's perspective, not all MSM are created equally. In

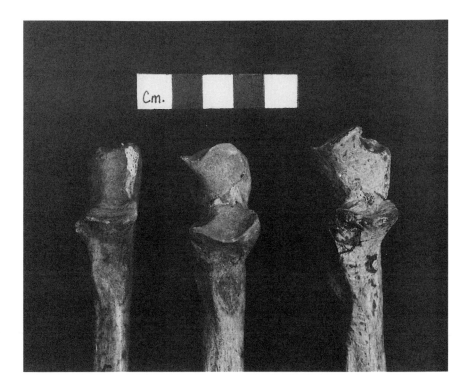

Figure 4.2. Varying robusticity scores on the proximal ulna. Robusticity scores for the biceps brachii insertion site (L to R): 1.0, 2.5, 3.0 (photo by the author).

general, insertion sites, rather than origin sites, appear to be better functional indicators (Benjamin 1993; Hawkey 1988). Even so, among insertion sites, some do not appear to display sufficient variability to break down into meaningful categories, and some have morphologies that are too complex or ambiguous to be measured by a single ordinal score (Robb 1994). Still other sites regularly fall victim to destruction from the array of post-depositional processes.

Given what we know about the formation of MSM, it is also clear that we must control for the age of the individual to the extent possible. Simply stated, it does not make sense to make MSM comparisons between a group of females in their fifties and a group of males in their twenties. The relationship between age and muscle score are strongly correlated (Hawkey 1988; Robb 1994).

Once age, sex, and MSM measurement data have been collected, the search for patterning can begin. In terms of identifying gender-specific

Figure 4.3. Examples of stress lesions on the medial clavicle. Costoclavicular ligament site on medial clavicles (photo by the author).

patterns, there are a number of ways to make sense out of the data. The different types of analyses can be divided conceptually into two categories: on one hand, those that attempt to identify gross patterns of activity or workload, and on the other, those that try to make specific activity reconstructions to explain the MSM patterns. The possibility of pinpointing certain activities (hunting or cereal processing for example) has captured the imaginations of many researchers. However, the realities of many archaeological situations suggest that we might more productively spend our energy exploring ways of measuring activity at less detailed scales.

Lateralization

The extent to which MSM scores from the right and left sides of the body differ is significant data. If activities regularly involve strenuous muscle use involving only one arm, that pattern of use should be reflected in noticeable bilateral asymmetries in the MSM scores. Think, for example of a stonemason who holds the chisel in one hand and repeatedly pounds it with a hammer in the other. Compare that to another individual who spends four to five hours a day processing cereal grains using a two-handed mano or pestle. Analysis of lateralization does, however, have to take into account natural asymmetries that occur as the result of right- or left-handedness (Stirland 1993). Differences in lateralization patterns between females and males are potentially significant in suggesting patterns of sexually segregated or integrated task systems as well as building cases for specific activity reconstructions that involve uni- or bilateral forces (Hawkey and Merbs 1995; Peterson 1994, 1997; Stirland 1993).

Generalists Versus Specialists

So too, we can try to identify the degree of task specialization between males and females within a population. The linking arguments and use of bivariate analysis in this context were first laid out and described by Robb (1994:5–6). If individuals are performing at about the same activity level, muscle scores will show low variability between individuals. By contrast, if some individuals are highly active while others are less active, average muscle scores will be much more variable. Variation within a skeleton derives from task specialization as well. Individuals with a generalized activity pattern, even if highly stressful, will have lower within-skeleton variability than those performing a more limited number of specialized activities (who should exhibit higher within-skeleton variability).

To my knowledge, Robb is the only researcher who has used bivariate comparisons of within- and between-skeleton variability for groups of males and females to assess sexual labor patterns. The characterization of musculature that this type of analysis provides, in terms of comparing the relative homogeneity and specialization of females' and males' activity-induced musculature, has a great deal of potential.

Cluster Analysis

Robb's (1994) analytical innovations include the use of cluster analysis. Using clustering techniques, groups of variables can be simultaneously compared between individuals of known sex to indicate underlying structure in labor organization. In another hypothetical example, four clusters were formed. Clusters 1 and 2 reveal high variability, which is a signal for specialized activities. In conjunction with high average scores, this result suggests that activities were labor intensive as well. The gender composition suggests that males were primarily, but not exclusively, responsible for these tasks. Cluster 3 suggests a more generalized activity pattern, but one that is still relatively labor intensive and composed exclusively of females. Cluster 4, the most mixed in terms of gender, suggests relatively low and unspecialized activity patterns. In the context of an early agricultural village, these clusters suggest several interesting sexual labor patterns.

Rank Ordering

Other researchers have found it informative to arrange the MSM scores for males and females in order from high to low score to examine the different rankings of specific muscle sites (Hawkey 1988; Hawkey and Merbs 1995; Peterson 1997). Points where the rankings differ suggest muscles or muscle groups used differentially between females and males. Rank-order muscle patterns that are very similar for females and males might indicate a labor system in which tasks were typically shared or where tasks of similar muscular demands were undertaken by males and females. Attachment sites that have noticeably different rankings can be compared statistically to measure the significance of those differences. Many such analyses attempt to take the results a step further to identify specific activities that might explain a few well-developed muscle sites.

In the example provided in Table 4.1, Natufian males and females have pronounced differences in the rank ordering of many important MSM sites on the upper appendicular skeleton, suggesting some marked activity differences. The high rankings for triceps brachii and anconeus in males were linked with overhand throwing motions, in conjunction with pronounced right-side lateralizations (Dutour 1986; Kennedy 1983; Peterson 1997).

Activity Reconstructions

A different issue is the inference of specific activities in individuals or groups of individuals. How fine-grained can we hope to be in our goal of sexual task differentiation? Ideally, we would like to be able to answer a variety of very detailed questions. Were males doing the majority of hunting? Were females primarily responsible for plant cultivation? However, we should proceed with some caution. Activity inferences must take into account that muscles do not operate in isolation but as synergistic groups. We cannot reconstruct a particular activity based on either subjective observations of "marked" development or high muscle scores for a single muscle attachment site.

For certain activities the synergistic muscle signatures, and the skeletal

Table 4.1 Largest Differences Between Sexes in Rank Order Scores for Periods

	Rank Score[a]		
Muscle/Ligament	Female	Male	Rank Difference
Natufian Period			
Lateral Dorsi[b,c]	*20.0*	9.0	11.0
Coracobrachialis[b]	*10.0*	2.5	7.5
Triceps brachii	4.5	*12.0*	7.5
Teres major	*19.0*	14.0	5.0
Anconeus[b]	7.0	*11.0*	4.0
Neolithic Period			
Lateral dorsi	9.0	*16.0*	7.0
Extensors	*7.0*	3.0	4.0

[a]Italic type indicates the higher MSM score.
[b]MSM scores are significantly different using Mann-Whitney test.
[c]Calculated using left-side MSM scores.

stress patterns that result, are fairly well understood. Throwing motions are an example due to the emphasis on treating injuries in sports medicine. Thus, kinematic and eletromyographic studies of throwing motions abound. As a result, MSM inferences from prehistoric contexts are often well supported (Dutour 1986; Kennedy 1983; Peterson 1994). To reiterate, these are not based on patterning of a single muscle site but across a group of well-understood synergistic muscles.

But analysts must confront the reality that many activities utilize similar muscle groups. It is unrealistic to think that MSM patterns resulting from repetitive downward blows made when tilling the soil will be distinct from those made by felling trees. Equifinality is a familiar issue for archaeologists, and one that applies to interpreting MSM patterning.

However, some activities are idiosyncratic enough in terms of the muscle activity to have relatively distinct signatures. Rowing and paddling activities, for example, have been reconstructed from skeletal data with some confidence (Hawkey and Merbs 1995; Lai and Lovell 1992). In this case, the success in inferring these activities derives from the immense muscle demands placed on a unique suite of synergistic muscles.

My research suggests that there are many activities and activity regimes that probably do not result in MSM signatures sufficiently unique or idiosyncratic to allow specific activity reconstructions. This realization has implications for how we approach differentiating sexual tasks in many prehistoric contexts. Finding innovative ways of characterizing more general patterns between the sexes may, in the long run, prove more productive than trying to squeeze observed MSM patterns into specific activity reconstructions.

Musculoskeletal Stress Markers in the Study of Gender Roles

The range of activities represented by material remains does not represent the complete activity spectrum for a group. Artifacts can be valuable guides in building activity inference, but many strenuous activities do not yield readily identifiable material correlates. For example, recreational and ritual pursuits can certainly be both habitual and rigorous in nature, yet may involve few identifiable artifacts (e.g., dancing).

Using MSM markers can be one way to infer past activity, but we must take care that our inferences that do not simply reflect our own gender categories. Robb (1994:1) notes, for example, that MSM patterning among males is typically ascribed to weapon use; while evidence of patterned behavior among females is attributed to processing activities. Our inferences from MSM data are no more objective or sophisticated than the mindsets we bring to them.

It is clear that the most convincing and valuable studies combine both general assessments of workload with specific reconstructions in contexts that warrant them. The use of independent lines of artifactual data and skeletal data (e.g., patterns of trauma and osteoarthritis) helps bolster activity pattern reconstructions (Lai and Lovell 1992; Molleson 1994).

A case study will reinforce some of the points discussed above. My goal was to identify temporal changes in patterns of sexual divisions of labor as human groups increasingly relied on domestic plants and animals. This issue is quite relevant in the southern Levant because it is here, in modern Jordan and Palestine, where plant domestication led to the establishment of the first settled agricultural villages.

I examined skeletal remains from a number of time periods ranging from the Natufian (c. 12,500–10,500 B.P.) through the Middle Bronze II (4,000–3,500 B.P.) (Table 4.2). An interval scoring technique described twenty-five attachment sites on the arm and shoulder regions (Peterson 1994). Previously published accounts and museum inventories were used to compile age/sex determinations. Fortunately, many of the collections had also already been examined for evidence of trauma and pathology; in addition, various genetic traits were tracked through measures of craniofacial morphology (Ortner 1979, 1981, 1982; Smith 1989).

One of many working hypotheses was that a significant shift in sexual labor divisions could be anticipated beginning in the Chalcolithic period. During the Chalcolithic, the mixed agro-pastoral lifestyle became more entrenched, with households relying more on domestic plant and animal products. Significantly, the range of animal products utilized expands to include secondary animal products such as milk and wool (Doll-

Table 4.2 Archaeological Chronology for the Southern Levant

Time Period	Approximate Dates (Years B.P.)
Final Epipaleolithic	12,000–10,000
Pre-Pottery Neolithic A, B, and C	10,500–7,700
Pottery Neolithic	7,700–6,200
Chalcolithic	6,200–5,500
Early Bronze I	5,500–5,000
Early Bronze II–III	5,000–4,200
Early Bronze IV–Middle Bronze I	4,200–4,000
Middle Bronze II	4,000–3,500

fus and Kafafi 1986; Gilead 1988; Levy 1983, 1986, 1993; Perrot 1984; Stager 1992).

In many ethnographic examples, marked dependence on domesticated animals tends to remove women from the agricultural labor pool, as they spend more of their time caring for animals and processing animal products (Burton and White 1984; Ember 1983). Ember's (1983) research indicates that women's *total* workload does not decrease, only the amount of their efforts directed toward agriculture. A corollary suggests that men, who no longer hunt out of necessity, may increasingly be drawn into agricultural service. This pattern seems to be especially pronounced in more arid areas (Burton and White 1984). These ethnographic findings formed the core of an expectation that was tested using MSM data.

The first reasonably large skeletal population that fits this description comes not from the Chalcolithic, but from the following Early Bronze I (EBI) site of Bab edh-Dhra in West-Central Jordan (Fig. 4.4). This time period is characterized by its continuity with Chalcolithic social and economic patterns (Hanbury-Tenison 1986). Skeletal analyses of cranial and facial morphology of Chalcolithic and EBI specimens do not support a hypothesis of large-scale population movements into the Levant during this period (Smith 1989). Overall, indigenous development of the EBI from the preceding Chalcolithic seems most likely.

At Bab edh-Dhra, the inhabitants utilized wheat and barley (McCreery 1981); the high frequency of caries and dental attrition attests to the importance of such cariogenic carbohydrates in the diet (Smith 1989). Domestic animals included sheep/goats, pigs, cows, and donkeys. Evidence for significant losses of cortical bone in female sheep/goats suggests that they were milked intensively (Smith and Horwitz 1984). The presence of ceramic churns suggests that some of this milk was processed into yogurt, cheese, and other products less prone to spoilage, a conclu-

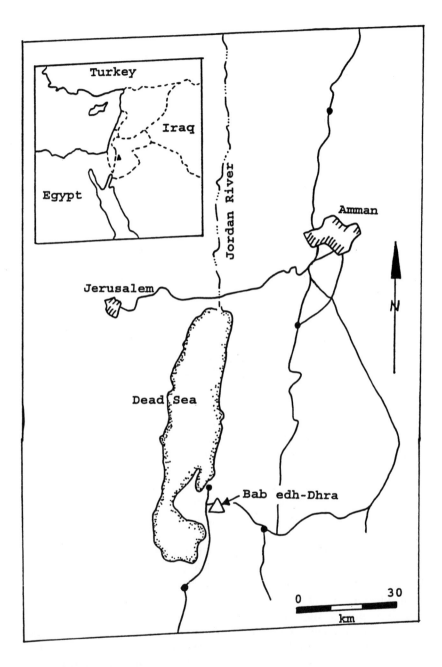

Figure 4.4. Location of Bab edh-Dhra, Jordan (redrawn by the author from Frolich and Ortner 1982).

Table 4.3 Significant Differences in Mean MSM Scores by Sex and Period
(Mann-Whitney Test)

Time Period	Muscle	High Score
Natufian	Deltoideus	Men
Natufian	Flexors	Men
Natufian	Anconeus	Men
Natufian	Supinator	Men
Natufian	Latissimus dorsi	Women
Pre-Pottery Neolithic	Brachialis	Men
Early Bronze I	Conoid ligament	Women
Early Bronze I	Brachialis	Women
Early Bronze I	Biceps brachii	Women
Early Bronze IV/Middle Bronze I	Flexors	Men
Early Bronze IV/Middle Bronze I	Latissimus dorsi	Men
Early Bronze IV/Middle Bronze I	Triceps Brachii	Men

sion that also coincides with a wealth of ethnographic data (Amiran 1970; Cribb 1991; Gilead 1988; Sherratt 1981).

The MSM data from this Bronze I site exhibit some unique and provocative patterning. In over half of the MSM sites, females' scores exceed males', often significantly so (Table 4.3). This represents an unprecedented inversion with respect to other time periods (Peterson 1994, 1997). This observation suggests that the workload for females relative to males increased during the EBI period. Even considering the relative discrepancies in muscle mass that males and females genetically possess, this pattern plainly documents significantly higher activity levels for females at Bab edh-Dhra.

These unexpectedly dramatic results required verification with independent measures. First, the entire collection was re-analyzed and the results confirmed. Next, several indices of arm robusticity were calculated using humeral mid-shaft diameter (Fig. 4.5) and least circumference (Fig. 4.6). Both measurements showed that the degree of sexual dimorphism decreased dramatically over time for the Bab edh-Dhra population. Females and males became less sexually dimorphic, due to the increased robusticity of the females. I suggest that drastically different activity regimes for males and for females may explain some of that convergence.

But what activities were females doing with such a vengeance? There are no clear activity reconstructions that match the observed muscle patterning among females (Peterson 1994). Bab edh-Dhra's adult females have fewer and less pronounced asymmetries than their male counterparts, which suggests that at least some of the demanding activities involved both arms.

A number of the high female MSM scores were associated with muscles

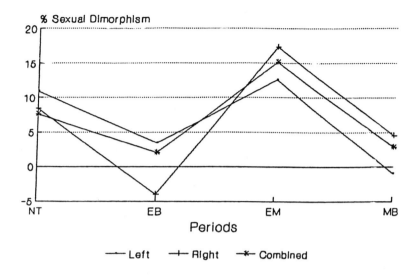

Figure 4.5. Percent sexual dimorphism in humerus mid-shaft diameter. The three lines differentiate between the right and left sides of the body and also show the combined score. The time periods noted are Natufian (NT), Early Bronze (EB), Early Bronze-Middle Bronze (EM), and Middle Bronze (MB).

that are active in extension and flexion of the forearm. And clearly there are many activities that require this type of movement: churning, grinding, and milking to name but a few. But marks representing the use of muscles stabilizing the shoulder and supinating the forearm — downward blows executed with some force — scored high for MSM development among females. These types of marks might be made by a variety of activities including chopping, harvesting, and tilling. In fact, female muscle patterning observed in the skeletal sample is consistent with a wide range of activities that we expect to have been a part of daily farm life. The lack of resolution in the MSM data may reflect that females continued to be active in both agricultural production and processing or, alternatively, it may reflect the problem of equifinality.

To specify that females were shifting their productive capabilities from the agricultural realm to the processing realm seems premature. Given the patterning observed for male remains, it is tempting to speculate that females maintained an active role in both spheres. However, it is also true that agriculture may have been practiced in a more opportunistic, limited fashion by the inhabitants of Bab edh-Dhra. Excavators have argued that during the initial period of EBI occupation, groups may have visited the site as part of a regular transhumant pattern. This conclusion is based

Periods

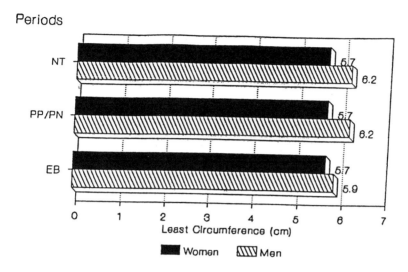

Figure 4.6. Temporal differences in sexual dimorphism in the least circumference of humeral shafts. The time periods noted are Early Bronze (EB), Pre-Pottery Neolithic and Pottery Neolithic (PP/PN), and Natufian (NT).

primarily on evidence for secondary, disarticulated "bundle" burials dating to this time period (Frolich and Ortner 1982; Ortner 1981; Rast 1981; Schaub and Rast 1984).

The next stage of MSM analyses for the Bab edh-Dhra population will focus on several more general monitors of sexual task differentiation: (1) identifying and characterizing activity clusters and (2) assessing relative task homogeneity/heterogeneity and generalization/specialization among aggregate male and female populations. In addition, radiographic evidence of cross-sections of humeri can provide independent data relevant to overall levels of stress on the upper arm. These should provide some additional insight into the structure of sexual labor divisions at EBI Bab edh-Dhra.

Conclusion

The methods and analytical strategies for MSM, though still being refined, have a productive role to play in "regendering" the past. These data can be used to identify sexual task differentiation, which is a preliminary stage in addressing a range of topics concerning gender roles and status.

Attempts to use MSM data benefit from a realistic view of their level of resolution, which is often not amenable to specific activity reconstruction. Integrating MSM data with bioarchaeological analyses of degenerative conditions, long bone structure (such as cortical thickness and diaphyseal dimensions) and other skeletal monitors of activity strengthens its potential for cultural inference.

Acknowledgments

I am obliged to Geoffrey Clark, Steven Falconer, Diane Hawkey, Charles Redman, John Robb, Katherine Spielmann, and Norman Sullivan for their help in various capacities with this research. In addition, thanks are extended to Donald J. Ortner and Bruno Frolich (Smithsonian Institution), who provided access and permission to analyze the Bab edh-Dhra collection. Costs associated with travel were defrayed by awards from the National Science Foundation (grant no. 9302853) and Arizona State University.

Chapter 5
Reconstructing the Lives of South Etruscan Women

Marshall Joseph Becker

Studies of women in the Classical world have long focused on their images and roles as depicted on works of art and on social relations as inferred from surviving texts (Fantham et al. 1995). Relatively new is the use of cultural models provided by anthropology in the interpretation of artistic and textual depictions of women. Similarly, the application of techniques from physical anthropology to identify the sex of skeletal remains and to investigate gender differences in health and disease incidence has only recently become another means by which we can learn more about the lives and status of these ancient women. Combining these approaches enables us to understand more clearly details in the lives of women in antiquity and to differentiate among the varieties of cultures in which they lived.

In the past decade, comparative studies of all the known ancient gold dental appliances together with discoveries in physical anthropology, archaeology, ancient literature, and social anthropology have enabled us to reexamine and better understand the functions of these appliances and what roles they played in the lives of South Etruscan women, as well as in the dynamics of change during the period of Romanization. These varied results, and the means by which they were achieved, are the focus of this chapter.

References in the Classical literature to gold dental appliances were well known long before the first actual example was recovered from an archaeological context. Toward the end of the eighteenth century a gold appliance was described (Böttiger 1797), but its origin remains unknown. Etruscan goldsmithing skills are well documented, but Etruscan primacy in applying these arts to "dentistry" has remained almost unknown. More than 2,600 years ago, skilled Etruscan goldworkers applied their talents in fashioning complex dental appliances. Two sets of skills were needed to make these pontics: a knowledge of goldsmithing and knowledge of the teeth around which an appliance was fitted.

Systematic mining of Etruscan tombs at the end of the nineteenth century revealed most of the known examples of ancient appliances. Since 1885, an extensive literature has emerged dealing with the score of ancient dental appliances, which exhibit an amazing variety of shapes and sizes (Becker ms. b). Recent evidence indicates that the earliest examples date from the seventh century B.C.E. (Waarsenburg 1994). While often cited by archaeologists, these ancient prostheses tend to be a subject more frequently noted by dental or medical historians. Aside from the serious efforts of Clawson (1934) and Johnstone (1932a, b), no detailed descriptions of any examples appeared before 1992. Previous descriptions of the prostheses were generally poor, contributing to the numerous errors that fill the literature (Becker, in press b). Without examining these appliances in detail, and in many cases studying only copies of the originals, several scholars generated "inventories" (Deneffe 1899, Sudhoff 1926, Casotti 1947). Tabanelli (1963) attempted a true catalogue (see also Emptoz 1987), but not until the recent review by Bliquez (1996) do we find specific information regarding the history of these prostheses in addition to many of the best available photographs of them.

These various difficulties can be remedied only by detailed study of the appliances themselves, careful study of the dental and skeletal materials found in association with these prostheses, plus reviews of the limited surviving field data (Becker ms. b). Because archaeological data relating to most of these prostheses are nearly nonexistent (see Cozza and Pasqui 1981; Waarsenburg 1994), the literary evidence is of great importance in understanding the cultural context within which these appliances were made and used. The relationship of practitioners of medicine to those who performed dental extractions (Becker, in press c) also helps clarify the gendered social context of their use. The manufacture of dental appliances clearly was a skilled activity of goldsmiths and other crafters, rather than the work of barbers or physicians.

The Use of Dental Appliances in Antiquity

Twenty examples of Etruscan gold dental appliances are known from Italy (cf. Bliquez 1996); an additional example was recovered from excavations at Tanagra in Greece (Becker ms. b). All of the surviving Italian examples have now been examined in detail (Becker 1992a, 1994a–d) with the specific intent of understanding where in the mouth they were placed and inferring their probable function. The relationship of medical practitioners to those who performed dental extractions (Becker, in press c) helps identify the social context within which these appliances were made and used. In addition, the minimal archaeological evidence associated with these pieces was also surveyed to determine if relevant information could be gleaned from notes associated with their recovery.

A brief summary of related history will help place these dental appliances in the context of medical developments in antiquity. The earliest records of dental care appear in Egyptian medical papyri of the seventeenth and sixteenth centuries B.C.E. (see Badre 1986). Guerini (1909: 28) notes that the Egyptians may have decorated teeth with gold after death, but concludes that they produced no dental prostheses before 500 B.C.E. (see also Emptoz [1987:546, Fig. 1] and Becker 1994c).

The first dental prostheses emerge in the Etruscan world in the seventh century B.C.E. (Johnstone 1932b: 448; see also Bliquez 1996 n. 18, citing Hoffmann-Axthelm 1985:28–31, 38–39). By 630 B.C.E. (Becker ms b), a high status resident of ancient Satricum was buried wearing a complex and sophisticated dental appliance. Over the next few hundred years the proliferation of gold prosthetic devices in Etruria is indicated clearly by the number of examples which survive, as well as by the frequency of references to them in Roman texts. These texts (Bliquez 1996) suggest that such appliances were still being made after 200 B.C.E., but no examples of gold bridgework appear to survive from the period of the later Roman Republic or of the Empire. The earliest Near Eastern dental prostheses, made from gold or silver wire, appear in the fifth century B.C.E. (Becker 1995b, 1996; Mesali and Peluso 1985).

Textual and Archaeological Evidence for Dental Extractions

We know about the practice of ancient dental extractions from a considerable literature on this aspect of "medicine," but we do not know how it relates to the "healing professions." In the early nineteenth century, Carabelli had already made a basic search of the Classical authors for information relating to ancient dentistry (Carabelli 1831). Heyne (1924) wrote a dissertation focusing on dentists and dentistry in the Classical literature. However, many authors, focusing on the early Greek texts and the Latin translations which followed, underestimate just how much Roman medicine had been influenced by the Etruscan tradition in surgery and dentistry (Tabanelli 1963:74–89) and the possible influences of Egyptian and Phoenician knowledge (Saunders 1963).

Medicine in ancient Rome had reached a high degree of sophistication by the second century B.C.E. Almost all aspects of general dentistry as it is now known, with the exception of tooth repair, seem to have become common medical knowledge by the Early Imperial period. The early development of dental bridgework, but not orthodonture, has a history which can be verified by archaeology to at least 630 B.C.E. and, therefore, may be presumed to have had its origins at an even earlier date.

Skilled practitioners of dental extractions are known from the literature to have been active by at least 500 B.C.E., and probably hundreds of years before. The proper removal of a tooth is a very skilled operation. Any bit of root remaining within the jaw after an unsuccessful extraction prevents proper healing and can have fatal consequences, a fact that ancient professional dentists knew quite well. The use of scaling instruments or specialized blades for cutting the gum and bone surrounding the tooth to expose and loosen the root, and to get a better grip with an instrument, was common by the first century B.C.E. (see Jackson 1990). Indirect evidence for the practice of tooth extraction in antiquity derives from references to dentists on tombstones, or the occasional depiction of what some scholars believe may be a dental forceps (Lanciani 1892:353).

Only one archaeological site provides unequivocal evidence for the "professional" practice of tooth extraction in antiquity. Excavations by a Danish team, as part of an international program coordinated by Dr. Irene Iacopi (Archaeological Superintendent for the Roman Forum), focused on the large Temple of Castor and Pollux in the Forum Romanum. These Danish excavations revealed an important series of small shops, or tabernae, built into the main temple platform and main stairway of the temple (see also Strong and Ward-Perkins 1962:25). One of these tabernae yielded large numbers of human teeth, indicating that dental extractions were one aspect of the trade conducted there (Nielsen and Zahle 1987; Guldager and Slej 1986:33; Guldager 1990; Poulsen 1992:56; Nielsen 1992:109–111). This shop provides the best archaeological evidence for dental extractions known from the ancient world. The effectively extracted diseased teeth found there demonstrate that dentistry was associated with the pharmaceutical aspect of the medical trades.

Textual Evidence for the Function of Dental Appliances

Several ancient sources refer specifically to the use of dental appliances, the preservation of loose teeth, or the replacement of missing teeth (Bliquez 1996; Becker ms. b). The section of the Hippocratic texts generally identified as "Dentition" as well as others (Hippocrates 1923, vol. 2:322–329; Jones 1946, 1953), however, provide no basic information on dentistry other than the references to the "wiring" of loose teeth. In fact, "Dentition" is not an independent text at all, but quite clearly an early scribal error (Hippocrates 1923, vol. 2:317–319) that relocated this brief section from *Aphorisms* 3 to a place between sections 25 (teething) and 26 (children's tonsils: see Hippocrates 1931, vol. 4:131).

Hippocrates (1928, vol. 3:258–265, *On Joints* 32–34) noted that teeth displaced or loosened through an injury to the jaw could be braced with gold [wire or bands?] or thread [fiber or gold?] until they were re-established or firmly fixed in place. Martial recorded that various materials were used in the replacements for missing teeth. Commonly employed were bone or ivory, and even the tooth of an ox. Pine and boxwood, often claimed (but never documented) to have been used for the dentures of President George Washington, are also said to have been used by the Romans (see Bliquez 1996: Text 10).

Loose teeth are a consequence of poor dental hygiene, of dental disease, or of trauma. Some appliances, the simple band type, can indeed help to stabilize teeth loosened by a blow or by periodontal disease. While most of the known dental prostheses appear to be cosmetic, the simple band variety probably could and did serve to hold in place teeth that were loosened by a blow or by disease. However, the possibility that such simple bands may have been purely ornamental cannot be discounted. More elaborate appliances, including dental pontics or bridges, include one or more false teeth. Even these cosmetic appliances, designed to fill the gap left by lost teeth, would serve to maintain the remaining teeth in their correct places. This would ensure continued proper articulation of the teeth and their continued efficient function, one of the principal goals of modern orthodontistry.

An Example of a Dental Pontic: The Copenhagen Appliance

The gold dental appliance in the Danish National Museum, Copenhagen (Fig. 5.1) is now the best described ancient pontic (Becker 1992a, 1994b, 1995a). This piece, one of four types of Etruscan appliances, is a good example of the ring-constructed variety, using a complex variation of the simple band technique (cf. Becker 1996). The Copenhagen specimen provides evidence for comparative dental wear and tooth size that enables us to ascertain that this pontic was worn by a female (Table 5.1), whose age was thirty to fifty years at death.

The Copenhagen appliance was made from three small, separate and seamless gold rings, or "loops," that have been cold-welded in a series. Three separate straps or bands were fashioned into loops, each to surround either a sound "anchor" tooth and the false tooth. The Copenhagen appliance was meant to be worn in the upper jaw of an adult female. The lateral loops were fitted over the upper left central incisor (1I) and the right lateral incisor (I2). Each of the loops is seamless, having been formed by drawing out a ring from a solid piece of gold rather than by making a loop from a strip of gold. These three loops, each custom-designed to fit one dental element, are joined at their adjacent

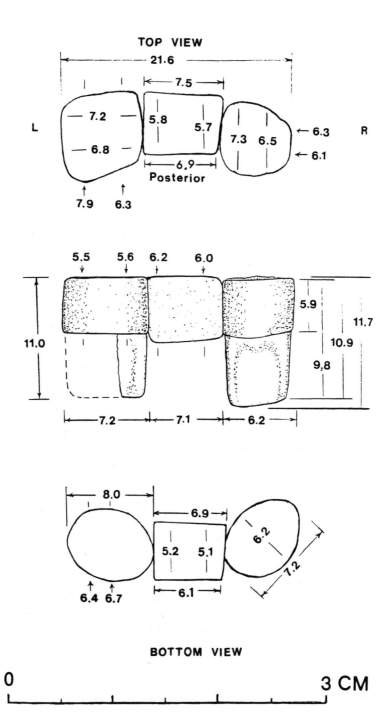

Figure 5.1. Location of measurements taken on the Copenhagen dental pontic (original in the Danish National Museum, Copenhagen; line drawing by the author).

Table 5.1 The Copenhagen Dental Appliance: Odontometric Data

	I2		*I1*		*I1*		*2I*	
	M-D[a]	*B-L*	*M-D*[a]	*B-L*	*M-D*[a]	*B-L*	*M-D*[a]	*B-L*
Orvieto/CPN	6.1	7.1	7.2	5.6	7.2	7.1	—	—
Valsiarosa	6.0	6.0	7.5	6.1	7.7	6.1	6.1	6.0
Bruschi III	7.2	6.9	6.1	5.9	5.3	5.3[b]	(7.9)	(4.5)
Liverpool I	?	?	6.2	7.2	6.9	7.5	?	?
Liverpool II	5.5[b]	—	7.0[b]	—	[8.7[c]]	[—]	—	—

[ ] Dimensions of "false" tooth.
( ) Bent and distorted band.
[a] Only the M-D length is important as an indicator of the space to be filled by the false tooth, presumably to M-D length of the tooth removed.
[b] Estimated.
[c] Appears not to be the original tooth in this appliance.

surfaces by invisible cold welds. The lateral loops were curved in such a way as to conform to the base of each dental crown, with specific fitting done after the false tooth had been set in place and the appliance was ready to be inserted.

While the lateral loops were designed to surround the curves of the natural teeth, the central band made to hold the artificial right central incisor (I1) has been bent into a sharply rectangular "box" to prevent the replacement tooth (of ivory or bone) from slipping in its collar. The false tooth set into this "box" would have been a "crown" only, with its upper and exposed portion carved to mimic the tooth that it replaced. The lower part or base of the false tooth would have been square-cut to fit into the "box" where the angular shape would prevent it from slipping in its fitted collar. No rivet (pin) is needed since the false tooth was held in place the way a gemstone is fixed in a setting. A small band was made and then fitted with the false tooth in the same fashion that a goldsmith would make any bezel setting. The rectangular setting would prevent rotation and facilitate a good fit, then the false tooth would be secured in place by pressing the gold tightly. With the lateral loops attached, the bridge is completed and has a design remarkably similar to modern examples. The bridge was worn by fitting the lateral bands around living teeth using pressure to mold the extremely pure, and therefore soft, gold band securely around them. This appliance was meant to be a permanent fixture.

Gendered Use of Dental Appliances

The conclusion that the Copenhagen appliance and similar appliances were worn by women comes from evidence of the size of the teeth that would have been included in such an appliance and the position of the pontic within the mouth. The gendered use of such pontics helps us understand the social status and role of women in this society.

Evidence from Appliance Size

That the use of these appliances was limited to Etruscan women is indicated by direct measurement of the surviving teeth or of the gold rings of the appliance that surrounded these teeth, reflecting their actual dimensions (see Table 5.1). The long history of odontometric research indicating sexual dimorphism (Goose 1963) has been brilliantly surveyed by Kieser (1990:65–70). The field studies of Ditch and Rose (1972) first demonstrated that dental size alone can be used to correctly evaluate sex in 93 percent of available examples. Their findings have been duplicated for a central Italian population of the first millennium B.C.E. (Becker and Salvadei 1992). While incisors generally demonstrate the least metric variability, Becker and Salvadei (ms. a) find that averages for the central incisor diverge between males (L=8.91 mm; R=9.04 mm) and females (L=8.26 mm; R=8.29 mm) in a central Italic population that was contemporary with the Etruscans.

The original research on the Copenhagen appliance provided only a suggestion that it might have been worn by a female. Subsequently, all of the known appliances measured have provided consistent evidence that they were worn by women. This conclusion can be inferred through comparison of the measurements with newly available anthropometric data from central Italy that provide evidence for gender differences in tooth size (Becker and Salvadei 1992). These data were correlated with gender as defined by associated tomb goods (Becker and Salvadei 1992:59–64, 113). Sexual dimorphism in tooth size also has been tested with a large sample of dental data from the south Etruscan city of Tarquinia (Becker 1990, 1993, ms. c), a site from which the greatest concentration of these appliances has been recorded.

Pontics with long bands that girdled several teeth do not reveal clear metric evidence for gender. However, those in which individual teeth were encircled by gold rings can provide measurements of tooth size, even in those instances where the actual teeth are not available (Becker ms. a). In addition to this odontometric data, which directly indicates that all of these appliances were worn by women, the limited archaeological data for the Satricum appliance (Waarsenburg 1994, cf. Becker 1994d) as well as the Valsiarosa appliance (Cozza and Pasqui 1981; Becker 1994a: 81–85) indicate that both of these people were adult females (see also Becker, in press a, b). These pontics also include gold bands, possibly used to stabilize loose teeth or, in some cases, worn as purely decorative status indicators.

Geographic Distribution of the Appliances

The evidence also suggests that the use of these appliances was not a cultural custom known throughout the Etruscan realm (see Becker 1992b). A distribution map of ancient dental appliances (Becker ms. b) demonstrates that this technology was concentrated in South Etruria. Unless there were radically different mortuary patterns in Central and Northern Etruria that might involve the removal of such appliances from the deceased, we must conclude that this technology was a part of the ornamentation used by women in South Etruria only. The few examples found beyond the borders of this specific zone of ancient Etruria can be explained by two factors relating to the movement of the Etruscan women wearing these appliances. These particular women may have moved beyond their native territories through high-status marriage alliances made between upper-class Etruscan mercantile families and foreign trading partners, or these women may have accompanied their Etruscan husbands beyond their homeland while the men were conducting business.

Gender and the Greek Connection

The discovery of an Etruscan style gold dental appliance at Tanagra in Greece can now be understood in terms that more specifically relate to ancient trade and social behaviors. The presence of this typically Etruscan artifact reinforces the hypothesis that the people from this Greek city had trade relations, or at least imported some artifacts, from Etruria. Assuming that the wearer of this appliance was actually present at Tanagra indicates that Etruscan people, as well as artifacts, were probably resident at the site. The linkage of these appliances with females only reinforces the idea that ancient, and not so ancient, trade was facilitated by marriage alliances (Buchner and Ridgway 1993). The discovery that these appliances were only a South Etruscan phenomenon helps us to locate the most probable origin for the woman whom I believe to have worn this ancient appliance, in life and in death.

Tooth Evulsion, Etruscan Gender Roles, and South Etruscan Pontics

After eight years of detailed studies, a consistent theme emerged regarding where these ancient pontics were placed in the mouth. Almost invariably they were designed to replace the upper central incisors of the women who wore them. However, during the 1980s, studies of the entire skeletal population at Tarquinia in South Etruria (Becker 1990, 1993, ms. c) revealed that the incisors would normally be the *last* teeth to be lost by old adults, being the most common teeth still in place at death. Women under sixty years of age almost never lost their incisors, and the more common early loss of the flanking teeth would make it impossible to wear an appliance. Therefore, the probability of an adult woman having lost one or both upper central incisors by natural means and being able to wear a pontic is extraordinarily low.

Leprosy is one disease causing early loss of upper central incisors and was considered as an alternate possible reason for the absence of these teeth. However, no evidence of this disease has been found in the surviving skeletal remains. Even if we posit that the social relations and proximity between Etruscan males and females generated unusually high levels of violence (cf. Robb 1997), the skeletal evidence demonstrates that these women did not lose incisors in the process. Loss due to violence or abuse would be detectable in the skeletal record; violent abuse is expected to result in loss of the left front teeth (since most males would have been right handed). In fact, for the women in this study, where a single tooth is replaced, it invariably is a *right* central incisor. It is also unlikely that loss of one tooth can be attributed to some task-specific activity.

Since use of pontics would require the deliberate removal of these incisors, one must infer that healthy teeth were removed in a process anthropologically documented from around the world and referred to as "tooth evulsion" (Becker 1995b). To date I know of no reference to tooth evulsion from the Classical world, nor of any possible examples from existing skeletal remains. Nevertheless, the evidence associated with Etruscan dental appliances clearly points to the deliberate removal of one or both upper central incisors among high-status Etruscan females expressly for the purpose of wearing a dental pontic.

That some of these deliberately removed teeth may have been "recycled," or used to serve as the "false" teeth in a dental pontic would solve the problem of size and color matches (Becker 1995b). In cases where damage to the extracted tooth was extensive, a replacement tooth would have been required.

South Etruscan Gender Roles and Eating Customs

This gendered use of dental appliances can be related to other Etruscan customs noted in the ancient texts. Several Roman commentaries indicate that Etruscan husbands and wives dined together in public, reclining together in their public life as they intended to lie together in death. Etruscan gender relationships thus differed from those of both Romans and Greeks, who practiced "gender avoidance" while eating and in other contexts. This "unusual" Etruscan social behavior generated considerable commentary from contemporary writers because it was perceived to be an abhorrent custom. Since polite Etruscan women dined together with men in public, their appearance provided an important reflection of family status. Gold dental appliances, like gold jewelry in general, provided an important display of wealth. The Etruscan use of decorative dental appliances disappeared (at least among the elite) as the Etruscan chiefdoms were absorbed into the Roman state during the first century B.C.E. in a process parallel to the demise of written Etruscan.

Makers of Pontics: Neither Dentists nor Physicians

The question of who made these prosthetic devices has been adequately answered by Bliquez and others (Guerini 1909:102; Hoffman-Axthelm 1985:30n). They conclude that goldsmiths, ivory carvers, and other artisans fabricated these appliances. I suggest that the makers fitted or applied these devices as a branch of cosmetology, as suggested by evidence from the Roman Forum. These professionals were independent of dentists, who did extractions, or physicians, who prescribed treatments for diseases of the mouth. It is also possible that these specialists, who made and fit women with dental pontics, were themselves women.

A brief review of the literature as it relates to dental practitioners and appliances is provided by Brown (1936) and Bliquez (1996). The earliest contemporary reference to a "dentist" may have been made about 409 or 408 B.C.E. by Aristophanes (Deneffe 1899: 10). The status of Roman dentists (tooth pullers?), possibly even lower than that of physicians, has often been discussed. Lanciani's (1892:353) note of the discovery in 1864 of the tombstone of the dentist Victorinus (or Celerinus), decorated with an instrument which may be a dental forceps, also provided an early clue as to means by which the status of some of these ancient practitioners could be inferred. Lanciani also noted the name of a general surgeon as well as an "Alexander" who is shown with a pair of pliers. This reference to a general surgeon appears to have led Jackson (1988: 119) to infer that extractions were performed by physicians and surgeons, but the data now suggest that this would have been the exception rather than the rule. Jackson (1988), in a revision of an earlier paper, suggests that by 100 B.C.E. Romans were taking over these medical trades from Greek immigrants (or their descendants?) or that Greek families were assuming Roman names. The status of these "new professionals" may have improved during this time.

Women working as "doctors" and/or "physicians" are noted in ancient Rome, in categories clearly distinct from midwives (Lefkowitz and Fant 1982:161–163). However, the specific activities that were part of the practices of these women, and of their male colleagues, remains unknown. Treggiari's (1978:162–164) sweeping examination of the activities and the status of laborers in ancient Rome, focusing on jobs described as "common" and "sordid" by the upper class, identified 225 specialized trades. Citing Cicero, Treggiari notes that numerous occupations were considered unsuitable for a free person. These included unskilled manual workers, retail traders, workshop employees and people providing pleasure (entertainers, food sellers, perfumers), all of whom operated from workshops (*officina*) of shops or inns (*tabernae*). Obviously people without formal establishments, such as street venders and some prostitutes, had even lower status.

Treggiari (1980:48) infers a low social status for people in the category of *opifices*, which included those who practiced manual arts (writing, building, healing) and probably also included physicians. She concludes that the surgeons and dentists, who were involved with blood and gore, would have occupied the lower end of this bottom end of the social scale. Treggiari (1979:82, n11) suggests that some of the goldsmiths of the period may have been women. It is therefore possible that women goldsmiths also assumed importance in the intimate contact needed for the fitting of dental appliances in the mouths of Etruscan women.

Summary

Emerging states in Etruria rarely employed writing for more than ritual and related religious purposes. Our knowledge of the details of Etruscan medicine and dentistry is therefore based on Roman writers, who incorporated into their texts what they knew of the medical and dental oral traditions of both the Etruscans and the Greeks. Similarly, our knowledge of the status of women in Etruscan society has depended to a great degree on the interpretation of artistic depictions (e.g., tomb paintings) and on a few references to the status of Etruscan women that appear in the Roman literature.

The study of dental pontics is thus important in that it represents another line of evidence that can be used to study gender roles and social relations in antiquity. This study has yielded three specific conclusions that have larger implications for our understanding of ancient Etruscan society. First, the metrical evidence of the available sample of dental pontics suggests that only women wore these appliances in ancient Etruria. Second, these dental pontics differed in function from another kind of dental appliance: the gold bands that have no false teeth attached. It appears that the long gold bands were intended to prevent the movement or loss of teeth loosened by a blow or by periodontal disease. The dental pontics considered in this study, in contrast, were not used to replace teeth that had been lost as a result of disease or injury. Rather, they represent decorative replacements for teeth that were deliberately removed (tooth evulsion). Third, the geographic distribution of these decorative dental pontics suggests that their use was limited to South Etruria.

The social relations between Etruscan women and men, and the power and prestige of women in various Etruscan cities, is only now becoming the subject of archaeological investigations (e.g., Nelson 1997). A similar approach to the study of gender relations and inequality has been used by Moss (1996, 1998) in a study of labrets among the Native Americans of the Pacific Northwest coast. In this area, labrets, decorative ornaments that were worn through incisions in the lips or cheeks, were commonly used as status indicators. Moss (1996, 1998) has found that the size of the labret, and the material from which it was formed, were particularly important in this system of status categories. In addition, even when the actual ornament is not present, its use by a person during life is indicated by the pattern of wear on the teeth, which also records the location of the device on the face and the size of the ornament (Moss 1996, 1998). This study of Etruscan pontics and Moss' recent work on labrets provide examples of how the use of dental appliances and ornaments can be identified and how the study of these objects can contribute to our understanding of the larger issues of social status and gender roles.

Acknowledgments

My most sincere thanks to Alison Rautman for her kind invitation to develop this paper for the conference. Thanks also are due to a great number of people who facilitated the individual studies of these Etruscan dental appliances at museums throughout Europe, to Dr. Mary Stieber for text translations, and to George Claghorn, Marianna Russo, and Ann Marie Smith for editorial and technical support. Special thanks are due Lawrence Bliquez for sharing his extensive data during all phases of this research. Funding for the first part of this research was provided by a series of small travel awards from the College of Arts and Sciences at West Chester University. The support of Douglas McConatha, Martin Murphy, Lynn Ruscheinsky, and Paul Stoller in particular is gratefully acknowledged. Thanks also are due to Adele Re' and many other Italian colleagues for their assistance at various points in these studies.

Chapter 6
Gender in Inuit Burial Practices

Barbara A. Crass

Arctic hunter-gatherer societies such as the Inuit are often described as having a strongly gendered division of labor (Burch 1988; Riches 1982; Watanabe 1968). This economic interdependency is, however, often portrayed in excessively simplistic terms, with men hunting and women staying home to process meat and tend the house and children. The actual relationship between economic organization and gender differentiation, as in any society, is considerably more complex. In Euro-American culture, for example, economic tasks are no longer strictly differentiated by sex, yet our names are quite gender-specific, and many activities are still viewed as "unmanly" or "unladylike." In contrast, in a hunting society such as the Inuit, where we might expect a high degree of differentiation in economic sex roles, there is little if any gender differentiation in personal names.

A simplistic man-the-hunter and woman-the-gatherer model obviously does not necessarily correlate with gender differentiation in other contexts, or, in fact, with actual performance of economic activities. Analysis of burial context and grave goods among Inuit burials shows that this lack of strong differentiation is also manifest in burial treatment. Apparently, in Inuit society, beliefs about the afterlife and about the economic complementarity of men and women are expressed in language and action as well as in the treatment of the dead.

Gender Differentiation in Inuit Society

The lack of strong gender differentiation seen in many aspects of Inuit society may stem in part from Inuit conceptions of the afterlife and the continued role of the dead among the living. In Inuit society, names are seen as holding part of a person's essence, or *inua*, which exists apart from that person's gender identity. When a newborn is given the name of a recently deceased relative or community member, the Inuit believe that the child acquires some of the wisdom, skills, and characteristics of the deceased, regardless of the deceased person's biological sex. In essence, the child becomes a living representative of the dead person (Weyer 1932:293). This practice results in the child assuming multiple roles and relationships with members of the community, regardless of the child's sex or age.

As one example, Stefansson knew an Inuit couple who had a seven-year-old son, "whose father called him stepmother and whose mother called him aunt, for those were their respective relationships to the woman whose soul was the boy's guardian" (1926:401). The use of relationship terms, such as "aunt" instead of "son," indicate that the nature of the relationship is more important than the sex of the individual (Giffen 1930:58). The lack of pronouns for specifying gender in Eskimo[1] languages (Barker 1995; Birket-Smith 1928; Fortescue 1984) is, thus, not surprising since individual people can have multiple gender identities. This idea that a person could have multiple gender identities, with no one of these identities paramount in importance, results in a lack of attention to the gender of English pronouns among bilingual speakers. For example, when speaking English, the Inuit commonly substitute "he" for "she" and vice versa (Barker 1995:90).

This lack of strong gender differentiation in Inuit society, demonstrated in the realm of language and personal names, is also apparent in people's activities. Even economic activities that one might suppose would be more strictly differentiated by sex are not assigned to mutually exclusive gender categories. A careful reading of early ethnographies reveals that activities such as hunting and domestic tasks are not ascribed solely to members of one sex. For example, Diamond Jenness noted that the division of labor in Inuit society was fluid and flexible. Despite a general attribution of domestic tasks as "women's work," he personally knew of a man who lived alone, hunted successfully, and managed to cook and mend his clothes (1957:140). He also met women who performed "men's work": they shot birds, hunted caribou with the men, and even stalked seals on the ice. Perhaps more important, Jenness commented, "The Eskimos seemed to consider this all natural" (1957:177).

Furthermore, activities that were commonly considered to be "men's work" or "women's work" were not ranked in terms of relative worth. For example, Patrick H. Ray, a member of the Point Barrow Expedition in 1885, reported: "The women as a rule seem to have an equal voice in the direction of affairs, when once admitted to the position of wife, and in each village there are a number of old women who are treated with the greatest consideration by all, they being credited with wonderful powers of divination, and are consulted in all important affairs. . . . The wife is invariably consulted when any trade is to be made, and the husband never thinks of closing a bargain of any importance without her consent" (1988:xcvi–xcvii).

These and other observations suggest that our models of the sexual division of labor among hunter-gatherers need revision. Native and non-native scholars have recently described the traditional roles of men and women in Inuit society not as a sexual division of labor but as two complementary forms of one function. This complementarity is expressed in a Yupik man's statement that "the man's success as a hunter was just as much her [the woman's] responsibility. They made up a team, complemented each other, and were very much equal in standing" (Kawagley 1995:20). Barbara Bodenhorn (1990) further describes the interdependent and complementary roles that an Inuit husband and wife must perform in order to have a successful hunt. According to her informants, the husband goes out and kills the game, but the wife is the one who attracts the game. The animals are pleased by the carefully sewn clothing that she makes for the hunter and are attracted to the woman's generosity and attention to ritual responsibilities. The animal is thus considered to give itself to the wife, even though the husband strikes the fatal blow.

Given the lack of strong gender differentiation in these linguistic, economic, and political realms, it seems likely that Inuit burial assemblages would also lack strong gender differentiation. Inuit burials are generally of two types: underground burials and burials in cairns. Burials are also often found with grave goods. This chapter examines the relationships between burial type and grave goods and the sex of the skeletal remains.

The Archaeological Data

In this study, only sites where the human remains were sexed by a physical anthropologist or other trained individual were selected. Burials for which the sex assignment was likely or possibly based on grave goods were eliminated. These burials date from the first century A.D. to the late nineteenth century, or within the Thule culture phase (Dumond 1987). Burials that date after the introduction of Christianity into this region were not included in this study.

The sites studied here include Ekwen (Arutiunov and Sergeyev 1975) and Uelen (Arutiunov and Sergeyev 1969) cemeteries from Siberia; the Gamble area of St. Lawrence Island, Alaska (Bandi 1984 and Hofmann-Wyss 1987); Igluligardjuk, Inuksivk, Kamarvik, Kulaituijavik, and Silumiut on Chesterfield Inlet, Canada (McCartney 1971 and Merbs 1964, 1967, 1968); Niutang and Tasioya on Baffin Island (Salter 1984) and Southampton Island, Canada (Collins 1955, Collins and Emerson 1954; Emerson 1954). From each of these sites (Fig. 6.1), all of the burials

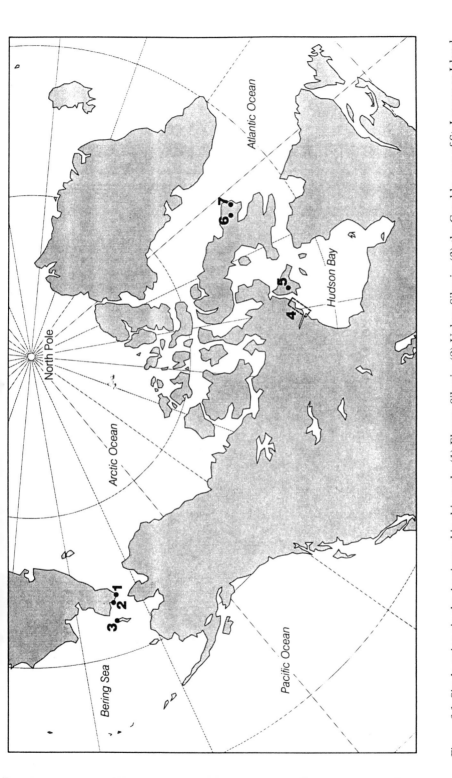

Figure 6.1. Site locations in the Arctic used in this study: (1) Ekwen, Siberia; (2) Uelen, Siberia; (3) the Gamble area of St. Lawrence Island, Alaska; (4) Igluligardjuk, Inuksivk, Kamarvik, Kulaitujavik, and Silumiut on Chesterfield Inlet, Canada; (5) Southampton Island, Canada; (6) Tasioya, Baffin Island, Canada; and (7) Niutang, Baffin Island, Canada (map drawn by the author).

containing sexed human remains were selected. Grave goods and skeletal orientation were analyzed, although the orientation was not known for all the burials.

The sites neatly divide into two ethnic/geographic groups: Siberian Yupik and Canadian Inuit. The Siberian Yupik lived in Siberia and on St. Lawrence Island in Alaska. The people lived in permanent settlements and used in-ground burials. The Inuit in Eastern Canada were seasonally mobile and buried their dead in above-ground stone cairns.

A total of 496 individuals were included in the study: 248 males and 248 females. Of these 496 individual burials, 326 (65.7 percent) had grave goods (164 males and 162 females). Obviously, the decision to bury someone with or without grave goods was not based on the deceased's sex. Approximately 150 different possible artifacts and materials were studied to see if any sexual differentiation existed. The artifacts represented all classes of goods; they included land and sea hunting items, sled and dog tack, lamps and household goods, sewing and skin processing tools, fishing gear, bird-hunting gear, containers, toys, ceremonial items, jewelry, figurines, and carving tools. Other items found as grave goods included worked bone, antler and ivory, ivory tusks, ochre, metal, soapstone, pyrite, graphite, jade, and quartz crystals. The number of males and females who had these grave goods was tested by the chi square test, with significance set at $p > .025$. Here, the total number of each item in any particular burial was not considered; rather, each grave was scored as having or not having an item.

Out of 150 possible burial items, only thirteen items showed any significant association with the sex of the individual: ten items were consistently associated with males and three items with females (Table 6.1). Although hunting items were all associated with males, not all male burials had hunting items, and only one hunting tool, a seal scratcher, was found exclusively with males (four males, no females). The only other item found exclusively in burials of one sex was a sinew twister (no males, two females). Only these two items were found solely in burials of one sex. All the other items and materials were represented with both males and females.

Although these data show that there were few differences in the types of burial goods included in male and female burials, there were some gender differences in the number of burial goods, particularly among the cairn burials. For burials in cairns, the mean number of grave goods was 2.5 per female cairn and 7.6 per male cairn. Four male cairns were exceptionally rich, however, containing 59, 73, 76, and 96 grave goods, respectively. If these 4 cairns containing 59 or more grave goods are omitted from analysis, the mean number of goods in a male cairn burial is 3.4 items. It thus appears that only a slightly greater number of grave

Table 6.1 Significant Items Found with Male and Female Burials

	Male	Female	Chi-square Significance
Harpoon head	60	36	>.01
Arrowheads	28	11	>.01
Drill parts	26	12	>.025
Adze	22	11	>.025
Socket piece	21	9	>.025
Ice probe	21	9	>.025
Shaft	17	6	>.025
Winged object	15	4	>.01
Wound pin	9	2	>.025
Ulu	14	29	>.025
Mattock	12	29	>.01
Needle	11	24	>.025
Antler	38	19	>.01

goods were generally placed in male cairns, although some males were apparently treated differently. A possible explanation for the male cairns with exceptional numbers of grave goods may be that these individuals had a higher status (such as shaman or whaling captain).

In-ground burials yielded greater numbers of items in both male and female graves, but the distribution of these goods by sex was more nearly equal. The mean number of grave goods in in-ground graves was 17.9 per female grave and 24.2 per male grave, a result that suggests that male burials in graves had more items. Again, however, several graves were exceptional: one female grave contained 167 items; two male graves contained 61 items; the rest contained 71, 78, 90, 92, 94, 101, 113, 116, and 136 items. If these exceptional graves are ignored, the mean number of items per burial is nearly identical: 16 items in female graves and 15.3 items in male graves.

In-ground graves, therefore, show slightly less differentiation between males and females both in terms of the numbers of items typically found in graves and in the representation of at least one female among the graves with exceptional numbers of items. It is also interesting that the one exceptional female grave had considerably more items that the richest of the exceptional male graves. The large number of burial items, as well as other unusual features of this grave, suggests that this woman may have had a special role during life, perhaps that of a shaman (Arutiunov and Sergeyev 1975).

The different types of burials (cairn and in-ground) are also associated with differences in the orientation of the body. Skeletal orientation in the cairn burials shows a distinct northeast-southwest orientation for male burials: 35 of the 57 males (61 percent) were oriented with the head positioned from north-northeast to east ($p>.001$). The majority of these burials were adult males. This preferred orientation is not as strongly expressed among the females in cairn burials, but chi square tests show that the orientation of females is nonrandom ($p>.025$). Females thus exhibit greater variety in skeletal orientation. In particular, a small number of female cairn burials were oriented with the skull positioned to the west or south-southwest.

Bodies in in-ground graves do not adhere to such a strong pattern of orientation. In addition, little difference is apparent between the male and female graves. However, for neither sex is the orientation of the body completely random ($p>.001$). Apparently, in-ground graves were constructed with less regard to a preferred orientation of the body, or else there were a number of acceptable alternative body orientations, no one of which was strongly preferred.

Inuit Belief and Mortuary Ritual

Some of this observed patterning in mortuary treatment makes sense in terms of Inuit religious beliefs. Early ethnographic data agree that the Inuit had no concept similar to a Judeo-Christian afterworld such as Heaven or Hell, but did believe in an afterlife (Weyer 1932). The afterlife was in another realm: at worst, filled with fewer hardships than life on earth; at best, filled with abundant game and warm, sunny skies. In general, Inuit groups had two afterlife realms, one in the sky and one under the sea or land. The destination of a soul to any one sphere depended as much on the matter of death as on the person's earthly conduct. Those who died a violent death, such as victims of murder, drowning, and hunting accidents, and women who died in childbirth, would go to the Land of the Day, or east. The Land of the Day is a supercelestial realm ruled by the Moon, which according to Inuit mythology is a male figure (Merkur 1991). The realm is filled with sunlight, mountains, rivers, warmth and herds of caribou. In contrast, those who died a nonviolent death would go to the Land of the Sea, or west (Merkur 1991). The Land of the Sea was envisioned as a dark, gloomy, monotonous realm ruled by the Sea Woman who also controls the sea mammals.

The orientation of the body after death would be important in that it would direct the soul to the proper afterlife realm. One of the early ethnographic reports suggests that orientation of burials adhered to this patterning, although several sources describe a more complex system in which the age of the deceased was also an important factor affecting grave orientation (see Lyon 1825:371). Merbs (1996) has recently argued that archaeological cairn burials near Chesterfield Inlet exhibit a preferred orientation that can be attributed to the violent or nonviolent nature of the individual's death.

The data presented in this study supports this proposed differentiation in skeletal orientation for bodies in the cairn burials. In the cairns, both males and females are most commonly oriented with the skull to the north-northeast to east. The majority of the males in this grouping are adult males, the age group at highest risk for a violent death. The women in this grouping are also primarily adults. While women can die violent deaths from drowning, murder, or hunting accidents, the most likely cause of violent death would be childbirth. An equal-sized cluster of adult women deviates from this pattern, with the skull oriented to the west or south-southwest. This group of women would presumably be those who died a nonviolent death.

Inuit mythology and beliefs about the afterlife can also help explain some of the patterned representation of different kinds of objects in the graves. Antler, for example, was found only in male burials. Other valuable material, such as ivory, was found with both males and females. McGhee (1977) has suggested that these items in particular have gendered significance, with ivory and antler symbolizing female and male respectively. The burials in this study did not exhibit such a simple correlation. I suggest that these two materials represent not just one or another sex or sex role, but rather symbolize the economic and social interdependence between men and women.

This suggestion is based on McGhee's (1977) elegant model of the Inuit worldview, in which the environment is centered around a dichotomy between the land and the sea. Taboos, such as the widespread prohibition against cooking caribou and sea mammal meat together, exist to keep separate land and sea mammals. Another example of such a taboo would be the prohibition against working on sealskin clothing during caribou hunts, and conversely, working on caribou clothing while on the sea ice.

Various myths also support this theory. As mentioned earlier, two afterlife realms are known among the Inuit: one on land, ruled by a male and filled with caribou; the other in the sea, ruled by a woman and filled with sea mammals. The myth of the origin of the walrus and caribou describes how during a famine an old woman (or sometimes the Sea Woman) took two pieces of fat and threw one on the water where it turned into a walrus that swam away. The other piece she threw onto the land, where it turned into a caribou and attacked her. She knocked out the caribou's teeth and has disliked caribou ever since (McGhee 1977:147).

In this model, seemingly dichotomous units are actually interdependent units. Thus, the sea and the land are separate, but together represent the world; in the supernatural world, the Moon Man and Sea Woman combined represent the afterlife realms. This interrelationship among seemingly separate and opposite characteristics is also expressed in every-day life: sea animals and land animals together represent food and other crucial resources. Thus, caribou and walrus, or their respective products, antler and ivory, together make human life possible. Similarly, man and woman together, separate but independent, represent a powerful team that can most effectively utilize these resources.

Conclusion

Hunting societies such as the Inuit are sometimes presented as societies with rigid economic sex roles that sharply distinguish male hunters from females who gather plant foods and process the results of male hunting. The ethnographic data presented here, ranging from ideology to reports of actual activity patterns, demonstrate the pervasive inaccuracies in such a simplistic view of this society. Analysis of burials also shows that there are no strongly significant differences in the treatment of males and females after death, whether they are buried in cairns or in below-ground burials. Some of the observed variation in skeletal orientation seen in male and female cairns can be explained not in terms of sex difference, but in terms of the circumstances of the individual's deaths. The orientation of in-ground graves reveals a more complex and yet unexplained pattern.

Inuit myths present a view of males and females being equally power-ful, yet forming an interdependent unit necessary for survival. This worldview seems to have structured actual economic activities, beliefs about male and female economic contributions, and mortuary ritual. Traditional life for Inuit hunter-and-gatherers was filled with uncertainty and risks. A tremendous degree of cooperation was necessary for sur-vival, so sexual differences had to be used advantageously. Unequal treat-ment in any form would only lessen the odds for survival. This principle seems to contribute to the general lack of distinctive mortuary assem-blage for male and female burials in this study.

A comment, made by Bilby in 1923 when discussing female representa-tion in Eskimo folk tales, was more insightful than he had realized: "One of [the tales] might almost point to a feminist movement in the Arctics! [*sic*]" (Bilby 1923:104). Apparently the Inuit female had more equality with males in her society than did American women of the 1920s.

Note

1. The term *Eskimo* is used to denote the Eskimo language family, which in-cludes Inupiaq dialects (spoken in Northern Alaska, Canada and Greenland), Central Yupik (spoken in Southwestern Alaska), and Siberian Yupik (spoken in Siberia and St. Lawrence Island, Alaska).

Chapter 7
The Status of Women in Predynastic Egypt as Revealed Through Mortuary Analysis

Stephen H. Savage

During the past decade considerable research has been focused on gender relationships and gender roles in both historic and prehistoric contexts (e.g., the papers in Gero and Conkey 1991; Walde and Willows 1991). And, although Wylie (1991a:31) has lamented that "there is no counterpart in archaeology to the vibrant traditions of research on women and gender" in other fields of social research, nevertheless, important strides have been taken. Particular themes have been addressed and found amenable to approaches informed by engendered themes. This appears especially true in the prehistoric domain. Conkey and Gero (1991:6) stress that "the tailoring of gender and feminist theories and insights to prehistory has the potential to radically alter extant notions about prehistoric humans and human evolution." They further state that "an engendered past addresses many longstanding concerns of archaeology: the formation of states, trade and exchange, site settlement systems and activity areas, the processes of agriculture, lithic production, food production, pottery, architecture, ancient art — but throws them into new relief" (1991:15).

One of the more fruitful research domains in the past decade has been the role of women in states. Silverblatt (1988:429) believes that feminist anthropology is moving toward new insights concerning this issue, including such central concerns as the role of women in state formation, state subversion, and the construction of social relations. Part of this concern clearly has to do with the origins of women's oppression in states; Engels believed that the overthrow of matrilinearity was "*the world historical defeat of the female sex*" (1972 [1884] 28:120, emphasis in original). Silverblatt stresses, however, that Engels's sweeping generalization has been replaced by approaches that favor specific historical circumstances, in part because such approaches "debunk essentializing categories" (1988:429). Taking a position somewhat between these two views, Lerner (1986) demonstrates how males learned to dominate other males by dominating women's reproductive and productive capacities. She describes a historical process in Mesopotamia in which "male dominance over women and children in the family" became manifest and then institutionalized, with "male dominance over women in society in general" arising as a result (Lerner 1986:239). According to Lerner, this creation of patriarchy in Mesopotamia took place over the course of several centuries. Lerner suggests that the adoption of agriculture may have been the most important factor initiating this process (1986:49) and that the development of patriarchy forms part of a pattern that encompasses the entire Near East, although the historic specifics may have varied from state to state (1986:8).

Lerner's study illuminates several broad themes that deserve exploration in additional historical settings. Pollock, too, sees a broad pattern that differs regionally in its specific details: "The undercutting of women's sources of power seems to be a common strategy and product of the formation of states, although neither the form nor the degree of women's subjugation is uniform from case to case" (Pollock 1991:383).

Silverblatt (1988) also sees patriarchy as a characteristic of states, but differs from Lerner (1986) in locating its origins not in the technological shift with the adoption of agriculture, but rather in the process of centralizing political power during the state development. For example, in Peru, Silverblatt (1988) shows how this centralization of power was accomplished by the formation of gender categories that were then assigned hierarchical value. These categories were justified by a new, male-centered mythology and were accompanied by shifts in the availability of roles for men and women.

The archaeological record of ancient Egypt presents a unique laboratory for examining the establishment of patriarchy, but in a different kind of state system. Egypt represents what was arguably the world's first territorial nation-state, whereas the Mesopotamian situation upon which Lerner focuses most of her attention is clearly an example of the segmentary, or city-state model (see Trigger 1993:8–14). Thus, there may be important differences in the specific circumstances that eventually led to the creation of patriarchy in Egypt. But it is only recently that specific studies have focused on women in ancient Egypt (e.g., Robbins 1993; Watterson 1991). Earlier works (James 1979; Kemp 1983, 1989; Lloyd 1983; O'Connor 1983; Trigger 1983) explored daily life or social relations in Egypt but essentially ignored women.

Lerner's (1986) and Silverblatt's (1988) ideas may be testable with Egyptian data from the Predynastic (c. 4000–3050 B.C.E.) and later periods. If the transition to agriculture acts as a prime mover in the development of patriarchy, we should see a reduction in women's status in Egypt by the early Predynastic period, for agriculture was already the dominant form of subsistence there by the Badarian period, about 5500 B.C.E. (Hassan 1988). However, if Silverblatt's (1988) ideas are extendable to the Egyptian case, it is more likely that we will see ideological shifts signifying the development of patriarchy occurring somewhat later, as the state was consolidated in Egypt during the first two dynasties.

Robbins's (1993) and Watterson's (1991) studies illuminate the richness of the archaeological and historical record in Egypt as it pertains to women, thus providing fresh insights into social relations in Egypt. What they reveal, however, is a sometimes bewildering array of textual and artifactual data from the historic periods. In doing so, these authors define a series of important topics, including the Egyptian attitude toward women, women's social and legal positions, female occupations and professions, health and childbirth, domestic life, women of power, and the like. The data are vast and sometimes contradictory. This contradiction is due in part to the fact that the data come from different time periods and may thus be expected to reflect different social circumstances. In addition, the data are biased in favor of the elite classes (Robbins 1993:17).

The archaeology of the Predynastic period (c. 4000 to 3100 B.C.E.) may shed light on these issues through the analysis of mortuary remains. Many cemeteries have been explored in the past hundred years or so (e.g., Adams 1987; Brunton and Caton-Thompson 1928; Debono and Mortensen 1988; Kroeper 1988; Lythgoe and Dunham 1965; Mond and Meyers 1937; Petrie 1900, 1901a, 1901b, 1902, 1903; Petrie and Quibell 1896) and inform our understanding of the development of patriarchy in ancient Egypt. Of these, some are clearly better resources than others. Many of the cemeteries were excavated nearly a century ago; their materials have been distributed to museums throughout the world, the field notes have often been lost, the publications are descriptive rather than analytical, and demographic data were frequently not recorded. Some excavations, however, were surprisingly "modern" in their data recovery methods. Of these, the Predynastic cemeteries at Armant (Mond and Meyers 1937) and Naga-ed-Dêr (Lythgoe and Dunham 1965) provide the most thorough data. This study will present data from Cemetery N7000 at Naga-ed-Dêr, which will be used to investigate the timing of some aspects of the development of patriarchy in ancient Egypt.

The Status of Women in Predynastic Egypt

Mortuary evidence from the Predynastic may shed light on the status of women in early Egypt. The evidence from Cemetery N7000 at Naga-ed-

Dêr suggests that women were of equal status with men, at least as far as the mortuary ritual was concerned. In addition, women may have had more social roles available to them than they did during later periods. Following a brief discussion of the relevance of mortuary analysis to this inquiry, I present descriptions of the various data domains and summarize the findings.

Mortuary Analysis

The analysis of mortuary populations is thought to provide more information about the organization of a society than any other set of behaviors and, therefore, creates unique opportunities to learn how a given society is structured (Brown 1981; Braun 1981; Chapman and Randsborg 1981; O'Shea 1981, 1984; Saxe 1970; Tainter 1978). Through an analysis of how the archaeological dimensions of space, form, and time are patterned with regard to the biological dimensions of age and sex, an understanding of the social organization of a society can be achieved (O'Shea 1984). The search for information about social organization is essentially a multivariate search for patterns in the archaeological record, as they intersect spatial, formal, temporal, and demographic variables. By examining a number of different "data domains" and observing how they are structured vis-à-vis the sex of the individuals interred, I believe an understanding of the social status of women in the Predynastic may be approached.

The Predynastic Cemetery N7000 at Naga-ed-Dêr

The village of Naga-ed-Dêr (Fig. 7.1, inset) is located on the east bank of the Nile about 160 kilometers north of Luxor, opposite the town of Girga, in what would have been the Thinnite nome during the historic period in Egypt (dynastic Egypt was divided into administrative districts called "nomes") (Butzer 1976). The area around Naga-ed-Dêr is at the center of (and perhaps even represents the "capital" of) one of the "proto-kingdoms" that Kemp (1989) believes existed in upper Egypt prior to the political unification of the country. Thus, it is an extremely important region, and the Predynastic cemetery represents the largest group of burials from this area. Graves in the cemetery range from the end of the Amratian/Nagada I period through the Gerzean/Nagada II, and a few might be dated to the Protodynastic/Nagada III period (Friedman 1981; Savage 1995; also see Kantor 1992 for a discussion of Predynastic chronology). The cemetery was excavated in 1902–3 by Albert Lythgoe, as part of the Hearst Expedition to Egypt (Lythgoe and Dunham 1965). Approximately 883 individuals were discovered in the 635 numbered graves (Podzorski 1990). Most of the grave goods were packed and shipped to

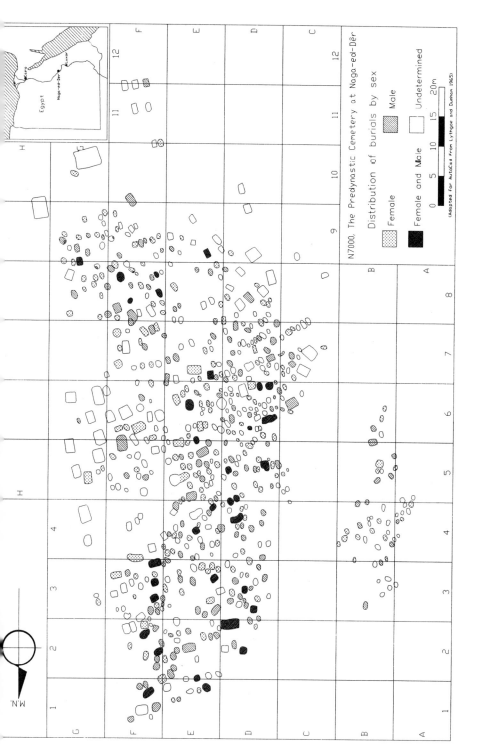

Figure 7.1. The Predynastic cemetery at Naga-ed-Dêr, Egypt. Location of burials, distinguished by sex (drawing by the author).

the Lowie (now P. A. Hearst) Museum of Anthropology at the University of California, Berkeley, where they are still curated. This research has been conducted over the past four years with the curated materials, notes, photographs, and published descriptions (Savage 1995).

This study presents data from a number of different domains, including demographic information, patterns of plundering the corpses, grave architecture (including grave shape, size, and architectural elaboration), ritual equipment placed in the graves, and artifactual data relevant to the assignment of various social roles to the burials (based on presence/absence of different classes of artifacts). Most of these data domains are not significantly associated with the sex of the burial. In most cases, tests for association between different classes of data and the sex of the burial were performed through G-square analysis.[1] A brief discussion of each type of data used is included below, along with a summary of the individual analyses.

Demographic Data from Cemetery N7000

The demographic data used here were recorded in the field by the excavators and compiled mainly from Lythgoe and Dunham (1965). The sex of the burials (and the age at death) was provided mainly by three researchers. Lythgoe, as the excavator, seems to have performed most of this task, assisted by G. E. Smith, a medical doctor associated with the expedition. Smith's notes record specific anatomical information not given by Lythgoe, frequently commenting about the preservation of soft tissue which made sex identification positive. Podzorski (1990) has provided additional age and sex data on skeletal remains housed at the Hearst Museum at Berkeley. Her assignments frequently confirm those of Lythgoe and Smith but sometimes differ; where they differ, I have used her evaluations.

Figure 7.1 illustrates the distribution of burials in Cemetery N7000 by sex. It is immediately clear that the cemetery is not spatially segregated into female and male areas. Burials of both sexes occur in all parts of the cemetery and sometimes occur together in what are probably family-group burials. The burial assignments by sex are used below to test the distribution of other classes of data.

Grave Plundering in Cemetery N7000

Tomb robbing is a practice that has occurred in Egyptian society from the Predynastic to the modern era, but most of the plundering at Cemetery N7000 seems to have taken place in the Predynastic period. Lythgoe suggested that while the Copts (Christianized Egyptians) did "root into the graves to some extent, yet it is certain that not one percent of the disturbances [in the cemetery] was due to them" (Lythgoe and Dunham 1965:96). The burials which the excavators thought were plundered in Dynastic or later times were excluded from this analysis, as were those burials which were likely disturbed by later expansion of grave sites.

Plundering leaves clues about how a body was adorned for burial, even though the specific objects themselves are missing. Damage was observed at specific locations on the body, thus suggesting that specific types of adornment were originally there. For example, a disturbance to the neck is probably indicative of the recovery of a necklace; damage to the waist/ pelvis suggests the corpse was buried with a belt or girdle that attracted the grave robbers. By paying attention to the locations of damage and the number of locations plundered on the bodies, we can determine whether female or male burials were adorned in different ways or to different degrees.

Plundering occurs in different locations on the body, but can be generalized into six primary loci: head, neck, arms and hands, legs and feet, chest, and waist and pelvis. A special notation was made if the body was missing to distinguish between bodies that are completely rifled, but whose bones are still present, from those that were removed from their graves. The locations of plundering and the number of different locations disturbed serve as nominal variables in cross-tabulations by the sex of the body, and significance is assessed through G-square tests.

None of the G-square tests of plundering and sex produced improbable results. Apparently, items of worth were buried with both females and males in Predynastic Egypt in about equal numbers and in about the same places. Neither individual locations, combinations of locations, or the number of locations on the bodies were significantly associated with the sex of the body. Although it is possible that the items themselves might have provided clues to the different status of females and males, their absence renders such a determination impossible.

Grave Architecture

The analysis of grave architecture includes grave size, shape, and architectural elaboration. The floor area of the graves was determined by using the dimensions from Lythgoe's field notes. Grave shape was recorded as circular, oval, sub-rectangular, rectangular, or irregular, based on Lythgoe's map of the cemetery (see Fig. 7.1) and individual grave plans. Only single interment graves in which the sex of the burial was observed are included here.

There are no significant differences in grave shape or floor area between the sexes. A G-square test of grave shape by sex achieved a value of only 1.6 (probability = .45). A T-test for unequal mean floor area also suggests that the means of the two groups are not significantly different (T = -1.08, $p = .28$). Tukey diagrams of grave floor area by sex confirm these results.

Lythgoe and Dunham recorded a number of architectural elements which can be represented as presence/absence variables for each element by grave. The architectural elements include the following: bough and mat roof, twig-lined walls, wooden tray below the body, wooden tray above the body, wooden box (around the body—an early form of coffin), twig roofing, plank roofing, bench or shelf (sometimes a boulder), pot burial, and mat-lined walls. The total number of elements was also recorded for each grave. G-square tests showed that the sex of the body is not significantly associated with either the number or the kind (either singly or in combination) of architectural elements.

Ritual Paraphernalia in Female and Male Graves

Although all grave goods may be argued to have some relationship to the mortuary regime, several kinds of artifacts seem to be more closely linked to rituals performed at the funeral. These include the remains of apparent animal sacrifices, grain offerings, liquid offerings (visible as residue in pots), ash filled jars, charcoal sprinkled in the bottom of graves below the lower matting, deliberately broken finely flaked chipped stone tools, balls of hair from the corpse, mud-filled jars, and dummy bread offerings (made of mud). Of the 883 bodies interred in the cemetery, only 136 have any of these nine types of remains. These inclusions seem to represent behaviors over and above those usually practiced at Naga-ed-Dêr. They qualify as indicators of elaboration of the funeral ritual because they appear to be associated with the preparation and consumption of funeral meals and, perhaps, with ceremonies conducted on the corpse for the benefit of the ka (something like the spiritual double of the body), such as the Ceremony of Opening the Mouth. Known at least from the time of the Fifth Dynasty, this ceremony probably has Predynastic antecedents (Budge 1972 [1909]:v–vi). According to Budge, the purpose of the ceremony was to reconstitute the body and restore the heart-soul (the ba) and the spirit-double (the ka).

Two bulls were sacrificed during the ceremony, and their left forelegs and hearts were offered to the deceased person or the ka; two gazelles were decapitated and presented (whether whole or in part is not known), and then a goose was similarly presented. The slaughter was performed with finely flaked flint knives which were produced in Egypt from Predynastic times but used for this purpose even after metal knives were available (Wilkinson 1992:189). Animal remains in Cemetery N7000 that are similar to those offered during the ceremony include parts of oxen (graves 7097, 7113, and 7519) and parts of gazelles or other small animals (graves 7235, 7296, 7454, 7480, 7484, 7497, 7519, 7583, and 7597). Flint knives from graves 7151, 7304, 7454, 7539, and 7595 are identical to those used in the ceremony. All these blades were broken deliberately, suggesting that they had been ritually "killed" following their ceremonial use (in contrast, less formal flint knives and other flint tools are never broken). Other possible correlates of the Ceremony of Opening the Mouth are the various bread offerings, jars of food, and jars of ashes present in many of the graves.

Only single interment burials of known sex are included here. The number of ritual indicators does not appear to be associated (G-square, p=.79) with the sex of the burial. These results are consistent with those observed for the other analytical units in this study.

Only two ritual items, dummy bread offerings and mud filled pots, were significantly associated with the sex of the burial. Dummy bread offerings are associated with female burials (estimated G-square, p=.05). Mud-filled pots are associated with male burials (estimated G-square, p=.03). However, in both these cases, the number of graves with dummy bread offerings (three) and mud-filled pots (seven) which could be identified by sex were so small as to render these findings little more than interesting.

Social Roles Represented in Cemetery N7000

Traditional mortuary studies in archaeology have attempted to recover social organization through an analysis of roles as defined by Goodenough (1965). According to Saxe and Binford, the funeral was the occasion where a number of the social identities, that is, the *social persona*, held by the deceased in life would be given symbolic expression (Binford 1971:17; Saxe 1970:6). Expanding on this notion, Tainter infers that "death and mortuary behavior call forth a fuller representation of an individual's social identities than does any occasion during life. Hence, the archaeological record of mortuary ritual should contain a greater range of information about the social identities present in the past than does any other category of information" (1978:110). Most mortuary analyses have accepted this position, either explicitly (Brown 1981; Goldstein 1976, 1981), or implicitly (Peebles 1971).

Hodder, in contrast, has stated that "burial ritual is not a passive reflection of other aspects of life. It is meaningfully constructed and our crosscultural generalizations must take the ideational and ideological into account" (1982:141). Hodder believes that mortuary behavior does not constitute an unambiguous reflection of social organization. Morris agrees with this position when he writes that the funeral "affirms order in the face of disorder, but the order affirmed need not be the same as that which members of society follow in everyday life. That is, the roles and relationships enacted in the rituals and detected by the archaeologist may not so much mirror real life relationships as distort them" (1987:39). Morris follows Pader (1982) in drawing upon Leach's (1954) distinction between social organization and social structure. Social organization refers to the "empirical distribution of relationships in everyday experience," while social structure forms an ideal model of social relationships (Morris 1987:39). Morris continues this line of reasoning by noting that the structure of society which is enacted in ritual can differ from that of the society in practical (nonritual) social action. Different forms of ritual (mortuary or otherwise) may deny, reflect, or exaggerate social structure.

According to Morris, "the ideal norms of the social roles of the survivors and the dead are played out with the greatest clarity, "capturing" something of the ideal social structure" (1987:32). Thus, the roles which are symbolized through mortuary ritual are idealized roles — they tell us about how a society views itself, not necessarily about how it actually was. So there is not necessarily a one-to-one correspondence between a role as expressed in the mortuary regime and a role in everyday life.

Presence/absence information for each of sixteen different artifact classes was collected for single burials of known sex. All burials with two or more artifact classes associated were included in the analysis. The artifact categories included the following: animal bone (other than animal sacrifices); beads (other than lapis and metal beads); ceramic cups and bowls; restricted rim ceramic jars; open-mouthed ceramic jars; special ceramic vessels (those with unusual shapes, such as hourglass-shaped jars or zoomorphic jars); metal (including metal beads); flaked stone tools; ground stone (including jars, maceheads, and probable jar blanks); ivory; lapis beads; minerals (galena and malachite); palettes; shell (except shell pendants and beads, which are included with beads); rubbing or polishing pebbles; and ritual items (as discussed above). Presence/absence is used here rather than abundance because using abundance would tend to conflate issues of wealth or prestige with those of role (Braun 1981). One hundred eleven graves are single-burial interments with positive sex identification and two or more artifact categories present.

Correspondence analysis was used to reduce the number of dimensions of variability from sixteen to eight. This procedure creates a series of scores for each case along principal axes of variation (called "eigenvectors"). It analyzes the variables as well as the cases. The output from the correspondence analysis is a table of values for each eigenvector, for each case and variable. These data were used as input in a k-means cluster analysis, and the resulting clusters can be loosely interpreted in much the same manner as componential analysis (Brown 1971; Morris 1987; Saxe 1970; Tainter 1973, 1978).

These methods suggest that there are twelve clusters, which may be interpreted as social roles, represented in the cemetery. Table 7.1 indicates which artifact classes are significantly associated with which role by reporting a value called "Allison's Z." This statistic calculates probability measures for each cell against the rest of the table and expresses them in terms of cell Z-score values based on a binomial model of cell probability, that is, of each cell versus anything else (for further explanation of Allison's Z, see Kintigh 1994). High positive values (highlighted in Table 7.1) of Allison's Z represent those artifact classes which are significantly associated with specific roles. High negative values represent artifact classes that are definitely not associated with specific roles. By reading down the columns (roles) in Table 7.1, the specific artifact classes associated with each may be clearly seen (an absolute value of 1.67 would have an associated probability of .05).

Female graves are associated with eleven different roles (role 10 could not be included, due to the lack of sex data). Male graves, on the other hand, are associated with only seven of the eleven roles analyzed. The G-square probability of this cross-tabulation of roles by sex was .003, suggesting that it is unlikely that the observed distribution is the result of chance.

The roles which are represented by only female burials have a tendency to be associated with ivory (roles 2 and 7), shell and beads (role 11 — although three of these graves contained subadult burials, the individuals were of sufficient age/preservation to make sexing possible), and possibly ritual (role 8, through the use of special ceramic vessels). Roles 7 and 11 are essentially aceramic. These results are intriguing, but must be viewed with caution in light of the small number of burials in some of the roles. Provisionally, this analysis seems to suggest that females were able to fill all of the social roles available to males, plus additional roles which were not filled by males. The Predynastic situation seems clearly different than that in dynastic Egypt; Robbins (1993:111) states that the distinction between male and female occupations was "already entrenched in Egyptian society by the Old Kingdom and continued throughout pharaonic Egypt."

Interpretation of the Data

The evidence from the mortuary record at Cemetery N7000 seems to indicate that women enjoyed a status equal to that of men and perhaps had more choices with regard to social roles. In some respects the Egyptian situation conforms to Lerner's expectations, which would predict

Table 7.1 Value of Allison's Z for All Roles by Artifact Classes

	Role Number											
Artifact Class	1	2	3	4	5	6	7	8	9	10	11	12
Animal Bone[a]	-1.63	1.13	0.51	-0.74	**8.63**	-0.82	-0.94	-1.38	-0.74	-0.75	-0.70	**3.03**
Beads[b]	-2.60	0.76	-0.09	-0.87	0.12	**9.19**	1.43	-1.56	0.34	0.22	**2.89**	-2.06
Cups/Bowls	**4.70**	0.13	-2.11	-0.52	-1.58	-0.24	-0.90	0.03	-0.76	-0.34	-2.04	-0.81
Restricted Jars	**4.92**	-1.37	-0.93	-1.91	-1.29	-1.93	-1.78	-0.80	0.17	0.47	-0.45	-0.66
Open Jars	**3.80**	-1.49	-2.35	2.51	-0.14	0.47	-1.41	-0.58	-1.10	-0.60	-0.35	-1.39
Special Vessels	-2.50	-0.98	-0.83	-1.47	-0.56	-0.84	1.11	**10.66**	-1.47	-0.77	-0.72	-0.39
Metal[c]	-1.35	-0.53	0.18	-0.79	-0.30	-0.45	-0.52	-0.76	-0.79	**11.60**	-0.39	-0.66
Flaked Stone	-2.34	0.18	0.75	-1.37	-0.52	-0.78	-0.90	-1.32	-1.37	0.67	-0.67	**9.45**
Groundstone[d]	-2.70	-0.11	**4.52**	-1.58	-0.60	-0.90	-0.08	-0.21	-0.95	0.37	-0.78	0.98
Ivory	-2.61	**2.92**	-0.60	-1.53	-0.58	-0.87	**11.96**	-0.79	0.45	-0.80	-0.75	-1.26
Lapis	-1.61	0.63	**3.46**	-0.95	-0.36	-0.54	-0.62	-0.91	0.11	1.51	-0.46	-0.78
Minerals[e]	-3.24	-1.26	**7.27**	-1.89	-0.72	-1.08	-0.44	-0.72	-1.36	-1.00	0.15	-0.29
Palettes	-2.33	**10.32**	-0.02	-1.58	-0.60	-0.90	-1.04	0.45	0.32	-0.83	-0.78	0.22
Shell[f]	-1.70	-0.98	-0.83	-1.47	-0.56	-0.84	**3.19**	0.01	0.78	-0.77	**11.81**	0.44
Polishing Stones	-2.75	-1.07	-0.48	-1.61	-0.61	-0.92	-1.06	-0.26	**11.46**	-0.85	-0.79	-1.33
Ritual Items	-2.19	-2.10	-0.32	**7.44**	**2.17**	-1.23	-1.58	0.30	-0.90	-0.44	-1.54	0.87

[a]Does not include animal sacrifices (which are listed under "Ritual Items").
[b]Does not include metal beads (which are listed under "Metal").
[c]Includes mostly copper wire, beads, and tools, plus two occurrences of gold beads.
[d]Includes maceheads, ground stone jars, and probable jar blanks.
[e]Includes galena and malachite.
[f]Does not include shell beads (which are listed under "Beads").

that women's status declined over time as patriarchy developed. However, the timing may be problematic, for Lerner suggests that the creation of patriarchy is a Neolithic phenomenon (Lerner 1986:9, 145). How are we to interpret these data? Are the Egyptian and Mesopotamian cases fundamentally different? Two alternatives seem possible: it is simply a difference in timing (patriarchy took longer to develop in Egypt than in Mesopotamia); or, the difference lies in the nature of the territorial state versus the city-state. Each of these alternatives is discussed below.

A Question of Timing

Many of the propositions discussed by Lerner have clear relevance to historic Egypt. For example, she suggests (1986:145) that the creation of a strong patriarchal kingship necessitated the overthrow of Neolithic creator-mother-goddesses in favor of male creator/storm gods. Ions (1982:32) thinks that a universal mother-goddess was worshipped in Predynastic Egypt; many of the later historic goddesses, such as Hathor or Neith, may be manifestations of this earlier "Gerzean goddess." She further states that this deity may well have been revered as the creator of the world. But according to the Heliopolitan cosmology, by the time of the Old Kingdom the act of creation was in the hand of the male god, Atum (Rundle-Clark 1959:36). Other rival creation stories of the Old Kingdom or later, such as the Memphite, Hermopolitan, and Theban cosmologies, emphasize the male role in creation, while subordinating the female (Ions 1982:25–32). The female deities become consorts of the male gods.

The Egyptian case thus presents clear evidence that corroborates one of Lerner's (1986) main theses, but the timing of these changes does not follow her proposed model. Lerner proposes that the erosion of women's status begins far back in the Neolithic, as a consequence of the development of agriculture (1986:154). If this were universally true, we should see the effects in the archaeological record (especially the mortuary record) of the Predynastic, perhaps as far back as the Badarian period (c. 5500 to 4000 B.C.E.), when agriculture first became widespread in Egypt. But the evidence from Naga-ed-Dêr does not appear to bear this out.

Silverblatt's (1988) model, in contrast, suggests that a reworking of ideological concepts such as these is a function of the process of centralizing state power. The shift in ancient Egypt described above occurred in the Archaic and Old Kingdom periods, while the Naga-ed-Dêr evidence indicates parity in mortuary treatment of females and males during the Predynastic. This evidence suggests that Silverblatt's explanation may be preferable. The burials seem to indicate that patriarchy developed later in ancient Egypt, probably during the late Predynastic and Archaic periods (Dynasties 1 and 2, c. 3050 to 2695 B.C.E.), when rulers were still consolidating their authority and establishing the institutions of the early state.

I have argued elsewhere (Savage 1997) that Archaic-period Egypt cannot yet be considered as a state, in an anthropological sense, because many of the commonly accepted indicators of statehood are not present in 3050 B.C.E. The unification of Upper and Lower Egypt is only a midpoint in the process of the consolidation of state authority (Savage 1997). Part of this process was the imposition of centralized artistic styles and forms of worship (Davis 1989; Kemp 1989). Another part was the development of the male-oriented cosmologies discussed above. In addition, a third part may have been the creation of patriarchy in the manner that Silverblatt (1988) describes. The reason this process may have occurred later in Egypt than in Mesopotamia may have to do with the differences between territorial and city-states.

Territorial State Versus City-States

The most compelling evidence that Lerner (1986) offers to support her theses is drawn from Mesopotamia and Classical Greece, both of which exhibited city-state political configurations. Herodotus, who was shocked by the way Egyptian women behaved, would probably have been much more comfortable in Babylon, where the attitudes toward women were more similar to those in his native land. In territorial states, however, the creation of patriarchy fit more closely with Silverblatt's (1988) model.

Trigger suggests that territorial states may have emerged in areas with lower population densities relative to the amount of arable land. Under these circumstances, a disadvantaged population would have been able to move to a more remote area, making it more difficult for the state to exert dominating influences over them (1993:13). In such states, Trigger believes that a two-tiered economy developed, divided between urban and rural sectors. And because of their large size, peasant communities may have been able to retain many of their traditions which originated before the time of state emergence (1993:11).

In contrast, the city-state appears to have developed in areas which were essentially resource-poor. When arable land (or irrigable land) is at a premium, disadvantaged groups have little recourse but to put up with their situations. Because city-states were frequently very small and resources internal to a given polity were scarce, competition between different city-states was often intense. The different polities often shared a common symbology and frequently made alliances with each other through mate exchange (principally the exchange of females). Agricultural labor was more rigidly organized and agricultural practices frequently more intensive, so that the city-state could often support large cadres of craftspeople (Trigger 1993:9).

Thus, the relative scarcity of land and resources in regions later dominated by city-state systems may have set inhabitants on a competitive course before their counterparts in areas which would later be incorporated in territorial states. Circumscription and all its consequences (see Carneiro 1970) would, therefore, seem to be more feasible and its effects more intrusive upon some elements of society in city-states than in territorial states, where state mechanisms may have been less intrusive (Trigger 1993:38).

Summary

The framework that Lerner (1986) and Silverblatt (1988) provide for understanding the creation of patriarchy certainly seems to apply in the Egyptian case, even though the status of women in the historic periods was relatively higher than in other parts of the Near East. The primary departure of the burial data from Lerner's thesis concerns the question of timing. Whereas Lerner (1986) postulated that the reduction of women's status is associated everywhere in the Near East with the introduction of agriculture, the mortuary evidence from Cemetery N7000 does not seem to bear this out. In Egypt, the Badarian period (c. 5500–4000 B.C.E.) witnessed the widespread adoption of agriculture in the Nile Valley for the first time. Based on ceramic evidence, cemetery N7000 appears to date to the late Amratian to the late Gerzean (c. 3500–3200 B.C.E.). Yet there are no discernible differences between female and male graves in the cemetery. Thus, it would appear that, to the extent that the mortuary ritual reflects Predynastic social conditions, women held a status greater than or equal to men. I believe the processes that Lerner (1986) discusses were not well under way in the early and middle Predynastic. Rather, they seem to have begun somewhat later, in the Protodynastic and the Archaic periods. This delay seems to suggest that the changes in women's status were the result of the process of centralizing state power. Early pharaohs may have created or expanded hierarchically ranked gender categories by reworking the Predynastic cosmology into a new, male-centered mythological system, thereby reducing the number of social and political roles available to women. The mortuary evidence discussed here thus presents clear parallels with the changes that Silverblatt (1988) finds in Peruvian state development.

The archaeological record of Predynastic and Dynastic Egypt is rich with information that may be examined through gendered approaches. This chapter has shown that significant similarities and differences exist between Egypt and the rest of the Near East. It is hoped that recent work investigating the status of women in these areas will not represent the end of the investigation of women's status, but only the beginning.

Notes

I would like to thank the P. A. Hearst Museum of Anthropology at the University of California, Berkeley, for permission to study the collections, photographs, accession cards, and field notes pertaining to Cemetery N7000. Thanks are also due to Steven Falconer, Charles Redman, Keith Kintigh, and Robert Wenke for invaluable assistance and advice during the preparation of my dissertation, from which this chapter was drawn. Chris Carr's graduate seminar in mortuary analysis provided much of the theoretical and methodological background of this and other of my studies. Joan Gero, Carol Redmount, and Kathy Bolen made specific comments on the first draft of this chapter; I have incorporated many of their suggestions, and I am grateful for all of them.

1. The G-square test may be interpreted as the more widely used chi-square test; its underlying frequency distribution is quite similar. However, it presents some advantages over chi-square that render its use more desirable. First, it is computationally easier to perform now that calculators have "log" keys. But more important, the results of G-square tests may be added or subtracted directly, which allows the analyst to measure the improvement in fit between different models (see Sokal and Rohlf 1981:692–765; Shennan 1990:89–99). Though I make no such comparisons here, I am in the habit of using G-square rather than chi-square, because G-square allows the development of more complex models.

Part II
Reading the Body from
Representations of the
Human Form

Chapter 8
The Human Form in the Late Bronze Age Aegean

Senta C. German

Work on gender has expanded exponentially in the last two decades, resulting in a wealth of important information and provocative theory. The study of gender now embraces many different and differing discourses. For example, Joan Scott (1996) posits gender as a basic and ever-present element of social interaction, stimulated by the recognized differences between the sexes, and argues that gender is a means by which power dynamics are described (Scott 1986:1067). Thus, gender can be viewed as a larger category of social knowledge, representing a major organizing principle of society. But what of sexuality? Certainly ever since Foucault's work (1976–84) the notion of sexuality's subtle yet formidable subtext in society has sparked much interest. The single most important result of Foucault's work has been a fundamental intellectual and political reconstitution of sexuality itself. Long thought of only as the biological reality of two different sets of genitalia, sexuality is now recognized as a personal and sociocultural negotiation of the circumstances of this equipment. This broad perspective has generated much fruitful discussion, ranging from the politics of sexual intercourse to rites of passage, the body, straight and gay politics, and reproduction (Davidson 1987; Padgug 1979). What has also emerged is the inevitability of gender to discussions of sexuality, and vice versa. As Kampen (1996:1) has said, the edges between sexuality and gender are altogether blurred; our task as scholars is to explore the fuzziness of this boundary, not to force it into false focus.

Exploration of these boundaries between gender and sexuality in the cultures of Western antiquity has only recently begun. Moving beyond the erotic and explicitly sexual, scholars now treat sexuality as a critical element of gender in a more general sense, including topics such as the meaning of the body clothed and unclothed, rites of passage marking sexual maturity, the politics of sex, and the psychosexual persona. The vast majority of these studies among Classical archaeologists have been limited to later Classical antiquity. This chapter extends this study of the body to earlier time periods of the Aegean, to the prehistoric cultures of the Minoans and Mycenaean dating to the later Bronze Age or second millennium B.C.E.

Unfortunately, an interest in fuzziness is not a hallmark of the field of Aegean prehistory. More comfortable with pottery chronologies and ty-pological studies, scholars who study the remains of the Minoans and Mycenaeans find their methodological inspiration from the field of Clas-sical archaeology rather than gender studies. These more conservative approaches have long been a fundamental part of the study of glyptic art among Aegean prehistorians, despite the potential for the investigation of more provocative questions with these unique archaeological remains.

Here, I examine one kind of glyptic art, a sample of seal stones from Bronze Age Greek culture. The hundreds of examples of the human form found carved on these seals constitutes the greatest body of visual data regarding gender and sexuality from this largely nonliterate culture. I specifically examine three topoi upon which gender and sexuality con-verge as representations on the seals: the body, performance, and erotic representation. The relationship between gender and sexuality in these three cases demonstrates how the sexualized human form simultaneously defined and charged gender construction in Late Bronze Age Aegean society.

Aegean Bronze Age Seals

Seals were used in a system of administration during the late Bronze Age in Greece, connecting palatial sites to periphery areas and even foreign peoples in the more remote areas of the Aegean. They have been exten-sively studied in terms of their forms and uses in administrative contexts (e.g., Weingarten 1986, 1988, 1992; Hallager 1988, 1995). Stamp seals consist of a lump of clay covering the lid of a jar or the string which secured a box or a door. The clay could not be removed or replaced without detection if it were stamped with a seal; the resulting stamped clay impression, the positive impression of the negative carving on the stone seal, is called a sealing. In an age before the invention of locks, seals or engraved gems offered a way of identifying property and preventing access to it. Critical to this security system is the uniqueness of the pattern carved on the seal and an understanding of the image itself.

The study of the seals and sealings of the Aegean Bronze Age began in the mid-nineteenth century and, within the field of glyptic art, stands at a reasonably sophisticated level. My concerns here are not typical of glyptic studies; however, much of the nomenclature, dating methods and stylistic approach that I employ are part of this field. For example, all notations regarding the identification of seals and sealings here follow the organizational system established by the *Corpus der Minoischen und Mykenischen Siegel*, begun in 1964.

There are severe dating problems with the majority of the Aegean Bronze Age seals, however, which has limited their utility in other archaeological investigation. I have, therefore, limited my study to include only seals and sealings with confirmed contexts and in a good state of preservation. However, even this select sample is susceptible, as are all archaeological materials, to biases affecting their retrieval and preservation. This latter point is especially poignant for sealings, which are nothing more than lumps of clay which have accidentally been fired in destruction contexts. Because sealings were only accidentally, and often only partly baked, they often lack the periphery of the image or even larger portions; thus, the full extent of a scene is often lost. An additional problem stems from the small size of seals and sealings and the constraints of size on the representations. Although some images found on seals seem to parallel those found on other media, by no means can all images be translated from one scale to another.

It was an innocent curiosity in the origin of these small carved stones that led Sir Arthur Evans to Crete at the end of the nineteenth century; ultimately it also led him to excavate one of the most important Bronze Age sites there, Knossos. The excavations and eventual publication of the remains of Knossos (Evans 1921–35) would prove to be of paramount importance to our understanding of the history of Bronze Age Greece; the history of Knossos provided the backbone for all relative chronologies in the Aegean.

The seals in this study come from the Second and Third Palace Periods, named after major reconstructions at Knossos. The Second Palace Period is regarded as the pinnacle of Minoan civilization on Crete. This period is marked by great population expansion, a high level of craft production, administrative control tabulated by Linear A documents, and a wide trade network across the Aegean. During this period, Crete also began engaging in extensive contact with the mainland Mycenaean Greeks from sites such as Mycenae, Thebes, Athens, and Pylos. These sites were already long established, although markedly less sophisticated, than Knossos. The demise of the Second Palace Period at Knossos is alternatively attributed to Mycenaean conquest or to social disruption following the eruption of the volcano on the island of Thera. At this same time, several other sites on the island of Crete were destroyed and never reoccupied. At Knossos, the palace was rebuilt during the Third Palace Period, and the written language of administration at the rebuilt Knossos changed from Linear A to B, a pre-Greek mainland script. By the end of the Third Palace Period at Knossos, large sites on the mainland as well as on Crete seem to decline; this period is marked by a reduction in the use of metal and the expansion of the production of less expensive commodities.

Images of the Body on the Seals

Beginning in the Second Palace Period on Crete, the female form is illustrated with an elegantly long and curvaceous body and elaborate costume. Breasts are large and exposed atop a narrow waist. An elaborate, often flounced, skirt covers the outline of full hips and thighs. The torso is held in a pose that suggests swinging of the hips and shoulders (Fig. 8.1). Women are often situated near or in association with architecture and landscape that includes large stones, trees, plants, flowers, and animals. Less frequently, women are associated with armaments and textiles. Performances in which women are represented exclusively form seven groups: women pictured alone totemically; women pictured in groups of two or three in identical poses as if dancing; women carrying objects or animals; women occupied with plants; formal presentation scenes where a woman is seated receiving an object, other women, or an animal; and women riding on boats.

Representations of men on Crete during the Second Palace Period are slightly more numerous than those of women. The men seem to represent just two types, a younger and an older male figure. The younger male is characterized by a narrow waist, broad shoulders, and swelling musculature. He wears either a very short skirt (which covers the buttocks) with a penis sheath, or a long skirt which ends in a great swoop in the front. His posture is rigidly erect, often with both arms up and hands placed at the chest. He is frequently associated with weapons, architecture, or landscape, as well as with items such as textiles and the double axe (Fig. 8.2). In contrast to this younger male figure, the body of the older male cannot be seen: he wears a great bulky robe with elaborate fringes at the bottom. He is bearded and often is depicted wearing a hat and carrying an axe over his shoulder.

Performances with male figures are more numerous than those featuring females of the period. Male figures are depicted with animals in scenes of bull-leaping, animal husbandry, or scenes of males standing heraldically with animals, usually lions. They may interact with other males, including the older bearded male; some of the scenes depict hand-to-hand combat with either men or animals. Male figures are also depicted walking or running together in pairs, carrying objects such as textiles and double axes in a procession-like circumstance, and driving chariots.

Figure 8.1. Female figure on a sealing, from Knossos, Crete, during the Second Palace Period (photo by Ingo Pini, printed with permission).

Figure 8.2. Young male figure on a sealing, from Knossos, Crete, during the Second Palace Period (photo by Ingo Pini, printed with permission).

Mainland sites during the Second Palace Period show fewer representations of males and females. Female physical attributes are largely identical to those used on Crete: the women's narrow waists are surmounted by large pendulous breasts, and they wear great flounced skirts. Women's bodies are again represented with a curve or sway, and the gesture of one hand to the head and one to the back is included. However, there are two notable differences in the mainland repertoire of female representations. First, there are far fewer representations of women compared to men; second, women are depicted in association with fewer things. Female figures on the mainland are associated only with animals, landscapes, and what are traditionally thought to be cultic accouterments (such as the double axe or sacred knot). Performances consist of totemic representations with an animal, a frontal view of a woman with arms raised and out, holding an animal at either side (referred to as the "mistress of the animals") and presentation scenes.

Representations of males on the mainland during this period are also strikingly similar in their physical elements of gender to those representations found on Crete. Two generic types, an older and a younger male, are again represented on the mainland. The older character wears a robe and carries an axe as on Crete; on the mainland, however, he is depicted with a great griffin. The younger male again has a narrow waist, broad shoulders, and bulging muscles; on the mainland in this period, however, his dress is more restricted in style: he wears only a short skirt. These younger males are depicted with weapons and animals, but unlike the Cretan examples, they sport elaborate helmets, some complete with plume, and they are sometimes placed in what appears to be a cave setting. Mainland performances that feature males in this period are commonly scenes of animal combat. However, scenes of hand-to-hand combat, men on chariots, and heraldic scenes of men with animals are also found on the mainland and are quite similar to the Cretan repertoire.

In the following Third Palace Period on Crete, little changes in the visual construction of the female gender. Large breasts, narrow waist, and wide hips clothed in an elaborate skirt are still the sole way of depicting the female form. However, objects associated with females are fewer: females are still depicted with animals, landscape, and architecture. During this period, weapons are no longer a part of the female repertoire, nor are boats. The types of performances that feature women exclusively are similar to those from the preceding period: women again appear alone or in identical pairs, in presentation scenes, and are occupied with plants and other women. New to the Cretan repertoire during this period is the "mistress of the animal" form with upraised arms, and entirely new to this type are examples in which the "mistress" wears a double-horned crown with a double axe.

Representations of men during this period on Crete maintain the same construction of the male body, and the same two age groups appear. The younger male has a narrow waist, broad shoulders and erect posture; the older figure wears a bulky robe and carries an axe. Male performances, however, are expanded during this period. Animal combat scenes, bull-leaping and heraldic depictions with animals, and scenes of hand-to-hand combat are all similar to those the preceding period, but added to this repertoire is a male counterpart to the figure of the "mistress of the animals." This scene shows a man standing frontally with both arms out, holding an animal in each hand. Men are also shown in lines, wearing battle armor and holding shields. Another quite striking image depicts a frontal face view of a male, who is shown either surrounded by animals or else atop a frontal bull's head, between its horns.

Images of women found on seals and sealings on the mainland from the Third Palace Period are more numerous than the previous period, yet the variety of images is still limited compared to those on Crete. The female form is, again, very similarly described, and females are associated with similar things. What is striking is the extremely limited repertoire of performances depicted for females; essentially all representations of females are of only two types. One type of scene depicts groups of either two or three women standing before architecture (some examples of which have foliage growing from it); the second type depicts the "mistress of the animals." Two examples from this latter type feature the double-horned crown with the double axe.

Representations of males in the Third Palace Period on the mainland fall into the now-familiar two categories, the older robed character and the younger male. Representations of the older character are unique and few; one seal shows him seated, receiving a great griffin; on another, the older male is seemingly attending to an animal sacrifice. The younger male figure is associated with the same sorts of objects, animals, landscape, and armaments. Male performances are similar to those found during the Second Palace Period, including scenes of animal combat, hand-to-hand human combat, bull-leaping, chariot driving, and heraldic posturing with an animal. A new figure, however is a youthful "master of the animals" similar to that found in the Cretan seals. Other new male figures include a lone male standing erect, and a scene in which a man is shown with architecture in a landscape with a goat.

The Body

The figures described above represent, first of all, depictions of the body, the first of the three topoi I discuss upon which the body and sexuality converge. Much scholarly, and to a large extent theoretical, attention has been given in recent years to the topic of the body, including philosophy of the body, the body and society, history of the body, psychology and the body, and the body and AIDS. However, as Caroline Walker Bynum notes in a recent article, "there is no clear set of structure, behaviors, events, objects, experiences, words [or] moments to which the body currently refers" (Bynum 1995:5). Further in the article she laments the body "dissolving into language" and asks where the studies are that deal in more formal ways with the corporal body. My concern is with the corporal body in this sense is strictly formal. What do bodies look like, how are they clothed, what parts are emphasized?

With this modest query of the body in mind, what useful observations can be made? First, there is a striking consistency in male and female bodies respectively between Minoan and mainland Mycenaean remains during the Second and Third Palace Periods. It is clear, however, that male bodies are featured more often, especially in the Second Palace Period on Crete and the Third Palace Period on the mainland. These periods are significant in that they represent the periods during which political power was concentrated in those two areas. It is also interesting to note that there are, in both periods, fewer representations of women from mainland Greek sites.

Looking more at the details of the body, women's bodies appear to be strategically clothed to reveal and accentuate certain parts, namely the breasts, waist, and hips. The general shape rather than the anatomic detail seems to be most important in the representation, and little or no attention is given to formal features. Men's bodies are by far more exposed, with minimal clothing of codpieces indicated by sculpted belts and skirts. Corporal details are often included, most especially seen in the musculature and physiognomy of the chest. The representation of men's and women's bodies is similar in that secondary sexual characteristics are emphasized, while primary ones, such as the penis and vagina, are hidden. Lastly, both the bodies of women and men on these seals and sealings are of unrealistic, Barbie-doll-like proportions, exemplified by waist-to-shoulder measurements in representations of men, and waist-to-breast measurements on women. As with the modern Barbie doll, the body depicted seems tenable at first glance; measurement of the body proportions, however, reveals the fantasy behind the image.[1]

What, then, do these bodies tell us about gender and sexuality in the Aegean Bronze Age? These bodies are unreal in shape and are dressed in highly impractical clothing. In so far as the body helps to construct gender, the representation of it in this culture is a fanciful and extraordinarily homogeneous. The fact that the parts of men's and women's bodies that are emphasized coincide so exactly with secondary sexual characteristics could perhaps mean a strong correlation between constructions of gender and sexuality. The attention paid to women's costuming may be a symbol of social power or status displayed upon the body.[2]

An emphasis on youthful men's bodies is seen in attributes suggesting physical strength, which may identify young males with potential power or action.[3] The older men's robe and axe no doubt indicate some rank, although their status in relation to the younger men is difficult to say. Similarly, facial hair may denote more than just age. The distinction in ages between these two types of men could indicate the presence of strong social divisions between age groups, here defined by secondary sexual characteristics such as musculature and facial hair.

Performance

The performances illustrated on the seals also help construct gender and sexuality. Performativity as a critical idea has enjoyed some popularity lately (for example, Parkin et al. 1996; Diamond 1996), but Judith Butler (1990c) is largely responsible for the application of the idea of performance to the study of gender, or "performative gender." She looks at performance as the culturally recognized "natural" performance or act of maleness or femaleness; she views this act as essential to the social construction of "abiding" masculinity and femininity (Butler 1990c). This is a provocative and potentially useful idea, even with the attendant problems in its application to a nonliterate archaeological culture such as that of the Bronze Age Aegean. In the present study, the body's "performance" concerns the way in which the body is depicted moving, being carried, posed, and displayed. These conventions of performance help construct gender and sexual identity.

I noted above that performance is apparently different between Minoan and Mycenaean men and women and that these performances change from the Second to the Third Palace Period. In general, men perform more than women, and scenes with males display greater variability. For instance, there are a number of activities that men perform exclusively, such as bull-leaping, chariot riding, and fighting with men and animals. Dancing is the only performance that is exclusive to women. Looking diachronically between the Minoan and Mycenaean material, we see the "mistress of the animals" appearing in the Third Palace Period on Crete, presumably derived from similar earlier depictions on the mainland. Conversely, the Minoan bull-leaping scene, found first on Crete, appears later, in the Third Palace Period, on the mainland.

What can these performances tell us about Aegean constructions of gender and sexuality? Despite the fact that men are found engaged in a greater variety of performances, the two genders in fact share similar performances. Despite claims to the contrary among Aegeanists, scenes with animals, scenes depicting so-called "cult" activity, and scenes show-ing an isolated figure in heraldic pose are not restricted to either male or female figures. Both are found performing these dynamic activities (Ma-rinatos 1995; Rutkowski 1986). Furthermore, both men and women per-form in relationship to similar things such as animals, foliage, weapons, and architecture.

Sexuality is another aspect of performance, conveyed here in the way in which the body is carried. The Aegean figures' different performances emphasize secondary sexual characteristics: men's bodies are held erect emphasizing the broadness of the chest and narrow waist, and women's arms are held back to thrust the breasts forward. Women often stand in a swaying posture which accentuates the hips and breasts. Men lunge for-ward in battle with one muscular leg fully extended back and one arm raised behind the head, opening the whole body for view. All these poses perform a subtle subtext of sex and help to construct sexual identity.[4]

I further argue that some scenes of formal performance such as bull-leaping or dancing may describe rites-of-passage ceremonies, ceremonies that acknowledge sexual development.[5] The ways in which the represen-tation of performances fell in and out of popularity across time and were dropped or picked up between the Minoans and the Mycenaeans may speak to their differing currency in the construction of gender and sex-uality during that period.

Erotica

The careful reader will note that I have not yet included erotic represen-tation, despite a promise for such at the beginning of this chapter. There are two reasons for this omission. First, it was useful to become familiar with more common representations before looking at the exceptional ones. Second, the erotic representations are few and very different in character from most representations; they deserve their own introduc-tion and explication.

The entire group of erotic representations described here come from Crete during the Second Palace Period. Furthermore, these images are exclusively sealings (Levi 1926), and all come from the same site, Zakros, on the far eastern coast of the island (Platon 1971). Curiously, Aegean art historians and glyptic specialists have in general ignored these seals ex-cept to hold them up as examples of "bad art" or cultural contacts with the eastern Mediterranean or the Near East (see particularly Weingarten [1983] for a discussion of the latter view). The erotic representations found on these sealings are particularly fascinating in that they feature figures that are half-human and half-animal, representing a kind of sex-uality and gender definition very different from the majority of other

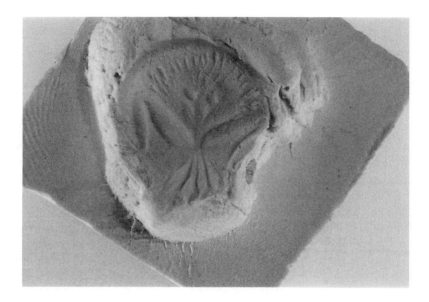

Figure 8.3. "Erotic" depiction of a female human-bird figure from a sealing, from Zakros, during the Second Palace Period (photo by Ingo Pini, printed with permission).

images. The first group includes representations of a human's spread legs, with a head of some kind, possibly a bird, poking out from between the legs (Fig. 8.3). There is another half-human, half-animal creature with a large penis protruding from its belly (Fig. 8.4). Equally strange is a deer-headed winged female with what appears to be a long penis protruding from between her legs. Another seal features an ox-headed winged beast with bare breasts and outspread legs, which are covered with bird feathers (Fig. 8.5). Lastly, a pig-faced human character cups her exposed breasts while turning to the left. She wears a boar's tusk helmet, which is typically worn only by men.

The chaotic mixture of genders and species represented in these images provide clues to understanding the gender system and sexuality in this culture. Unlike the images on the majority of the seals, the primary sexual characteristics, the penis and vagina, are chosen for gendering, and they are manipulated in fantastic ways. Penises are not just seen, they are disproportionately large; female legs are spread wide. Moreover, these primary sexual characteristics, usually hidden, are found in combination with agitated animals, thus heightening the sense of disturbance and disequilibrium.

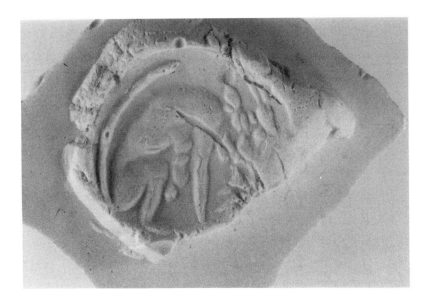

Figure 8.4. Human-animal figure with exaggerated phallus, from a sealing, from Zakros, during the Second Palace Period (photo by Ingo Pini, printed with permission).

It is notable that these are the only clearly erotic representations in all of Minoan and Mycenaean art. It is therefore possible that a certain amount of deviance might thus be attached to ideas of the erotic during this time. This association leads one to wonder how sexual activity in general was regarded. It may be the case that Bronze Age Greek society was one in which unambiguous circumstances of sexual excitement and intercourse were suppressed. Certainly it seems true that sexual organs and sexual activity are rarely represented, and when they are, they are portrayed in unnatural sizes, situations, or juxtapositions with animal body parts.

Gender and Sexuality in Aegean Seals and Sealings

In conclusion, let me return to the idea of fuzziness. I have tried to explore Aegean ideas of gender and sexuality found in the representations of humans through careful attention to the body, performance, and the erotic, as shown in depictions on seals and sealings. Gender and its construction as expressed through the body appear remarkably consistent throughout both periods surveyed and between Minoan and My-

Figure 8.5. Ox-headed winged female with tail feathers from a sealing, from Zakros, during the Second Palace Period (photo by Ingo Pini, printed with permission).

cenaean remains: the depiction of men's and women's bodies is relatively uniform, although represented in unreal (but superficially plausible) physical proportions.

The performance of the body, however, reveals greater complexity in the construction of gender. Subtle performances such as stance and posture are consistently associated with either maleness or femaleness, but overt performances such as presentation scenes, chariot driving, or dancing shift in popularity. Over time, female performances become more restricted in variety, a trend that is especially apparent on seals from sites on the mainland during the Third Palace Period. Erotic forms, known only from the Second Palace Period, include representations which feature males and females, or often only parts of bodies, found on half-animal figures. Erotic scenes are not gendered as uniquely or exclusively male or female.

Physical clues of sexuality are closely tied to the secondary sexual characteristics that identify bodies as male or female, and thus we might assume that these clues are also closely tied to ideas of gender in Aegean culture. We might further suppose that sexuality was displayed on bodies and was enhanced by the subtle performance of posture and pose. More formal performances represented on some seals and sealings may have been meaningful as ceremonies or rites of passage, such as those that mark sexual maturity and membership in social groupings. In addition, the very different representations of the older male character may reinforce the idea that some social groups may have been differentiated by age. The decreased number of female performances in the Third Palace Period suggests that women's sexual or social freedom of expression may have been curtailed at that time. And last, the presence of atypical representations, with their exaggerated presentation of primary sexual characteristics and their association of human sex organs with animals, may indicate the emergence of a different attitude about sex and sexuality in Second Palace Period Cretan society.

This paper represents only the beginning of the exploration into issues of gender and sexuality in the culture of the Aegean Bronze Age. The most important next step would be an expanded investigation into representations of bodies and performances in other media, such as wall painting, pottery, small scale sculpture, and metal work. Examinations of gesture and personal adornment in these media would no doubt be quite valuable as well. Modern studies of the limited sample of skeletal remains might also offer important insights into the biological realities of gender and sexuality of Minoans and Mycenaeans. Until these and other similar studies are undertaken, however, more probing questions about the roles of Minoan and Mycenaean men and women cannot adequately be answered. It remains for future generations of Aegean prehistorians to contribute additional details to the picture of Bronze Age Greece that was sketched out by Arthur Evans so long ago.

Notes

1. See Urla and Swedlund (1995) for a discussion of Barbie dolls and unreal bodies with special attention to anthropometric measurement.

2. Joyce (1998) and Marcus (1994) both discuss how representations of dress and adornment serve to construct gender and display social rank in the cultures of Mesoamerican and Bronze Age Iranian art respectively.

3. Connections between representations of the youthful strong male body and power have been made in various cultures including by Winter (1996) in Mesopotamia and by Potts (1990) in eighteenth century France. Various essays on bodies, power, and ideology can be found in Adler and Pointon (1993).

4. Marcus (1996), Robins (1996), and Laqueur (1990) all discuss how the representations of sexualized bodies help to construct ideas about sexual identification and behavior in culture. Although I do not see these images commenting so much on sexual behavior, I believe they do elaborate on sexual determination.

5. Koehl (1986) has identified rites of passage scenes elsewhere in Minoan art

and is presently working on a study of the representation of these rituals elsewhere in the Bronze Age Aegean. He outlines the participation of youth, physical exertion, and the witnessing of events by large groups as likely markers of rites of passage in Bronze Age Greek culture. I believe that the representations of the activities outlined above could be included in these ceremonies.

Chapter 9
Deciphering Gender in Minoan Dress

Mireille M. Lee

The famous Minoan "Snake Goddess" figurine (Fig. 9.1) and her "priestess" or "votary" (Fig. 9.2), both from the Temple Repositories of the palace at Knossos on Crete, have been central to many hypotheses about women's status and roles in late Bronze Age society (c. 1700 to 1450 B.C.E.). These remarkable figures of bare-breasted women, one with snakes twining over her arms, shoulders, hips, and head, the other holding wriggling snakes in the air, have aroused interest not only for their apparently powerful postures and curious (possibly cultic) occupation as snake-handlers, but also for their dress. Soon after their discovery around the turn of the twentieth century, Lady Evans, sister of the excavator, Sir Arthur Evans, noted that the Goddess's proportions "are those considered ideal by the modern corset maker rather than those of the sculptor" (Evans 1902–3:81), prompting Evans himself to suggest that the overall effect of the figure was that of a depiction of "a fashionable Court lady" (Evans 1921:503). Half a century later, in an age of glamorous movie stars and "nudie" pinups, Charles Seltman observed that in the "priestess" figurine: "Emphasis is almost entirely on sex-appeal, and one is aware that the artist, in making this enchanting little figure, was representing a typical fashionable young woman of his day who was out to captivate by means of such allure as she was fortunate to possess. The firm, well-formed breasts, the long, stray lock of hair caressing the armpit, the wasp-waist and wide hips . . . all these calculated details were meant to entice the male" (Seltman 1956:51). Whereas Evans' interpretation implies a Victorian ideal of femininity, Seltman's commentary construes the image as a 1950s icon representing a safe sexuality. Both interpretations trivialize the figurines.

In contrast, in the late 1960s, at the advent of the modern women's movement, Jacquetta Hawkes interpreted the figurines in feminist terms. According to her, such "provocative" dress would have been "appropri-

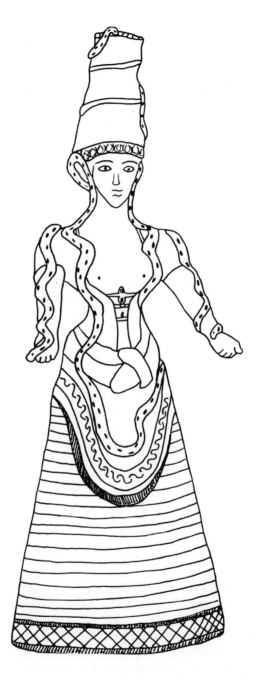

Figure 9.1. "Snake Goddess" faience figurine from the Temple Repositories of the palace at Knossos, Crete (line drawing by the author).

Figure 9.2. "Priestess" or "votary" faience figurine from the Temple Repositories of the palace at Knossos, Crete (line drawing by the author).

ate to the high status of women in Minoan society, to their uninhibited liveliness in public and the freedom with which they mingled with men" (Hawkes 1968:110). The notion that women enjoyed high status in Minoan society has had a strong appeal for many, and the idea that Minoan Crete might have been a matriarchy, although now discredited by archaeologists, remains pervasive in the popular literature.

Clearly, each of these interpretations reflects the cultural milieu in which it was written, as well as certain personal and intellectual agendas of the author. More important for this study, these interpretations betray an assumed relationship between dress and gender, and the authors have extrapolated sexual and social roles, including social status, from the artistic imagery. In the past quarter-century there has been little scholarly interest in developing new interpretations of the Snake Goddess and votary figurines and their dress, and many of the old ideas about the figurines continue to be cited. A few scholars have considered the meanings associated with the iconography of Minoan dress, particularly in relation to issues of rank and status in Minoan society.[1] But the relationship between Minoan dress and gender systems has not been examined by archaeologists, despite the fact that dress has long been recognized in other disciplines (such as anthropology, art history, sociology, and social psychology) as a reflection of, and means of maintaining, social constructions of gender. In this chapter I argue that there is a need for the systematic study of masculine and feminine dress as a means of deciphering gender constructions in Minoan society.

The Functions of Dress

A basic premise of dress theory is that dress functions as a primary means of nonverbal communication or "signaling."[2] The essential components of dress, including clothing as well as jewelry and other accessories, hairstyles, cosmetics, body painting, and body piercing (Roach-Higgins and Eicher 1992:1), emit constant, complex social messages that would have been intended by the wearer and understandable by the viewer. The primary messages of dress are social membership and social event (Enninger 1984:79; Kaiser 1983–4:2; McCracken 1987:105). Through dress, then, both the identity and the situation of an individual are communicated without any verbal exchange (Kaiser 1983–4:2). If dress is understood as "a collection of *material* 'systems of difference' which encode a set of parallel *conceptual* 'systems of difference' " (McCracken 1987:105), it follows that a universal function of dress is signification of gender (Vicary 1988:299). Dress may be considered a particularly appropriate medium for communicating social constructions of gender because the social messages constru(ct)ed in dress are often of the type that would be inappropriate, or cannot be articulated, in verbal language; for example, social inequities (Kaiser 1990:413), including those of gender.

How does dress signal social information to the viewer? It has been noted by sociologist Fred Davis that dress codes are of "low semanticity," so that, as with music, it is often not obvious how dress evokes meanings (Davis 1992:5–6). As is true for all material culture, dress does not carry any inherent meaning, but is ascribed social meaning in a particular cultural context. These meanings are arbitrary and socially specific, complicating the task of the archaeologist who is removed temporally and spatially from the original ancient "coding community." Although as modern viewers we lack direct access to ancient dress codes, it is possible to reconstruct them from the artistic iconography by analyzing their constituent parts and patterns of use and by considering certain fundamental principles that are applicable to all types of dress systems.

The iconography of Minoan dress is known from the remains of wall paintings that decorated the palatial centers of Crete, from the iconography of carved seals and finger rings, from various small-scale figurines, and from other objects in bronze, faience, ivory, stone, and other materials. These various images have been found all over the island but primarily in palatial and sanctuary contexts.[3] The wall paintings are our best source of evidence for dress, not least because they preserve the colors and decoration of the garments. The paintings also are in larger scale than the small-scale figurines or the representations shown on seals and, therefore, show greater detail. Few of the wall paintings are well preserved, however; almost all are quite fragmentary, and most were restored early in the century, many quite fancifully. The seals are also problematic because the pictorial images are at such a small scale that it is often difficult to read those details of the iconography that are crucial for a study of dress. The figurines, especially the large corpus of bronze votives, are particularly useful because they illustrate fairly consistent patterns of masculine and feminine dress that might serve as a reference for the pictorial representations. Among the figurines too, however, there are problems of questionable restoration.[4] For example, the so-called "priestess" or "votary" faience figurine (see Fig. 9.2) has been reconstructed with a cat on her head, even though it was not found attached.

Minoan Figurative Art

Virtually all the human figurative art from Crete is believed to be religious art, or at least to have "ritual, ceremonial, or symbolic significance" (Dickinson 1994:164), because almost all paintings, seals, and figurines were found in sanctuaries or in palatial complexes that seem to have served a religious function. Certain images apparently illustrate performances of rituals. The so-called "Sacred Grove fresco" from Knossos depicts a group of women wearing elaborate skirts who make gestures of worship toward an outdoor shrine (Davis 1987:158)[5] while crowds of spectators look on. Another Knossos fresco, the so-called "Grandstand Fresco," has been interpreted similarly as representing a crowd of spectators gathered to witness a ritual event, perhaps bull-leaping, an activity also depicted in Minoan iconography. Images on seals and finger rings depict more intimate scenes of worship, such as a small group of devotees gesturing toward a goddess or priestess, or individual suppliants performing rites in the presence of a goddess or priestess. Individual worshippers also seem to be represented by a large number of bronze votive figurines displaying gestures of prayer or adoration. These votive figurines were left at sanctuaries by the faithful in order that they might be in the perpetual presence of the deity. Finally, ritual objects, such as *rhyta* for pouring libations, are decorated with apparently ritual scenes, including ritual athletic events or a procession in celebration of the harvest.

Within the broad and varied corpus of Minoan art, the iconography for males and females is highly conventional and distinctive for each sex. In polychrome images such as wall paintings and the faience figurines, males are represented with dark skin and females with light skin. This distinction is also characteristic of contemporary Egyptian art, which is probably the source of this Minoan convention. The dichotomy of dress for males and females is equally explicit.[6] Male figures in Minoan art are in most cases relatively sparsely clad (Fig. 9.3). Males are typically represented wearing a phallic sheath or codpiece, either alone or in combination with a loincloth or breechcloth. There is much variation in the length and shape of the loin- or breechcloths, but two primary types are discernible. The first type is open at the sides, leaving the buttocks uncovered; the second type is closed at the sides, fastening at the front somewhat like a kilt. These garments are sometimes decorated with an allover woven or embroidered design, but more often in this period they are plain or simply decorated with a border (Barber 1991:315).[7] Males frequently wear a tight-fitting belt that appears to cinch the waist. Some male figures, perhaps only those of high status, also wear a dagger and/ or "sacred knot" tucked into the belt. A few figures wear pointy-toed, laced shoes.[8] The males frequently wear jewelry, examples of which have been preserved in the archaeological record. Masculine hairstyles are varied and are often quite elaborate, with long serpentine locks descending from the top of the head and sometimes knotted at the back.

In contrast to the male figures, female figures are covered from neck to the feet, with only the forearms and the breasts exposed (see Figs. 9.1 and 9.2). The short-sleeved bodice is a form-fitting garment laced across the

Figure 9.3. Depiction of the "priest king" from a fresco (reconstruction) from the palace at Knossos, Crete (line drawing by the author).

front.[9] The fabric of the bodice is often woven with a decorative pattern, sometimes also with a band extending along the tops of the sleeves, across the shoulders and behind the neck. Three types of fabric skirts can be distinguished, all of which are held in place with a rather bulky belt that rests on the hips. A few females wear a tight-fitting belt that cinches the waist, similar to those worn by males. The faience votary wears this belt in combination with a sort of double apron over the skirt, with one panel in the front and one in the back, analogous to the loin- or breech-cloth worn by some of the male figures. The feet are usually hidden by the skirts, but when they are visible they are always bare. In contrast to the males, most females are represented wearing relatively little jewelry, and those pieces that are depicted are restricted to a few simple necklaces and bracelets similar to those worn by males. Only a few of the frescoes depict females wearing elaborate jewelry. Feminine hairstyles do not generally differ from masculine hairstyles, and they might have been considered indicators of age and/or ethnicity rather than gender.[10]

Dress in Minoan Society

The iconography of male and female dress indicates quite different conventions of dress for each sex. Most items of dress are worn by one sex or the other; very few are shared by males and females.[11] Male dress covers very little of the body compared to female dress, which extends from neck to feet. The fact that so much of the body is left uncovered by Minoan male dress gives the costume the effect of a kind of "uniform" that is represented by the male anatomy and emphasized by the differential skin color. In contrast, female garments exhibit more variety and more elaborate decoration. This variation in form and decoration of female garments in comparison to the relative uniformity of male garments suggests that Minoan dress functioned to mark females as differing from a male norm.

A similar construction exists in our own culture, in which there exist multiple categories for women and not for men. For example, the titles "Mrs." and "Miss" categorize women in terms of their marital status, and the title "Ms." intended to confound the other two categories, nonetheless implies an adult female. Men are not defined according to age or marital status but are referred to by the generic "Mr." In our own culture the norm is masculine, and the feminine is constructed as differing from that norm; the multiplicity of constructed categories for females is not indicative of high status for women. In the Minoan artistic idiom the uniformity of masculine dress and the variety of feminine dress would suggest a parallel construction of male-as-norm and female-as-other.[12]

The differentiation of gender in Minoan dress is emphasized further by the fact that both masculine and feminine dress draw attention to external sexual characteristics. The phallic sheath or codpiece covers and protects the male sexual organ, yet calls attention to it, while the feminine bodice emphasizes the breasts by exposing them. The ambiguity of both concealment and exposure as means of emphasizing the external sexual characteristics does *not* indicate that social constructions of gender were ill defined, but rather the opposite; the categories of masculine and feminine were strict social constructions that were perpetuated on an everyday, individual level through dress. It is also not legitimate to assume that emphasis of the penis and breasts necessarily connoted specifically sexual meanings in Minoan culture as they do in our own. Although these organs function biologically in procreation and lactation, many cultures ascribe them other meanings as well, such as virility and nurturing. But while the specific *meanings* attached to these aspects of male and female dress elude us, the *structure* of the Minoan dress system suggests that male and female were primary social categories that were maintained through dress.

A high degree of social control was exercised in the Minoan dress system. Because both masculine and feminine garments were constructed and not draped, potential variation was limited except through the addition or removal of accessories.[13] Another level of behavior codification may be adduced from the apparent physical restrictiveness of Minoan garments. In Minoan artistic iconography, males and some females are represented wearing the tight-fitting belt that appears to cinch the waist. But whereas males are unencumbered by garments on their lower legs, arms, or torso, females wear tight-fitting bodices and full skirts that might have restricted their physical activities. Minoan dress would have had a psychological effect on the wearer, serving to enforce social and gender constructions.

The decoration of Minoan garments also seems to follow gendered constructions. Elizabeth Barber has noted that in this period of Minoan art females are represented wearing much more elaborate fabrics than those worn by males.[14] Because feminine dress covers so much more of the body than does masculine dress, the potential for social marking through both the form and the decoration of Minoan garments is much greater for females than for males.[15] Barber suggests also that women were responsible for the production of these garments on the basis of textual evidence provided by Linear B tablets from the succeeding period on Crete (Barber 1991:283–84). Indeed, textile production constituted "women's work" in many early societies, as it could be done concurrently with child care (Barber 1991:289). If Minoan women were responsible for textile production and garment fabrication, women may have been active participants in the (re)production of gender constructions for Minoan society.[16]

Additional evidence for the significance of dress in Minoan society may be derived from representations of garments that seem to have had a ritual function. Votive garments made of non-perishable luxury materials such as faience and ivory, as well as images on seals depicting rituals involving the dedication of garments, suggest that the dedication of real garments was part of Minoan religious practice, as is the case in traditional modern Greek culture (Gullberg and Åström 1970:45). Entire ensembles, including a chemise, belt, and skirt specially decorated with crocuses (which probably had religious significance) were recreated in faience and deposited together with the Snake Goddess figurines at Knossos; two belts, made separately, were dedicated as well. "Sacred knots," apparently the same as those worn by some of the males in the artistic iconography, were also recreated in faience and ivory and dedicated as votives. Multiple images of persons bearing "sacred" garments are extant among the seals and sealings (Demargne 1949:283–85). It has been suggested that such garments were used in a rite in which a priestess was dressed to appear as an epiphany of a goddess (Niemeier 1987:166). Clearly these garments, particularly the flounced skirt, had a religious significance. Meanings associated with these garments may also have extended to those who made them and those who wore them.

Textiles had religious significance in Minoan culture, but they were important for economic reasons as well. The widespread distribution of loom weights and spindle whorls in the archaeological record in the Neopalatial period suggests intensive production of textiles, probably exceeding the immediate needs of individual households. Linear B tablets from the subsequent period reveal that textiles were required as tribute to the palatial centers of Crete, a practice that was probably a continuation of earlier practices (Barber 1991:284–85). Under the control of the palatial elite, these textiles became part of much larger trade networks that extended throughout the Eastern Mediterranean. Although actual textiles have not been recovered, evidence for their trade is found in Egyptian tombs from the same period. Images of Cretan tribute-bearers bringing textiles and other Minoan objects are found in Thebes in the Eighteenth Dynasty tomb of Menkheperresneb, and Minoan textile motifs appear to have inspired Egyptian ceiling decoration in several other contemporary tombs (Barber 1991:338–51). Clearly, the importance of Minoan textiles extended far beyond the island of Crete.

Consideration of the economic and religious importance of Minoan textiles illuminates the significance attached to Minoan dress. Elaborate textiles were required by the palatial administrators for their participation in an elite trade network. That women were required to make and provide these textiles to Minoan palatial centers is suggested not only by the later Linear B tablets, but also by the ritualization of this practice, illustrated by the dedication of votive garments to a deity. The ritualization of the bestowal of textiles is important because it codified the need for these textiles and might have ascribed women a high degree of social worth, at least in this particular realm. Artistic representations of females wearing elaborate garments reinforced the integral association between women and textiles. Whether Minoan women actually wore such elaborate dress on a regular basis is unknown, although it seems reasonable to suggest that such dress was worn on ritual occasions, perhaps only by the elite. What is clear from the artistic representations is that the differentiation of the appearance of males and females reflects a conceptual difference between masculine and feminine that was derived from the social roles ascribed to men and women, particularly the role of women in textile production.

Summary

The meanings ascribed to the Snake Goddess and her votary are clearly more complicated than earlier scholars assumed. To understand these objects we must resituate them in their cultural context. In the past quarter-century, we have greatly increased our understanding of many aspects of Minoan society, including political organization, social organization, production, economy, trade, and religion. Advances made in these areas can in turn help us to understand the more ideological aspects of Minoan culture that are depicted in wall paintings and figurines, including the construction of gender and its role in social differentiation.

Notes

1. In her study of the bronze votive figurines from Crete, Colette Verlinden considers the iconography of dress as indicative of social status (1984). A recent survey of Aegean male costume by Paul Rehak (1996) associates different costume types with differences in age, status, and activity, and Robert Koehl (1986) has studied the relationship between hairstyles and rank and status. More has been written about dress and social rank and status in the frescoes from the site of Akrotiri on the Aegean island of Thera, which appear to have been influenced by Minoan art (e.g., Davis 1986; Morgan 1988).

2. Semiotician Werner Enninger (Enninger 1985: 85) argues that rather than *communicating* like spoken language, dress more accurately *signifies*, like a traffic light, for example. Sociologist Fred Davis also cites sociologist Herbert Blumer's observation that " 'while clothing may "speak," it seems rarely to engage in dialogue' " (Davis 1992: 8). Several scholars have taken issue with the correlation of dress and language (e.g., Davis 1992: 3; Gottdeiner 1986: 252–253; Kaiser 1990:

239; McCracken 1987: 110–123; Schevill 1993: 6–7). Within any given community, however, individuals emulate the dress of others, which suggests two-way communication rather than one-way signaling.

3. The iconographic corpus under consideration here has been limited to the Neopalatial period (Middle Minoan III through Late Minoan IB, about 1700–1450 B.C.E.) and to objects found on the island of Crete. These are artificial spatial and temporal boundaries that serve to "fix" the iconographic system in time and place. Of course, all cultural systems, including iconographic, dress, and gender systems, are dynamic and are best studied both diachronically and across regional boundaries. The present study is intended only as a test for the applicability of certain principles of dress theory to a particular set of evidence.

4. Given the problems associated with specific objects in terms of state of preservation, quality of restoration, and amount of observable detail, this study is limited to general patterns discernible in the iconography of masculine and feminine dress. The use of artistic iconography as evidence for ideological construction does not *necessarily* imply that the dress system represented in the art reflects actual dress worn by Bronze Age men and women. It is assumed, however, that since the images must have been comprehensible to their ancient viewers, the iconography must have had some basis in reality.

5. The previous interpretation of this image as representing a group of dancing women has proved incorrect following the restoration of a white masonry structure in the left part of the painting.

6. The typology of Minoan dress is derived primarily from Verlinden's study (1984: 98–112). Males and females appear to share garment types in two examples of Minoan art, the Agia Triada sarcophagus and the Toreador fresco. Neither will be considered in this study because they postdate the period in question.

7. Elizabeth Barber (1991) distinguishes between the *Classical Minoan* period of dress and the succeeding *Transitional/Ritual* styles of dress dating to Late Minoan II-IIIA when Crete seems to have come under Mycenaean influence. In the latter period male dress becomes more elaborate, with more elaborate kilts and extensive surface decoration. Our best-preserved example of male dress from this period is the "cupbearer" from the procession fresco from Knossos.

8. Males are also represented wearing other garments, including robes, tunics, "shorts," cloaks and capes, much less frequently than the standard Minoan dress.

9. Barber describes the Minoan bodice as a constructed garment that was cut and sewn to fit the wearer (Barber 1991:318). Rehak contends that such "implausibly elaborate patterns of cutting and stitching" (1996b:39) are unlikely for Minoan dress, given the fact that later (Archaic and Classical) Greeks wore simple draped garments.

10. Verlinden notes that the Minoans were known in the Mediterranean world for their long coiffures and were depicted with elaborate hairstyles in contemporary Egyptian tomb painting (1984:94).

11. Both the form-fitting belt and the double-paneled apron worn by some of the females, which resembles the masculine loin- or breechcloth, may in fact represent ritual garb that was not usual feminine attire.

12. Among the bronze votive figurines, patterns in dress of masculine uniformity and feminine multiplicity are also discernible in the types of gestures performed by the figurines (Lee 1994, 1996).

13. For an ethnographic example of the expressive capacities of a draped garment see Messing (1978).

14. There seems to be a reversal in the relative ornateness of female and male dress in the succeeding period of Minoan culture. See note 7.

15. In his study of folk dress in the former Yugoslavia, H. Martin Wobst found that all types of female dress carried messages reflecting women's social status within a group, whereas male dress included items (particularly the headdress) that specifically carried intergroup messages. Wobst suggests that "this is to be expected in a strongly patriarchal society where males determine most kin affiliations, where most public activities are in the hands of males, and where the movement of women is restricted to the context of the local group" (1977:335).

16. Although gender constructions are reproduced in every act of dress, I wish to emphasize here the active social contribution made by women's *production* of the dress items themselves.

Chapter 10
Fear and Gender in Greek Art

Timothy J. McNiven

One of the strongest contrasts between men and women made by the ancient Greeks was between manly courage and womanly cowardice (Gilmore 1990). In Greek literature, this distinction is made repeatedly. For example, in Xenophon's Socratic dialogue *Oikonomikos*, the narrator Ischomachos assures his new wife that the gods gave women a greater share of fear so that they would be happier staying safely at home (vii.25). Indeed, the ancient Greek word for courage is *andreia*, which literally means "manliness" or "virility" and clearly has gendered connotations (Hall 1989:121; Loraux 1995:10, 154). Greek art also reinforces this stereotyped dichotomy between men and women. This study examines the portrayal of fear in Greek images to gain some new insights into this aspect of ancient Greek gender ideology.

Emotions are not usually dealt with in iconographical studies of Greek art. Emotions are most easily read from facial expressions, and it is just such expressions that are generally avoided in Greek art. Rather, the artists worked to achieve the controlled, emotionless visage that was a distinguishing characteristic of the heroic ideal. A good example of this ideal is the figure of the god Apollo, the model of rationality and restraint, as he presides over the riotous battle between the Greeks and the centaurs on the west pediment of the Temple of Zeus at Olympia (Ashmole and Yalouris 1967:Plate 105). Women are also usually rendered in this expressionless way and sometimes face the most appalling situations with no reaction displayed on their faces. Again the Olympia pediment supplies an example in the figure of the bride Deidameia who shows no emotion even though she is being violently assaulted by a half-horse monster (Ashmole and Yalouris 1967:Plate 111). Women were included with Greek men under the canon of beauty that dictated that self-control is the highest sign of the noble, and the noble is equated with the beautiful.

It is only the marginal figures, the Others, who distort their faces with emotions. The monstrous centaurs from Olympia, for example, show emotion on their faces, but they of course are only partly human (Ashmole and Yalouris 1967:Plate 92). Nevertheless, emotional facial expressions are surprisingly rare, even in the case of monsters.

Lacking facial indicators of emotion, we have to look at the other aspects of body language, especially to gestures (McNiven 1982), in order to "read" the emotional content of the image. Gestures are used to display a wide range of expressions, often in contexts where the circumstances are known, and, therefore, reasonable conclusions concerning the emotions being displayed can be drawn. In particular, the depiction of fear is very much a gendered phenomenon in Greek art.

Women are depicted expressing fear surprisingly often in Greek art. In contrast, adult men are never depicted expressing fear. In many scenes, a woman's basic response to a man is fear. In others, the woman's only role in the image seems to be to react in terror. In a much smaller number of scenes, males exhibit fear, but these males are never adult Greek men of the heroic type. Boys, old men, half-human monsters and other anti-heroic opponents of the great Greek heroes show their fear. Their display of fearful behavior links them with women, and their marginality only reinforces the basic gender division between "heroic males," on the one hand, and "women and other individuals" on the other.

The data for this investigation come mainly from the pottery painted in the city of Athens in the sixth and fifth centuries B.C.E. Athenian pottery presents us with a vast storehouse of easily datable images that are painted on vessels whose function, and consequent audience, are fairly well understood. However, the data must be interpreted with caution. The large number of images preserved on pots has led earlier scholars to take the images at face value, treating them as a vast pictorial archive of ancient life and myth. It is important to keep in mind that painted images are not documentary photographs but rather artistic creations, produced to satisfy buyers' demands. They do not present an objective measure or a random sample of reality. The images found on Athenian pottery are projections of the assumptions, preconceptions, and ideals of their makers and of Athenian society at large (Bérard et al. 1989:8). These images, then, functioned as vehicles for the ideology of ancient Athens, and are some of our best evidence for that ideology.

Greek Femininity and the Iconography of Fear

The most common gesture of fear is made by extending both arms outward, either parallel to each other or spread wide. Sometimes only one arm is used. The gesture is one of alarm, or perhaps prayer, and the abandon with which the gesture is made indicates the strength of the emotion. Most of the figures making this gesture are reacting to some obviously terrifying event. Often they are observers, acting as a sort of tragic chorus watching a hero kill an opponent, as seen, for example, in the scene depicting Herakles wrestling the giant Antaios on Euphronios's krater (Beazley 1963:14.2; Boardman 1975: Fig. 23). Here, as often, the males act in the foreground, while the females react in the background. These women show their unmanliness by the gestures that reveal their fear, by the motion that betrays their lack of decorum, and by the lack of effective action that contrasts with the feats of men.

In other examples, women directly involved in the event make gestures of alarm. They are often women who are escaping while a hero or god pursues their sister or friend, such as the companions of the Leukippids on a krater by Polygnotos in Ferrara (Beazley 1963:1689; Alfieri and Arias 1958:Plate 68).

In many of these scenes of flight the women flee to an old man, making a further contrast to manly behavior. On a hydria at Bowdoin College by the Niobid Painter, for example, Oreithyia's sisters escape from her kidnapping and run to their father Erechtheus (Beazley 1963:606.68; Buitron 1972:118). He stands calmly by, wrapped in his mantle, carrying a scepter, while his daughters flee in terror, throw up their arms, and even make direct supplication to him. One might expect a father to respond to the abduction of his daughter with some strong emotion — anger, surprise, perhaps even fear. Instead, Erechtheus displays decorous and controlled behavior, what the Greeks called *sophrosune* and regarded as the highest virtue (North 1966). The variety of the women's poses, the varied directions they face, their wide-flung arms, and their open palms in these scenes signal the women's susceptibility to emotion in contrast to the men's rationality (Bremmer 1992:19).

Most of the women who are depicted making gestures of fear are figures on the margins of scenes. They comment upon, but do not take part in, the action portrayed. The woman being pursued, however, also displays fear, an emotion almost required by the situation in which she finds herself. This general kind of scene, conventionally called an "erotic pursuit scene," "abduction," or "rape," is familiar enough to seem rather common in Greek art. In a recent discussion, Andrew Stewart tabulated 700 examples from Athens in the fifth century B.C.E., but he calculates that this is less than four percent of the vases known from the period (Stewart 1995a:87–88).

These scenes do, of course, depict a common motif in Greek mythology (Lefkowitz 1993; Zeitlin 1986). While the basic story is not the invention of the artist, the depiction of these scenes is the artist's choice, and understanding that choice gives us insight into the workings of the Greek ideology of gender.

The interpretation of pursuit scenes on Athenian pottery has been much discussed. Sophia Kaempf-Dimitriadou (1979) interpreted the pursuit scenes that involve gods as depictions of divine intervention in human affairs. This interpretation seems rather more symbolic than Greek art tends to be (Cohen 1996:118–119) and does not explain the other scenes where a hero or mortal pursues a woman. Eva Keuls (1985: 51), on the other hand, sees these scenes as "dramatizing the power of the male over the female," the perfect embodiment of what Keuls calls the "Reign of the Phallus." Stewart (1995a:86) seems to accept Keuls idea, in a more politic form, for he sees pursuit scenes as "nothing more nor less than the projection of male desires on the heroic world" in order to "promote the cause of Athenian masculine self-assertion." Ada Cohen (1996) makes a forceful argument for keeping the issue of rape in the foreground when discussing these images. She suggests that depicting pursuits and abductions to the exclusion of actual rapes may have allowed the Greek artist to show heroic men in control of women and also of themselves (Cohen 1996:119).

Another dimension to understanding these scenes as an expression of men's control over women is given by Christiane Sourvinou-Inwood (1973; 1987a; 1987b), who connects abduction scenes with the Greek belief that an unmarried girl is a wild thing that must be tamed by marriage. Pursuit and abduction scenes thus refer to this taming process. This interpretation is supported by the appearance of these scenes on vessels that were given to the bride as part of the wedding ceremony. Depictions of mythical and actual weddings often parallel the pursuit scenes on such vessels (Oakley 1995; Reeder 1995:229–231). All of these scenes refer to the ritual abduction which was a central element in an ancient Greek wedding (Jenkins 1983).

The woman being pursued often throws out her arms in a strong expression of fear, but sometimes the gesture is more controlled. Usually she attempts to move away: at times her pace is slow and stately, other times both participants are running. She is never willing, accepting, or even coy because such a response would violate the modesty which the Greeks considered one of the greatest virtues of a woman (Reeder 1995: 123–124). Some scholars have read coyness, or even seductiveness, into the returned gaze of the woman, but the accompanying gestures are unanimously negative (*pace* Frontisi-Ducroux 1996:81–84; Reeder 1995: 125–126; Sourvinou-Inwood 1973). Such portrayals of fear seem a strange message to send to a girl about to be married. Yet perhaps as heroic paradigms for the present event (that is, the wedding in which the bride is about to take part) these scenes were intended to reassure her that fear is a natural reaction, and perhaps they were intended to suggest a potential positive outcome (famous children, even apotheosis) (Lefkowitz 1993).

Abduction scenes may show only the couple, providing a direct comparison between the male and the female, for the male abductors are the active subjects, and the female victims the emotive objects. The gender split parallels the power differential, which is even more evident when the pursuing male is a god, as seen in images of Zeus pursuing Aegina, or Poseidon pursuing Amymone (Kaempf-Dimitriadou 1979:Plates 12–20).

In some mythical abduction scenes, the status and power of the female are greater than that of the male. According to Greek myth, the mortal hero Peleus was permitted by Zeus to wed the goddess Thetis if he could capture her. As a sea deity, she had the power to change herself into many forms, but Peleus held on, and eventually subdued her. Among abduction scenes, the subject of Peleus wrestling Thetis is relatively common (Krieger 1975; Reeder 1995: 340–349). Usually, Thetis is depicted as relatively calm, raising her skirt gracefully with one hand and extending her other hand (Reeder 1995:341, figure 106, but note 107 also). The snakes which curl off her arms and leg to bite the hero and the miniature lion which crawls down his back, indicate her power and, perhaps, her transformations. The message is still the same, however: whether the woman displays her fear or not, the man conquers in the end. Because she is an immortal, however, Thetis loses her composure to a lesser degree than mortal women would. She can, therefore, be seen as a model for womanly behavior, even though most women will not have shared her situation.

The only pursuit scenes in which a woman is able to defend herself successfully are those which involve maenads, the mad women of Dionysos. Maenads are usually associated with the half-human, half-donkey satyrs. A series of images from the fifth century B.C.E. shows a satyr accosting a maenad, who turns her ritual staff, or *thyrsos*, against him (McNally 1978). These militant maenads sometimes also show the fear expected of a normal woman, but usually they are more courageous because they are invested with the power of the god Dionysos. In Euripides' *Bacchae* (lines 714–768), a band of maenads even defeats a group of armed men who attempt to capture them.

Satyrs, on the other hand, occasionally show their horror that a maenad would fight back. For all their exaggerated maleness, satyrs are less than human, and often represent the opposite of the normal world (Lissarague 1990). Scenes of the satyrs' failed pursuits portray a world upside down, where women take action and men are afraid.

Amazons are another class of women who do not fit the norm (Bothmer 1957; Stewart 1995b). The majority of these warrior women are shown fighting and dying like their male opponents. Only rarely does a defeated Amazon submit, reduced to begging for her life, another unmanly gesture that I have discussed elsewhere (McNiven 1996). Only one

Amazon appears in an abduction scene, on a cup by Oltos in Oxford (Beazley 1963:62.77; Bothmer 1957:Plate 68). She is Antiope being carried off bodily by the hero Theseus, whom she later married. Such scenes are not common. Amazons deserved more respect than normal women; they were armed. In the end, however, they were still women, and barbarian women at that, and so would be defeated by men.

Greek Masculinity and the Iconography of Male Fear

The opposite of *andreia* (the ancient Greek word for courage) is *anandreia* ("unmanliness") a word that is more strongly gendered than the English "cowardice." In the Greek tendency to think in terms of binary opposites, either one is a man, or is not. That is, the dichotomy was not between Man and Woman, but between Man and Other. Women were the most numerous group, but to an ancient Greek (that is, a freeborn adult male Greek), the Others were all alike. Consequently, we need to broaden the focus of this discussion to include the much rarer examples in Greek art where male figures exhibit gestures of fear.

Some pursuit scenes involve not women but boys, as on an amphora in Boston by the Pan Painter showing Zeus pursuing Ganymede (Beazley 1963:553.39; Kaempf-Dimitriadou 1979:Plate 2.3). In these scenes, the same vocabulary of gestures indicates the boys' fear, and thus spells out the parallel nature of women and boys. There is, however, one important difference, as a quotation from Aristotle (1972) shows: "Women have the ability to make choices, but that quality is inoperative. Boys have the ability to make choices, but the quality is undeveloped" (*Politics* 1260a:13–14). In other words, unlike women, boys can grow up and if properly trained as men, they can move to the other side of the power inequality (Golden 1990).

An interesting reversal of the norm exists, however, in depictions of the goddess of the dawn, Eos, pursuing and carrying off boys. In myth, she is cursed to fall in love only with young mortals, and both the huntsman Kephalos and the schoolboy Tithonos attract her desire (Kaempf-Dimitriadou 1979:16–21, Plates 8–11; Stehle 1990). Eos, as a goddess, has the power to act on her desires, but she must do so like a man, pursuing boys, the standard objects of Greek male homoerotic desire (Dover 1985). Robin Osborne actually sees her as a reverse role model for Greek women (1996:68). Evidently the Greek artist could only conceive of active desire in masculine terms. Similarly, he could only conceive of the boy's reaction to that desire in passive, emotional, that is feminine, terms.

Another group of male figures who show their fear like women are old men (Falkner 1989). The aged Priam, for example, throws up one arm in fear when the Greek hero Neoptolemos attacks him during the fall of

Troy (Beazley 1956:362.35). Even though he is the king of Troy, leader of the legendary enemies of the Greeks, Priam is treated respectfully in depictions of most incidents from his story (Miller 1995). His emotional reaction to imminent death signifies his loss of power, his woman-like situation.

Another old man, the "Old Man of the Sea" (probably the sea god Nereus) is wrestled by Herakles, whom we must understand as the model of Greek heroic manhood. Nereus, despite his divinity, runs and throws up his arms rather than standing and fighting like a man (Beazley 1956: 361.18; Boardman 1974:Fig. 202). Like Priam, his old age makes him as susceptible to fear as a woman.

Other opponents of the paradigmatic Herakles, such as centaurs, also throw up their hands (Beazley 1956:283.9; Boardman 1974:Fig. 197). This is not surprising since, like the satyrs, they are part animal. As personifications of the uncivilized and bestial, they are often the aggressors in abduction scenes, but, like the neighborhood bully, not courageous enough to oppose a threat from a man.

Herakles' nemesis, Eurystheus, is a more surprising member of this category. As a king and a member of Herakles' family, he should behave like a heroic Greek man of the noble class. Instead, Eurystheus shows that he is a coward. When Herakles brings him the monstrous Erymanthian boar, Eurystheus hides in a storage jar. Faced with the prospect of having the boar dropped on his head, he waves his arms frantically in a comically unheroic manner (Beazley 1956:279.47; Boardman 1974:Fig. 192).

Another, less common type of figure who shamelessly displays fear is the barbarian. An example is the Egyptian king Busiris and his followers, depicted on a pelike by the Pan Painter in Athens (Beazley 1963:517.7; Boardman 1975:Fig. 336). The Greeks often criticized non-Greeks for their womanliness, for wearing luxurious clothing and jewelry and using perfume (Hall 1989:79–83). Here the parallel is made not just by their flight, but also by the extreme emotion they so clearly display. Busiris is not just a barbarian, however. He is killed for attempting to offer Herakles as a human sacrifice, a serious violation of Greek hospitality and religious norms. As such, Busiris symbolized the capricious, tyrannical despot who was very much a bugbear of democratic Athens. By showing Busiris behaving like a woman, the Athenian artist provided political justification for the government Athenian men had made for themselves (Bazant 1987).

The signs of fear examined here, therefore, are the signs of the non-Man. Made by the monstrous opponents of Herakles, these gestures symbolized a nonhuman lack of control that was quite opposite to the dominant virtue of self-control. Made by the barbarian transgressors of everything the Greeks held sacred, the gestures signified the weakness of a non-Greek people. Made by the distraught victims in erotic pursuit scenes, they signaled female emotional passivity in a world that valued male action. Looking at these signs of fear, the Greek man could say, paraphrasing Thales of Miletos (in Diogenes Laertius, 1.33: [1966:60–65]), "There are three reasons to be grateful to the gods: that I am human; that I am Greek; that I am male."

Chapter 11
Mississippian Weavers

Alice B. Kehoe

> . . . here in this place called Quiché. Here we shall design, we shall
> brocade the Ancient Word.
> — Opening of the *Popol Vuh* (Tedlock translation,
> quoted by Berlo 1991:445; alternative translation is
> ". . . we shall inscribe, we shall implant.")

Sitting back on her heels as women do when weaving at indigenous American horizontal and backstrap looms (O'Neale 1945:47; Sperlich and Sperlich 1980:45), the "Keller figurine" from the American Bottom near Cahokia (Illinois) has an open, pleasant expression on her face, her lips parted as if singing (see Emerson 1982: Plate 5). This female figurine of red fire clay was found inside a substantial structure at the BBB Motor Site (11MS595), three kilometers northeast of Monks Mound at the center of Cahokia. The excavator, Emerson (1989:49), interpreted the building as a temple not only on the basis of the figurine, but also the presence of Ramey Incised fine ceramics, mica, galena, red cedar, and remains of the hallucinogenic Datura plant, in combination with an absence of domestic debris. The site was occupied during the Stirling phase of the Mississippian period, from about A.D. 1100 to 1200 (calibrated radiocarbon dates [Hall 1991]).

Half of the figurine was found in a shallow pit inside the apparent temple building, the other half in a garbage pit outside (south of) the building. A second red fire clay figurine of a woman, the Birger figurine, had been deliberately buried in a small pit outside, and east of, the same building (Emerson 1989:50). Three more reconstructable fire clay figurines of women (and, possibly, fragments of more figurines) were recovered from a comparable probable temple location in the Stirling phase Sponemann site (Fortier 1992). Emerson interprets the BBB Motor Site as the local center of a farming district, and the figurines as symbols of fertility and water and of the Underworld that is associated with these themes (Emerson 1989:90–91; Knight 1986).

It appears to me that the Keller figurine found inside the BBB Motor Site "temple" may be interpreted as a weaver, based on the characteristics of the figure itself as well as on other evidence regarding the importance of weaving in Mississippian society. First of all, the common occurrence of fabric-impressed ceramics in Mississippian sites attests to the general importance of fiber work and weaving, despite the fact that this fabric is conventionally ignored under the rubric "cord-impressed" (Drooker 1989, 1992). Second, a variety of prehistoric fabrics have been recovered from the few locations in which they could be preserved (e.g., Spiro [Brown 1996:619–631]). Third, chroniclers describe the importance of textiles (including mats [DePratter 1991:94]) in Southeastern kingdoms of the sixteenth century. Weaving was likely to be both economically and metaphorically powerful for Mississippians, even though this task is slighted in standard general publications on Southeastern Indians (e.g., Hudson [1976:267] who includes one paragraph on "women's work" among five hundred pages).

The Keller figurine is shown sitting on what may be a woven mat such as those described in the Historic period. Her arms are stretched out, and her surviving hand grasps a rod-like object. This object superficially resembles a mano or hand grinding stone, commonly used in the American Southwest and Mesoamerica. Use of a mano, however, is unlikely in the Midwest, where mortars and pestles were the standard means of pulverizing maize. It seems more reasonable to interpret this rod-like object as a batten or weaving sword that she is pulling toward herself to tighten the weft (cf. Hecht 1989:61). In this interpretation, the box-like object under the batten may be a horizontal loom, seen in a foreshortened perspective, its vertical stripes representing the warp.

The posture of the Keller woman, as well as her facial expression, is consistent with the task of weaving. She appears tranquil, engaged in a comfortable task. In this she contrasts with the stressed face of the Birger figurine (see Emerson 1982: Plate 3), a woman straining as she tugs her hoe.[1] Keller's open uplifted face reminds me of the generally relaxed air of weavers settled into their rhythmic repetitions.

Emerson (1989:90–91) has suggested that the Birger and the Keller figurines, both female, embody fertility themes (see also Knight 1986). This interpretation may be valid for the Birger figurine that was buried outside the temple. This figurine shows plants twining up around the woman from her burden basket, and she is engaged with a double serpent, icons suggesting the Hidatsa Old Woman Who Never Dies (Princi-

ple of Regenerating Vegetation) with her consort the serpent-tailed Un-
derwater Panther (Bowers 1965:334).[2] But Emerson and others may have
failed to see the complementarity signified by the pair of figurines. More
broadly, a neglect of the economic, social, and symbolic importance of
weaving, and a naïve readiness to assume that women embody fertility
(cf. Roth, this volume), exemplify two aspects of the male perspective so
pervasive in archaeology. It is this "male gaze" that persists in seeing a
pair of women's breasts in the Paleolithic Dolní Véstonice pendants that
indubitably represent male genitalia (Kehoe 1991b).

Weaving as a Sign for "Woman"

At the Southeast Iconography Workshop in Texas when I proposed identifying the Keller figurine as a weaver, the Muskogee members of our workshop (Mary Johns, Dan Penton, Charles Daniels/Sakim) commented
that their people consider that the Beloved Woman "weaves together" the
members of the community and that it was traditional that she actually
weave a fabric symbolizing this role. They also noted that each community
kept, in a woven box in the care of its ritual leader, a set of small objects
symbolizing the lineages of the community, and that the object in front of
the Keller woman might be such a box. I consider it possible that the
object represents both a horizontal loom and the woven box, the multi-
vocality giving more power to the image.

Spinning and weaving are commonly associated with women and with
female fertility in many Native American societies. Thelma Sullivan
(1982:13), for example, quotes from Sahagún an Aztec ruler's advice to
his daughter:

> Pay heed to, apply yourself to, the work of women, to the spindle,
> the batten.
> Watch carefully how your noblewomen, your ladies, our ladies, the
> noblewomen,
> Who are artisans, who are craftswomen,
> Dye [the thread], how they apply the dyes,
> How the heddles are set, how the heddle leashes are fixed.

Among the Aztecs, spinning also carried strong sexual innuendoes. Sullivan (1982:14) quotes, again from Sahagún, a riddle: "What is it that they
make pregnant, they make big with child in the dancing place?" Answer:
the spindles rotating in bowls as they fill out with thread. Setting the
spindle rotating in the bowl itself connotes coitus.

This same association of spinning and weaving with females and female
activities is also seen among supernatural beings elsewhere in Mesoamer-

ica. Thus the Huastec Mother Goddess Ixcuina (Nahuatl: Tlazolteotl-Ixuina [Tlazol=tla[n] *teeth* + zolin *quail*]), Lady Cotton, wears two spindles of cotton thread in her headdress. In addition she may also be depicted wearing the Quetzalcoatl headdress *coxoliyo huey itepol,* that is, "the great currasow-feathered phalli," black currasow feathers with four red feathers projecting from the headdress (Sullivan 1982:8).

Sullivan reports (1982:17) that Lady Cotton from the cotton-growing Huasteca later merged with the Aztec goddess Xochiquetzal, patroness of parturient women, of spinning and weaving, and of licentiousness. Xochiquetzal sometimes is shown carrying a batten as if it were a club, possibly referring to the idea that a woman giving birth is equivalent to a man going into battle—she brings into the community her "little captive" (Sullivan 1982:18). Chalchiuhtlicue, the Aztec goddess of water, is also associated with childbirth (representing the amniotic fluid) and was sometimes shown carrying weaving tools—a spindle and a batten (Sullivan 1982:22). Postclassic Aztec spindle whorls are decorated with the same designs used on shields (McCafferty and McCafferty 1991:31), again showing the association between weaving and warfare.

Similarly, Mayahuel, Lady Maguey, is shown in one codex wearing a headdress made from unspun cotton with two spindles, representing the use of maguey as well as cotton for spinning and weaving. Maguey was spun and woven into commoners' cloth throughout Mexico; in addition, its thorns were used as needles (and bloodletters), its leaves were made into paper, and its juice, unfermented, was used as an abortifacient (Sullivan 1982:23; the bark of the cotton plant was also used to induce abortions [Sullivan 1982:19]). Mayahuel was ruler of the day *tochtli,* "rabbit." Rabbits are, of course, exceptionally fertile animals; they live among the maguey plants, and in Mexico, the figure in the face of the moon is a rabbit. Maize and cotton are also related in Mesoamerica in that cotton was said to grow from corn silk, maize ears were said to grow "like thread on the spindle" and a spindle full of thread, as well as the ear of maize, is called *mazorca* in contemporary Mexican Spanish (Sullivan 1982:28).

The Maya goddess Ix Chel (Lady Rainbow) is similarly associated with weaving. She is usually shown in two aspects, youthful and aged (Stone 1990). Youthful, she is Sak na' kab, White Mistress of the Earth (or alternatively, of Honey, another meaning of *kab* in Yucatec) (Stone 1990:16). Stone also notes that *sakal* means "weaving" (Stone 1990:10). The young Lady is commonly depicted as playful, a party girl, shown in one painting with a rabbit grabbing her breast. In her appearance as an aged woman, the goddess is Chak Chel, Red (or Great) Rainbow, and she may be shown as a weaver (Stone 1990:17, 29). Youthful or aged, the Lady wears headdresses with serpents (the rainbow is a serpent [Stone 1990:24]), with spindles of thread, and with a figure-eight looped cord.

Here, as in central Mexico, weaving is the woman's occupation *par excellence*, particularly for the leisured noble lady. Exactly the same valorization of spinning and weaving for noble ladies was made among the Inca (Murra 1989:291) and in sixteenth- and seventeenth-century Europe, where portraits of a noblewoman engaged in spinning signaled the lady's virtue (Stone-Ferrier 1989:216–218).

Weaving as Dance

In the community of Roça Grande, in southeast Brazil, weaving was and still is women's work, their business, and their solace. According to Luciana Bittencourt (1996:125), these women are unusually articulate about the sounds and movements of weaving: "The shuttle dances in the cloth" just as people dance, and it carries the thread across, back and forth, as women walk back and forth carrying gossip and weaving interaction between families. The weaver plays her loom as the guitar player plays his instrument, her harness roller sings—indeed, the people call this part of the loom *garricha*, which is the name of a local bird said to sing the same song. Significantly, the garricha bird brings "tiny spiders to feed her children" (Bittencourt 1996:126), and "the spider weaves like us," the women say (Bittencourt 1996:128).

These women sing while they card, spin, and weave. They see textile designs as similar to the structure of verse, rhyme, and meter. The stanza form in verse is thought of as paralleling the repetition and balance in a woven design (a concept shared by the Maya, who compare textile design with formal oratory [Berlo 1991:441]). The women indulge in song duels, "throwing verses" as they throw shuttles in weaving (both actions are called *jogar*) (Bittencourt 1996:182–184).

In contrast, men in Roça Grande are not adept at throwing verses, they are believed to be poor singers. Instead of singing, when men are working in their fields they banter jokes. "There is no way to sing when we are sweating," explained a man. Men's provoking joking is opposed to women's singing and gossiping. The men are disruptive, but the women are weaving "something that comes and goes [from one person to another] like the shuttle" (Bittencourt 1996:146–154).

In the *Iliad* of the ancient Greeks, weaving and song are intertwined: Calypso and Circe sing as they weave. The myth of Arachne has the prideful young woman challenging the goddess Minerva, patroness of weaving, to a contest of their skill; the goddess normally occupies her noble self at her loom (Scheid and Svenbro 1996:133). For the Greeks, the three Fates—female, of course—spin thread to be the weft woven in and out of the warp that forms a person's life events. When the last weft thread is woven through, the fabric is cut from the loom and the person dies (Scheid and Svenbro 1996:158–159).

The Roman poet Pindar called the lyre a loom, the lyre strings its warp, its music weaving a headband to crown the victor of battle (Scheid and Svenbro 1996:116–117). In Latin, *texere* means "to weave" and also "to write," and in a fable in which a man frees a cicada caught in a spider's web, *textus*, the web, represents the singing voice caught in a written text (Scheid and Svenbro 1996:128–134). The dancelike motion of weaving is not lost to contemporary handloom weavers: "There is nothing more truly satisfying than being seated at a loom . . . the rhythmic swing of the body as all parts unite in the steady motion" (Gallinger 1950:xvii).

Weaving in the Archaeological Record

The perishability of fiber products and loom parts which are preponderantly made of wood (e.g., Rowe 1981:19) is only one factor that contributes to the invisibility of spinning, weaving, and fiber work in the archaeological record. Perhaps more important, the pervasive "male gaze" in archaeology has resulted in a widespread neglect of weaving and denial of its economic, social, and metaphoric importance in a wide range of societies throughout the world. In particular, this attitude has resulted in the neglect of a major economic activity among indigenous societies of the Eastern Woodlands. The abundant if tedious and frustrating evidence of weaving on pottery surfaces commonly called "cord-marked" is very seldom analyzed, bone weaving implements are unrecognized, and textile production is left out of discussions of labor and trade. This "invisibility" of weaving in Eastern Woodlands archaeology is matched by similar neglect of indices of fiber work throughout the course of human evolution. For example, early evidence of fiber working and weaving during the Upper Paleolithic in Eurasia has only very recently been addressed (Adovasio, Soffer and Klíma 1996; Kehoe 1990, 1991a).

Weaving is relevant to a gendered interpretation of the archaeological record because it has generally — but emphatically not exclusively — been women's work. In the European tradition, men were professional weavers, earning their living by producing for the market, and in this tradition these weavers kept pattern drafts on pieces of paper, exchanging drafts with other weavers (Atwater 1928:18). In Guatemala, gender differences are similarly related to men's full-time market production versus women's part-time domestic production (Anderson 1978:17). On the other hand, in Mesoamerica and in the Inca empire, women weavers formed a significant sector of the extra-familial economy (e.g., Brumfiel 1996b). A comparable gendered economic structure may have existed in the Cahokian state (Lincoln 1985). Whatever the organization of craft production, there can be no question that weaving was important to Mississippians. Identification of the Keller figurine as a weaver represents a first step in our efforts to understand the full range of economic activities in Mississippian society.

Notes

1. Might the hoe biting the earth also connote a hide scraper? These have heavy curved hafts similar to the implement in Birger's hand. One can speculate that tilling the soil may have been metaphorically conflated with the similar motion of removing flesh and gristle from hides with knocking blows. Birger's unsmiling face may represent a woman at either of two arduous, outdoor tasks — hoeing and hide scraping (a job Indian women say is both foul and exhausting).

2. The Hidatsa are a Siouan-speaking agricultural nation in central North Dakota. They are culturally related to Midwest Siouans, and quite possibly to Cahokia.

Chapter 12
Prehistoric and Ethnographic Pueblo Gender Roles
Continuity of Lifeways from the Eleventh to the Early Twentieth Century

Brian S. Shaffer, Karen M. Gardner, and Joseph F. Powell

Gender roles in the archaeological record have been discussed by several authors (e.g., Dobres 1995; Gero and Conkey 1991, and citations therein; Scott 1986; Wall 1994), although the roles described usually rely on historic period analogies without diagnostic archaeological support (Wylie 1991:33–34). Simply recovering and identifying prehistoric artifacts known to be used by a particular gender during the historic period, however, does not identify the gender of the prehistoric users. Many gender roles involve intangible behaviors and hence are archaeologically invisible. Therefore, except in rare cases (such as with mortuary data or art in which human activities are portrayed) it is difficult to convincingly assign gender roles or to identify gender-specific activities in prehistory.

In the American Southwest, archaeologists have argued that there is a general continuity from the lifeways of Puebloan peoples in historical times to the prehistoric past, citing the apparent similarity of artifacts, features, and architecture through time and across the region (e.g., Cordell 1984:5; Cushing 1896; Moulard 1984:xxvii; Scully 1989:1). Such extrapolations have often included gender roles. These assumptions were rarely tested with archaeological data; in fact, archaeologists have not been able to develop methods of identifying gender-specific artifacts or tasks (Cordell 1979:146; Wylie 1991a).

The material record of at least one prehistoric Pueblo group, however, does provide a clue regarding the role and significance of gender in its society. The realistically portrayed motifs painted on the interior of bowls created by the Mimbres-Mogollon provide an additional body of information regarding everyday life during the prehistoric period. These Mimbres motifs are particularly relevant to the study of gender because they often explicitly portray a variety of activities performed by males and females.

Use of Mimbres Pottery Motifs for Gender Research

The Mimbres Culture encompasses the area around the Mimbres River Valley and within the Mogollon region of southwestern New Mexico (Fig. 12.1). This desert-adapted culture is identified from pit house and, later, puebloan sites, and dates from about A.D. 200 to 1150. During the Classic Period (A.D. 1000–1150), the Mimbres people lived in above-ground pueblos and produced much of the pottery for which they are known. By A.D. 1150, the core area of the Mimbres was abandoned and the pottery was no longer produced (Anyon et al. 1981; Anyon and LeBlanc 1980; Brody 1977; Brody and Swentzell 1996; Gilman 1987; LeBlanc 1983a, 1983b:23–33; Shafer 1982; Shafer and Brewington 1995). People later reoccupied the Mimbres region but did not settle at the same sites nor produce pottery with the naturalistic designs that are so readily identifiable as "Mimbres."

Previous scholars have recognized the potential to use Mimbres pottery to reconstruct past behaviors (Brody 1977:203–207, 1983:123; Brody and Swentzell 1996; Carr 1979:4; Fewkes 1989a [1914], 1989b [1923], 1989c [1924]; Kabotie 1982; LeBlanc 1983a:120–137; Moulard 1984: xxiv–xxv; Shaffer and Gardner 1995a, 1995b; Shaffer et al. 1995; Snodgrass 1977). These studies have noted that, while painted pottery is produced throughout the American Southwest, naturalistic depictions of people and their artifacts are unique to the Mimbres culture. These depictions thus have the potential to shed light on many aspects of Mimbres society, many of which are not accessible from other archaeological data. Even so, no systematic analysis of Mimbres motifs regarding gender roles was previously undertaken.

Methods

This study examines photographs of nearly 6,000 Mimbres pottery bowls with painted imagery, most from the Mimbres photo archives at the University of New Mexico, Maxwell Museum of Anthropology. (The exact number of bowls in uncertain because some photo cards include more than one bowl, and there are several bowls that were depicted more than once.) While this research incorporated published sources (Anyon and

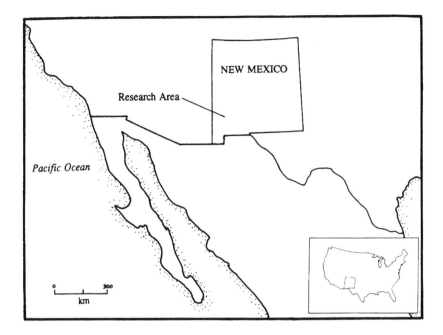

Figure 12.1. Mimbres area, New Mexico (line drawing by Karen Gardner).

LeBlanc 1980; Brody 1977, 1983; Brody and Swentzell 1996; Carr 1979; Fewkes 1989a [1914], 1989b [1923], 1989c [1924]; Kabotie 1982; LeBlanc 1983a, 1983b; Moulard 1984:xxiv–xxv; Shaffer et al. 1995; Snodgrass 1977), most of the photographs examined came from the University of New Mexico archives and from private collections documented by Laurel and Paul Thornburg. In addition, actual bowls were examined from the collections of the Maxwell Museum of Anthropology, the Colorado Springs Fine Arts Center, and the Dallas Museum of Art.

These photographs and the actual bowls were examined to identify those images that depicted humans with clear sexual anatomical traits. In this sample, nearly 500 images of human figures were identified. Of these, a total of 138 were classified as anatomically explicit, of which 90 were male and 48 were female. Males were identified based on two criteria, the presence of genitalia and/or a beard. Females were identified by the body attributes of genitalia and/or breasts, or by the depiction of pregnancy or giving birth. Cultural attributes such as clothing or hairstyles were not used to determine the sex of the individual portrayed because it is possible that some of the depictions might be of cross-dressed individuals (Lange 1959:415; Parsons 1939:38, 53, 90, 131; Roscoe 1991).

Within this chapter, the term "sex" refers to the biological sex of a person as indicated by primary and secondary sex characteristics of the body. "Gender" or "gender role" is used to refer to behavior commonly assigned to a person of a given sex. The distinction is important because biology does not necessarily dictate behavior. For example, anatomically, a person may be male, but by performing activities and assuming roles commonly associated with biological females, the gender of that person would appear to be a female from a Western observer's "etic" perspective (e.g., Angelino and Shedd 1955). Thus, in this study, the identification of the biological sex of people portrayed in Mimbres pottery is based only on observable biological attributes.

After identifying the sex of the humans portrayed on the basis of anatomical traits, we then identified the objects associated with, touched, or used by each individual, or the activity being performed. We then consulted historic period references for descriptions of humans performing similar activities or using similar items. In some cases, different activity types identified among the historic Pueblos are associated with either males or females, but not both. Puebloan gender roles were then inferred from this observed association, and these roles were then extrapolated to identify the prehistoric gender roles that may be portrayed by the Mimbres painted motifs. In this chapter, only single examples of each gender role are given. Only the portion of the motifs depicting humans and their tools is portrayed; the rim designs are not reproduced here because they do not appear to be associated with the activities portrayed in the naturalistic portion of the motifs.

The interpretation of Mimbres gender roles has been limited due to a variety of factors. First, the Mimbres painters themselves selectively portrayed only certain activities and lifeways. Many of the 138 Mimbres human motifs in this sample are shown as portraits without any activity represented. Furthermore, the artisans apparently did not portray every aspect of their society. For example, there are no reported depictions of Mimbres Pueblo structures, use of fire, butchery of animals, consumption of foods or liquids, or use of milling stones, even though other archaeological evidence documents the performance of these activities. Additionally, bowls with motifs that are available for study represent only a small part of the total possible archaeological sample; many bowls have been looted from Mimbres sites. Furthermore, many of the activities documented historically may not have existed during the prehistoric period; conversely, activities performed in prehistory may have had no historic analog. Even so, the graphic accuracy of many of the Mimbres motifs clearly shows males and females performing a variety of behaviors, many of which were documented historically for Puebloan peoples hundreds of years later.

Male Activities

Male activities represented on Mimbres bowls frequently involve aspects of food procurement and warfare. Game procurement activities such as hunting, trapping, and fishing, along with warrior roles, were also historically documented as male activities. The presence of only males in horticultural depictions, however, is not completely congruent with historic period descriptions since women and children assisted men in planting, tending, and harvesting maize (Lange 1959:99–101, 370; Parsons 1939: 39, 78).

Hunting motifs that portray males include solitary and communal hunting episodes (Fig. 12.2). Hunting motifs such as tracking and depictions of the successful completion of a hunt (see Fewkes 1989a, Fig. 13) correspond to historic descriptions from Pueblo and other Native American groups. Other similarities between these accounts and the prehistoric Mimbres motifs include hunt party organization (single and communal), the tools used (bows, arrows, staffs, crooks, rabbit sticks), and the association between males and hunting (e.g., Beaglehole 1936; 1937:18–19; Lange 1959:127–140).

Trapping has also been documented in the desert west and southwest as a male activity (Beaglehole 1936:17; Beals 1933:349; Cushing 1920:81; Du Bois 1935:13; Lange 1959:130; Spier 1928:113; Stephen 1936:188; Underhill 1991:63–64; White 1962:301–302). No Mimbres artifacts have been identified as traps or components of traps (Shaffer et al. 1996); however, snares were portrayed in at least three bowls in this sample, one of which is reproduced here (Fig. 12.3). This figure shows a male holding three snares. He is surrounded by four additional snares, three of which contain captured birds.

Given the limited water resources in the Mimbres River, one might not expect fish to be a significant source of food. Mimbres pottery, however, shows a variety of fish and fishing implements (Jett and Moyle 1986; Shaffer and Gardner 1995b). In the fishing scenes where the sex of the fisher-folk can be identified, the sex is male (see Brody 1977, Fig. 118). Historic accounts describe fishing as primarily a male activity, although it was documented that a "few women may do a little fishing" (Lange 1959:122, 140–141).

There is no reported archaeological evidence of warfare among the Mimbres; the paintings, however, do depict warriors on at least three bowls, of which Brody's (1977: Plate 14) is the best example. This warrior is shown with several weapons, including arrows in a quiver, a shield, and

Figure 12.2. Hunting motifs on Mimbres pottery (from a painted image on pottery; line drawing by Karen Gardner).

a lance. Since historic Pueblo societies commonly had warrior societies (e.g., Cushing 1920; Lange 1959; Parsons 1939; Stephen 1936), the Mimbres warrior depictions may indicate that warrior societies were maintained in the prehistoric period as well.

The depictions of plant remains in Mimbres pottery are rare; depictions of domesticated plants are even rarer. Domesticated plants are identified by the linear arrangements, or crop rows, that are depicted. In Bradfield (1931: Plate LXXIX, no. 187) and Moulard (1984: Plate 5) a field of such rows of corn are shown, along with several males holding sickle-shaped objects. These sickle-shaped objects may be similar to sickle and sword-like weeding tools which have been historically documented

Figure 12.3. Male hunter with three snares (from a painted image on pottery; line drawing by Karen Gardner).

(Cushing 1920:194–195; Lange 1959:99–101, 370; Parsons 1939:39, 78 Underhill 1991:26). Typically, Puebloan men were associated with this activity and these tools in historic times, but women often participated in horticulture as well (Powell 1972:16).

Female Activities

Paintings of females and female activities are not as commonly depicted as male activities; anatomically explicit females are portrayed about half as often as males. Four main female activities are identified. These in-

Figure 12.4. Female holding a child (from a painted image on pottery; line drawing by Karen Gardner).

clude caring for a child (or children), midwifery, carrying burdens, and assisting in game procurement.

Except for the attribute of size, few children can be distinguished in Mimbres pottery motifs. Most of the portrayed children are shown being held by adult-sized females (Fig. 12.4). No males are portrayed handling children in these motifs. This association of only females with children suggests that women were the primary caregivers for children, as they were historically (Babcock 1991; Beaglehole 1937:18–19; Dennis 1940; Parsons 1939:1, 109).

One example of female midwifery is documented in Mimbres pottery (Beaglehole 1937:19; Lange 1959; Underhill 1991). In this scene a woman giving birth is being attended by another female; see illustration in Shaf-

Figure 12.5. Female carrying a jar (from a painted image on pottery; line drawing by Karen Gardner).

fer et al. (1997: Fig. 3). Underhill (1991:133) noted that among the historic Pueblo, women helped with the birth unless there were complications; only then was a (male) medicine man called. For pregnant Cochiti females, another female, often the woman's mother, served as a midwife, in part due to "tardiness" of medicine men (Lange 1959:398–399).

Based on historic period data (Beaglehole 1937:18–19; O'Kane 1950: 54; Parsons 1939:54, 58, 143), females were responsible for the regular acquisition of water and transportation of water to the pueblo. Historically, this was done using jars. Often, these jars were carried on the tops of women's heads (see Babcock 1991:53, 74 for historic photographs; Parsons 1939:54). Figure 12.5 depicts this activity, showing a female carrying a jar on her head and carrying an artifact resembling a ladle in her left hand. The combination of artifacts and the carrying of the jar on the head is consistent with historically described water transportation.

The identification of females assisting male hunters is based on the depictions of females transporting game animals (Brody 1977: Plate 16). Females are never shown with tools such as snares, bows, or arrows and, therefore, do not appear to be the hunters themselves.

Activities Common to Both Males and Females

Both males and females are portrayed in foraging activities, in ceremonies, and in handling captive birds, all of which were also historically performed by either sex. Foraging activities include gathering nuts, wood, other plant materials, or catching small game. In Brody (1977: Fig. 113), for example, a pregnant woman transports a load of sticks in a burden basket, while a male in the background carries a single larger tree portion, stripped of smaller branches.

Both sexes are portrayed as participants in ceremonial activities, although identifying specific ceremonies or ceremony types is difficult. One ceremony appears to be representing the snake dance (Shaffer et al. 1995). The example in Moulard (1984: Plates 1 and 2) shows both males and females as participants; both are shown using artifacts such as decorated staffs, rattles (?), and mobiles.

Parrot or macaw handling is commonly depicted as a female activity on Mimbres vessels, although a male is also shown in Brody (1983: Plate 22). Apparently the boxes and spheres surrounding the birds represent cages, which were also used historically (Bourke 1984:26 [1884]; Parsons 1939: 29). Other bird-handling tools shown include staffs and crooks.

Gendered Roles Inferred from Mimbres Pottery

Mimbres motifs document gender-specific roles as well as non-gender-specific roles. Only some of these roles, however, show continuity between the ancient past and the historic period. Men's work appears to involve game procurement through hunting, trapping, fishing, and warfare. Women's work involved child care, midwifery, and the transportation of water in jars. Both men and women engaged in foraging and participation in ceremonies. All of these roles appear in historic times among Puebloan groups.

Other motifs depict aspects of men's and women's work that may not have continued into historic times. For example, the participation of women in hunting as transporters of game is not well documented in the historic period. In addition, the Mimbres motifs suggest that agriculture was considered to be men's work; historic documents indicate, however, that females and children also commonly worked in the fields.

The use of Mimbres painted pottery motifs for assessing prehistoric Puebloan gender roles has proven informative in several aspects. First, the association of many Mimbres activities with males or females coincides closely with the gendered activities documented among historic Puebloan society. This occurrence substantiates the diachronic continuity of basic Puebloan lifeways described by many scholars. Furthermore, the gender roles identified in Mimbres motifs correspond with historically documented roles, with no contradictions evident between the two. More important, however, because the Mimbres represent one of the earliest Puebloan cultures, comparability of such roles between prehistoric and historic times indicates that the observed gender roles are ancient in origin and that they span virtually the total Puebloan chronology.

While ethnographic analogy was used to interpret the activities portrayed in these motifs, the assignment of gender roles in prehistoric Mimbres society was based on the emic aspect of the motifs provided by the Mimbres artisans. The combined attributes of the motifs (sex of the individuals, artifacts portrayed or used, and the activities depicted) allow for a detailed identification of prehistoric Pueblo gender roles at a level of detail that previously could not be substantiated through the analysis of individual artifacts or through historical comparisons.

The interpretation of Mimbres gender roles from painted motifs is constrained by a variety of factors, most importantly by the fact that only a limited sample was available for study. As such, these studied motifs do not document the full range of the possible prehistoric Pueblo gender roles. Additionally, there are quite likely several aspects of Mimbres society that will not be able to be identified because there is no described modern equivalent, and vice versa. While these factors are limiting, it would have been nearly impossible to identify the gender roles described in this chapter with any degree of accuracy if it were not for the self-documented, explicit depictions provided by the Mimbres people approximately nine hundred years ago.

Acknowledgments

Barry W. Baker, Johnny Byers, C. Reid Ferring, and Debra McIlvain all provided comments on an earlier draft of this chapter. Special thanks goes to the Maxwell Museum of Anthropology at the University of New Mexico for granting access to the Mimbres cultural collections curated by the Museum.

Chapter 13
And They Said, Let Us Make Gods in Our Image
Gendered Ideologies in Ancient Mesopotamia
Susan Pollock and Reinhard Bernbeck

In a now classic essay on gender as a category of analysis in history, Joan Scott (1986) urged historians to place both gender and ideology squarely in the center of their research, arguing that gender is a primary, persistent metaphor for the signification and legitimation of relations of power. One reason for the centrality of gender and sexuality is that they are regularly referred to in contexts that have nothing directly to do with them (Godelier 1981). The pervasiveness of these metaphorical references serves to embed certain specific meanings of gender relations and sexuality deep within sociocultural reality.

Scott's arguments can be applied equally to archaeology. In recent years, archaeology has moved away from a major preoccupation with reconstructing past social realities by accepting the importance of ideology. Even more recently, feminist perspectives have begun to make their way into archaeology, bringing an insistence on the centrality of gender to archaeological understandings of the past. But studies that explore the relationship between ideology and social reality in explicitly gendered terms remain uncommon.

We venture into the terrain of relations between gendered ideology and social reality in this chapter by focusing on a particularly fascinating time in ancient Mesopotamian (pre)history, the late fourth and early third millennium, known archaeologically as the Late Uruk and Jemdet Nasr periods. It was a time of profound changes in economic, political, and social spheres, which surely had marked impacts both on gendered social reality and ideology (Bernbeck 1995). We begin by clarifying what we mean by the term ideology.

Ideology

Ideology means different things to different people. We use the term here in a Marxist sense to refer to the portrayal of the particular interests and values of certain social groups as if they were the interests of everyone in a society (Marx and Engels 1939). Ideology structures systems of beliefs, knowledge, and values so that they legitimize a particular set of interests (cf. Pauketat and Emerson 1991:920). The ways that ideology does this are many and varied. Ideology may mask, naturalize, or flaunt a particular view of the world. Susan Kus (1982) has distinguished two broad categories of ideologies in terms of the way they relate the social to the natural world. Some ideologies confound the social with the natural order, creating a semblance of social reality as inevitable and unchangeable because it is "natural." Other ideologies seek to decouple the social world from direct dependence on nature and portray social relations as legitimate products of historical change, innovation, and creation of order.

In recent years it has become common to argue that not all groups in a society share a single, dominant ideology (Abercrombie et al. 1980). While there is every reason to accept the notion that a dominant ideology rarely fully controls *all* ideological production in a society, we contend that major elements of a dominant ideology *do* dominate.[1] Ideology in the sense we are using it is based upon the idea that people accept at least the major elements of a (dominant) ideology even if they themselves do not belong to the dominant groups and even though, on an "objective" level, their acceptance of such an ideology works against their own interests. Ideology convinces people that it is ultimately in their best interests to comply. Indeed, the power of ideology is that it works by consensus rather than coercion (Hall 1986:14–15). The notion of a dominant ideology does not, however, imply something done consciously by a dominant group to subordinate groups. Ideology is an effective and needed means of promoting cohesion among dominant groups (Abercrombie et al. 1980; Hall 1986:14).

Social Reality: Mesopotamia in the Late Uruk and Jemdet Nasr Periods

Investigating ideology necessitates some knowledge of "actual" social relations. In other words, a critique of ideology is only possible by comparing an ideological view of the world with the underlying conditions of socioeconomic life. Such a comparison does not imply the ability of an observer/analyst to uncover "objective" socioeconomic relations.

Rather, a critique, with its underlying emancipatory goals (Habermas 1971:308), allows us to discern major discrepancies between an ideological sphere and social conditions.

We first present a brief synopsis of the Late Uruk and Jemdet Nasr periods (c. 3300–2900 B.C.E.) in Mesopotamia. We then examine some possibilities for engendering this picture, before turning to a consideration of ideology.

Although scholars are far from agreeing on the precise nature of the political, economic, and social changes that took place around the turn of the third millennium, few would deny their magnitude (Adams 1981; Nissen 1988). A trend toward urbanization that had roots centuries earlier took on new dimensions at this time, with massive movements of population and the dramatic growth of the city of Uruk, which reached a size of more than 200 hectares (and housed perhaps as many as 40,000 people). The Late Uruk period saw a geographically widespread adoption or emulation of southern Mesopotamian styles of artifacts and architecture in parts of northern Mesopotamia and western Iran, thought by some scholars to represent colonization or "informal empire" (Algaze 1993).

The broad similarities in material culture throughout the region broke down substantially in the Jemdet Nasr period when localized styles reappeared. A variety of administrative and bureaucratic developments characterize the Late Uruk period, most notably the widespread adoption of cylinder seals and the invention of writing. Other evidence points to escalating conflict, involving military engagements and the taking of prisoners. By this time there appeared stratified societies throughout Mesopotamia in which social, political, and economic inequalities were considerable.

Analyses of the limited available evidence pertinent to the organization of production suggest that the domestic unit continued to be a primary locus of production of mundane goods during the Late Uruk and Jemdet Nasr periods (Pollock 1999). At the same time, large households known in the scholarly literature on Mesopotamia as *oikoi* were being established. Oikoi employed large, highly specialized work forces engaged in production processes that were often subdivided into segments. Oikoi became a prominent feature of urban economies by the mid-third millennium.

The scholarly literature contains little in the way of gendered examinations of these periods (with the exception of Zagarell 1986). There are, however, two principal sources that can be used to begin such a project: written texts and pictorial evidence.

Written records in the form of clay tablets from the Late Uruk and Jemdet Nasr periods are collectively referred to as "archaic texts." The texts are extremely laconic, having been used primarily as administrative shorthands rather than prose (Nissen 1988:87–89, 135–38; Michalowski 1990). It is not even possible to specify with certainty what language is involved: signs are ideographic, containing no grammatical parts, and thus could have been read in any language. Approximately 85 percent of the texts are "economic," dealing with the receipt and disbursement of such things as grain, beer, animals, and their products. Although personal names are sometimes mentioned, we have no way of knowing whether they refer to females or males. The remaining 15 percent of the texts consists principally of lists of words or phrases, probably designed as scribal *aides de mémoires* or training devices.

Most of the texts were found in excavations in the Eanna precinct, the ritual/religious and administrative center of the city of Uruk. Although nearly all were recovered from tertiary contexts, it is assumed that they were written and used by oikoi within the Eanna precinct. In short, the archaic texts offer some insights into kinds of goods produced and controlled by major oikoi of the time, but attaching genders to specific activities is not possible on the basis of the texts alone.

Texts from the mid-third millennium offer much greater detail on gender-related issues, especially the gender of people engaged in particular activities. It is probably unnecessary to mention the dangers of extrapolating from material written five hundred years after the fact and assuming that it applies to the time period under consideration. However, where other evidence suggests specific continuities, it can support the use of limited inferences about gendered activities based on later references. Of particular importance is the connection of women with textile manufacture, a subject we will return to later.

More information concerning gendered activities is contained in visual imagery. The Uruk period is the source of the first extensive body of pictorial material known from ancient Mesopotamia, much of it in the form of designs carved into cylinder seals. Seal imagery is preserved either in the form of the seal itself or the impressions on clay made by using the seals. A seal holder signified his or her authorization of a transaction by the act of sealing, rolling the seal across a piece of moist clay. Clay sealings were used to close doors, presumably of storerooms, as well as a variety of containers, including ceramic vessels, baskets, reed mat packages, and bags. Seals were also rolled across tablets, signifying authorization or witness of the information contained therein. Finds of sealings and tablets in association suggest that they were used by similar people or in similar contexts.

Seals of the Late Uruk and Jemdet Nasr periods can be placed into two broadly defined categories: those with naturalistic designs that were finished using engraving tools (Fig. 13.1, top), and schematic seals worked

Figure 13.1. Seal imagery from the Late Uruk and Jemdet Nasr periods. The top three images show cultic/religious scenes; the fourth, bound captives being killed; and the bottom one, a scene of daily life (drawing after Amiet 1980).

solely with mechanical tools such as drills (Fig. 13.2, middle). Seals and sealings of these two categories are differentially represented: most seal impressions are of the naturalistic seals but few actual seals have been found, whereas numerous seals but few impressions of the schematic variety are known. Hans Nissen (1977) has argued that the naturalistic seals, which were usually larger and whose motifs exhibit considerable variety and distinctiveness, were used by individuals, whereas the schematic seals, which have quite repetitive motifs that are not always easily distinguishable, were used by "legal persons" on behalf of some institution (compare to Pittmann 1994).

Among those seals that have representations of people (and many do not), we can distinguish those that seem to represent cultic/religious scenes (indicated by depictions of temples or symbols associated with specific deities; see Fig. 13.1, top); those depicting political acts (e.g., killing bound captives, such as in Fig. 13.1, second from bottom); and images of daily life (including caring for animals, hunting, fishing, and textile manufacturing; see Fig. 13.2, bottom).

The figural images on seals offer important insights into gendered activities. In arguing from pictorial evidence, we make the assumption that *what* and *who* are depicted represent actual activities of particular groups of people in the past. In other words, depictions of women involved in textile manufacture are assumed to correspond to a portion of reality in which *some* women were engaged at least *some* of the time in the production of textiles. *How* these activities were portrayed is more indicative of their ideological content, as we will try to show later (cf. Marcus 1995). The existence of multiple, qualitatively different layers of meaning in pictorial images is well recognized by art historians (Panofsky 1955:26–41).

Who does what in the pictorial images?[2] Portrayals of people can be divided into four categories: men, women, "pig-tailed figures," and naked, hairless individuals lacking identifiable sexual features (see Fig. 13.3). The first two categories—men and women—are clearly identified as such by primary and/or secondary sex characteristics such as beards, penises, or breasts. Men, and certain women, invariably occur on naturalistic rather than schematic seals.

The pig-tailed figures are usually identified as women (Collon 1987:16; Pittman 1994:182), an identification that can be supported by their hairstyle, which is only occasionally seen on men in contemporary representations and is often seen on figurines that are clearly depicted with breasts (LeBreton 1957: Figs. 31/5 and 32/11; Harper et al. 1992: Figs. 25 and 31). Other pig-tailed figures wear garments that cover them from their shoulders to knees or below, a characteristic of women's but not men's dress (until the later part of the third millennium). Most seals with

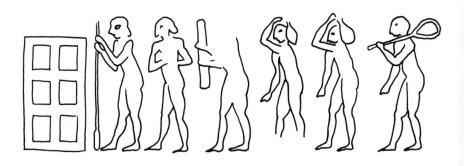

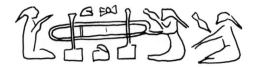

Figure 13.2. Seal imagery from the Late Uruk and Jemdet Nasr periods. The uppermost image depicts a procession; the other three represent scenes of daily life (drawing after Amiet 1980).

Figure 13.3. Examples of different types of figures from seal and relief imagery (drawing after Amiet 1980).

depictions of pig-tailed figures are of the schematic variety. The gender of the naked, hairless individuals is ambiguous; we will return to this point later. Seals portraying them are overwhelmingly of the naturalistic variety.

Prominent among the images of men are depictions of an individual with a beard and a rolled headdress, who is frequently dressed in a so-called net skirt (see Fig. 13.1). Representations of this man are found on seals, statuettes, a stela, a knife handle, and so forth, from a geographically widespread collection of sites. He engages in a variety of acts, including hunting and mastering wild animals, overseeing the slaughter of bound captives (or taking part himself), feeding domestic animals, leading processions, performing libations (Schmandt-Besserat 1993), and standing before an important person (see Fig. 13.1, top). In many of these scenes he is alone or accompanied by a single individual in the characteristic pose of an attendant. In the statuettes, he is portrayed standing in an unusual pose with fists clenched against his chest.

In several scenes, the net-skirted man is shown bearing offerings to or standing before an individual in a pose suggesting ritual attention. The most famous example is on the Uruk vase, which depicts the net-skirted

Figure 13.4. Imagery on the Uruk Vase (drawing after Amiet 1980).

man — albeit only partially preserved — at the head of a procession whose members carry containers filled with various fruits of the land (Fig. 13.4).

The focus of cultic attention in these scenes is always female. Needless to say, her identity has been of considerable interest. She has generally been interpreted either as the goddess Inanna — based on the reed bundle symbol of Inanna that is often present — or as Inanna's high priestess. Although her identity cannot be resolved with certainty, the weight of evidence points to her being a goddess. In a number of cases, she wears an unusual headdress; while not the characteristic horned variety known from depictions of deities in the later third millennium, it differs from any seen on other figures. Moreover, historical evidence indicates that the high priest/ess was of the opposite gender to the deity he/she served (Winter 1987:201 n. 44). If a similar practice prevailed in the late fourth millennium, we would not expect Inanna to be served by a priestess, but rather by a priest.

Table 13.1 Depiction of Figures Seated or Engaged in Repetitive Scenes

	Goddess	Man in Net Skirt	Other Men	Genderless Figures	Pig-tailed Women
Seated position	20%	7%	0%	30%	80%
Repetitive scene	0%	0%	29%	31%	70%

Note: Percentages are calculated with reference to the total number of scenes in which such figures are depicted.

Apart from the depiction of this important female, probably a goddess, women are almost invariably represented as pig-tailed figures. They occur in scenes markedly different than those just considered: they are almost never shown individually; in most cases they are seated; and they occur only on seals. In more than half of the scenes in which they are portrayed, they are engaged in repetitive tasks in which two or more figures perform the same activity (Table 13.1). The most commonly attested, recognizable activities are those involving textile production and something to do with vessels (Fig. 13.2). A similar connection between textiles and vessels can be found among the archaic lexical lists. The reason for grouping these seemingly dissimilar things together in one list remains unclear. It does, however, seem that vessels in the list were important principally because of their contents, which included beverages — especially beer — and various kinds of animal fats (Englund and Nissen 1993:31).

Portrayals of genderless figures share some characteristics of depictions of males, on the one hand, and pig-tailed figures on the other. They sometimes occur alone, usually when shown hunting. They are sometimes depicted seated, in which case they frequently engage in activities similar to those of pig-tailed figures. Involvement in repetitive tasks is less common than for pig-tailed figures (Table 13.1). Like them, however, genderless figures are often shown doing something with vessels (Fig. 13.1, bottom), but nearly as often are involved in animal tending, hunting, or participating in processions (Fig. 13.2, top). Less common activities depicted include agricultural tasks, food preparation, and filling of storehouses; only one scene seems to be related to textile production.

The intermediate nature of the depictions of genderless figures permits a number of possible interpretations. Some may have represented females and some males, but this begs the question of why they were distinguished from pig-tailed figures and depictions of other males by omitting their distinctive features. Possibly they were of different social positions than those whose genders are clearly portrayed. The fact that they are more often portrayed in activities in which males are shown lends some support to their identification as men, as do their bald heads, also seen on some depictions of men (Fig. 13.4). Another possibility is that they represent members of a third gender category. Or, the genderless figures may refer to other social identities, such as age groups, in which gender is unmarked.

How do the depictions fit with other archaeological and historical data? Oikoi were concerned with the storage, receipt, inventory, and distribution of goods such as grain, animals, and their products: many of the same kinds of goods seen in the pictorial images. Third-millennium texts indicate that women and children were by far the most important sources of labor in large-scale textile production enterprises (Waetzoldt 1972; Maekawa 1980). The pictorial connection of female figures with textile manufacture in the Late Uruk and Jemdet Nasr seals makes it likely that this connection was already established by that time (cf. Zagarell 1986). Later texts indicate that there were also at least some *elite* (mortal) women, including queens, known to have run households in their own names, carried on trade, and the like. Elite women, however, are not represented pictorially in the Late Uruk and Jemdet Nasr periods.

In summary, the imagery suggests that men and women engaged in quite different kinds of activities, based on their gender and social position (and no doubt age as well), but both women's and men's labor was instrumental to the political economy. Much of the evidence available speaks most directly to the organization of gendered and class-based labor within oikoi; the extent to which a similar organization prevailed in smaller domestic units is a question that is beyond the scope of this chapter.

Ideology in Figural Imagery

An examination of gendered ideology must rely on pictorial evidence because of the absence of indications of gender in contemporary texts. Studying *how* gendered activities were portrayed and the relationship among the people involved may offer insights into the workings of gender in ideological constructions in this past society.

Hierarchical relationships are portrayed in some seal scenes in which pig-tailed or genderless figures are depicted. One figure may, for example, sit on a special platform or mat while others sit on the ground (Fig. 13.2, second from bottom) (Collon 1987:16). Hierarchical relationships are shown within a single gender, rather than across genders. Indeed, most scenes involving pig-tailed figures and, to a somewhat lesser extent, genderless figures portray only a single type of figure and hence people of a single gender.

Hierarchical relationships are also evident in other kinds of scenes.

The man in the net skirt is invariably depicted killing people or supervis-
ing others doing so. We have already mentioned the attendant who frequently accompanies the man in the net skirt. Procession scenes are led
by the man in the net skirt, followed by others bearing offerings. Again,
these representations tend to be restricted to a single (human) gender,
in this case male. Let us look more closely at the most graphic of the
procession scenes, the one depicted on the Uruk vase (Fig. 13.4).

Irene Winter (1985:19) has argued persuasively that narrative depictions in early Mesopotamian art are to be understood as beginning at the
bottom and moving to the top. When we examine the Uruk vase in this
light, we see a clear, divided sequence, with water at the bottom, followed
by plants and domestic animals, then men bearing fruits of the land, and
culminating in the man in the net skirt. The man in the net skirt is both
followed and preceded by attendants, one of whom presents the first
offerings to the female whom we have argued is probably the goddess
Inanna.

That this sequence is to be interpreted as a hierarchical arrangement is
suggested by appeal to other narrative pictorial works, the increasing size
of the bands as one moves up the vase, and the clothing and poses of the
individuals portrayed. From the vase, as well as depictions of similar figures on seals, we see that at the top of the hierarchy stood a female, not a
mortal one but a goddess. At the top of the human hierarchy stands a
male, namely the man in the net skirt. Below him are other males and
below them are animals, plants, and water, in that order. Such a portrayal
can be understood as depicting hierarchical relationships with reference
to a naturalizing ideology. Mortal women are conspicuously absent from
this "natural" hierarchy; they are categorically excluded.

This hierarchical pattern can be extended using the information from
the Uruk Vase in conjunction with seals. Below the man in the net skirt
are other males, genderless figures of at least two hierarchical categories,
and pig-tailed women, also of two categories. Although not unequivocal,
there is circumstantial evidence to support the placement of the pig-
tailed figures at the bottom of this hierarchy. They are portrayed in ways
that are most dissimilar to the man in the net skirt and the goddess: they
are usually shown sitting, in groups, and engaged in repetitive activities;
they are never shown in scenes that contain cult symbols. Furthermore,
the seals containing pig-tailed figures are usually of the schematic sort,
small, quick to produce, and relatively infrequently used to seal and thus
authorize transactions.

Other values associated with gender can be discerned from the way in
which scenes are composed. Recall that the man in the net skirt, as well as
some other males and genderless figures, are shown hunting, mastering
animals, and killing people. Imagery from both earlier and later periods

indicates that the symbolism of mastering wild animals was associated with maleness and especially with important males. Weapons also have a long history of association with elite men, based on pictorial images and mortuary associations (Marcus 1994:11; Pollock 1983). With the exception of depictions of hunting and killing captives, the scenes in which the man in the net skirt is present almost invariably contain one or more reed bundles, the symbol of the goddess Inanna. There is, thus, good reason to understand the man in the net skirt as a symbol of a powerful ruler whose duties and powers combine political and cultic leadership that are at the same time associated with masculinity.

The importance of Inanna and of cultic scenes in the pictorial imagery in general raises the question of how the images fit into the larger picture of Mesopotamian religion. The Assyriologist Thorkild Jacobsen (1976) claimed to be able to disentangle the threads of fourth-millennium religious beliefs from later texts. While it is certainly appropriate to treat his reconstruction with some caution, it nonetheless offers compelling insights into possible underlying themes in Mesopotamian religion.

Early characteristics of goddesses, according to Jacobsen, include associations with fish, cows, grain, grapes, wine, and storehouses: all products resulting from the fertility of the land and a place where they are stored. Gods, on the other hand, were associated with water (which is semantically connected to semen in Sumerian [Jacobsen 1976:111]), marsh plants and animals, bulls, the moon, sun, wind, thunderstorms, floods, the hoe, shepherds, and so forth: powers that produce fertility and yield, as well as powers that cause their destruction. The sexual metaphor here is quite clear.

Inanna was one of the most prominent goddesses, not least because of her position as patron goddess of Uruk. As we have seen, she is frequently represented by her symbol, a reed bundle, which is an indication of her connection to community storehouses. In a series of stories concerning her association with and ultimate marriage to the half-god Dumuzi, who is usually said to be a shepherd, she is said to be attracted to him because of his qualities as an embodiment of fertility and yield. The wedding of Dumuzi and Inanna symbolized the power for productivity joined to the community storehouse and hence captured for the benefit of the community.

Conclusion: Gender Ideology and Social Reality in the Fourth Millennium B.C.E.

The various lines of evidence we have explored in this chapter show the complex relationships between ideology and social reality. The late fourth-millennium world was built to a significant extent on women: in reality on women's labor and ideologically on a powerful goddess who could claim the principal city of the time as hers. People at the time — as well as modern scholars — might have been tempted to assume that women's power in the human world would correspond to the power of Inanna in the world of the gods (cf. Westenholz 1990). There is, however, little indication that this was the case.

Instead, members of the upper social echelons, who were those most likely to be consumers of pictorial imagery on seals, statues, and the like, were treated to representations of women as menial laborers. Not all women *were* menial laborers; class differences among women may have been as sharp as gender differences (Sacks 1974:218). Men were shown performing various kinds of menial labor, too, but also attaining the highest political and cultic positions and a variety of positions in between. In other words, the same ideology that depicted a powerful deity as female also made clear that the epitome of human power was male. Sexually-laden metaphors connecting women to products that were engendered through the male power of fertilization were belied by social reality in which women were doubtless responsible for major portions of the productive labor, not least the manufacture of textiles which were among the most critical commodities in the political economy of Mesopotamian states. Human labor, both female and male, was portrayed to be in service of the deities, in particular Inanna, just as the most powerful human figure, the man in the net skirt, is depicted as being in her service. The ideological message that all people must labor in service of the goddess was a legitimation for labor in the service of powerful men. It is an ideological message that works to represent a world of human making as really the result of the acts of the gods and goddesses. It is surely no coincidence that Inanna herself exhibits an ambiguous combination of gendered characteristics. She is not in any way associated with motherhood or maternal characteristics (Hallo 1987:49), but rather is protectress of harlots, connected to rain and thunderstorms, and goddess of war as well as love.

Having a powerful goddess as principal deity of the major city of southern Mesopotamia was an ideologically potent symbol. At the same time that people in general, and perhaps women in particular, were being exploited as never before, they were confronted with images which at once reinforced the exploited positions of many women by portraying their socioeconomic position as natural and which proposed that, at least at the divine level, some females *were* in fact powerful. It was a way to legitimate the interests of elite men by suggesting that in fact both men and women had a share in power.

At the beginning of this chapter, we suggested that ideology can work in very different ways. In the Mesopotamian case we have examined, ideology represented hierarchical relations between people of the same gender as natural. However, for the most part, hierarchical relations *between* genders were denied by the simple expedient of avoiding portrayal of women and men together. Powerful men created the image of a world, which had very little place for women at all.

Notes

We thank Michelle Marcus, Henry Wright, and two anonymous reviewers for their comments on this manuscript, the participants in the Fourth Gender and Archaeology Conference at Michigan State University for stimulating papers and discussion, and Alison Rautman for her encouragement throughout. Susan Pollock would also like to thank the Department of Anthropology at University of California, Santa Barbara, for a lecture invitation that provided the initial stimulus for this chapter.

1. An example might be the consumerism that is an integral part of capitalism.

2. The sample used in this analysis includes both seals and impressions, as well as occasional other objects that bear images (for a total of 151 items). The sample included examples with one or more anthropomorphic figures and those fragments of impressions that were complete enough so that one could discern what was occurring in the scene. Sources of these images included Frankfort (1955), Le Brun and Vallat (1978), Brandes (1979), Amiet (1980), Strommenger (1980), Collon (1987). For discussion of seal themes, see Pittman (1994). The final publication of Chogha Mish (Delougaz et al. 1996) was available to us only after this chapter was completed, and those images, therefore, could not be included in the analysis.

Chapter 14
Beyond Mother Earth and Father Sky
Sex and Gender in Ancient Southwestern
Visual Arts

Kelley Hays-Gilpin

Hundreds of traditional Navajo sandpaintings comprise a complex system for healing illness and bringing the world into harmony. Contemporary artists reproduce some sandpaintings for sale. One of the most popular shows Mother Earth and Father Sky (Fig. 14.1), who are benevolent, "persuadable" beings (Parezo 1983:93). Unlike most sandpainting symbols, which are considered dangerous outside a ritual setting, Mother Earth and Father Sky can be painted without causing harm to the artist. Buyers also like them. Middle- to upper-class European and Euroamerican visitors to the Southwest find Native art and culture captivating for many reasons, but one is "The Indian's" reverence for Mother Earth. As Gaia, Mother Earth is also an ancient figure in European religious thought. She enjoys a revival in Europe and in North America in the many-faceted women's spirituality movement (e.g., Sjoo 1975). Those who look to "pre-patriarchal" European cultures for spiritual inspiration often say they feel a kinship with Native American traditionalists in the causes of ecology, human rights, and nonviolence because members of both groups respect Mother Earth.

The argument I present here does not deny the importance of Mother Earth in Native American traditions, nor in women's spirituality. Here, I explore the history of the concept of Mother Earth by examining a variety of depictions of female and male beings in ancient Southwest art, together with ethnographic accounts of their use. These data suggest that ethnographic evidence can be used to interpret prehistoric imagery and that prehistoric rock art and pottery provide a dated developmental sequence for some aspects of gender ideology in the Puebloan and Navajo cultures of the American Southwest.

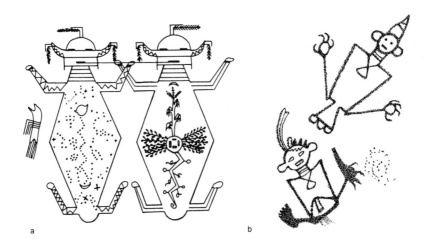

a   b

Figure 14.1. (a) Navajo commercial sandpainting of Father Sky (left) and Mother Earth (right) purchased in Holbrook, Arizona, in 1999 (tracing by K. Hays-Gilpin). (b) Petroglyph from the Middle Little Colorado River area, probably Pueblo IV period (drawing by Patricia McCreery, used with permission).

Specifically, although the Earth in prehistoric Southwest religion was probably both important and female, the Mother Earth figure was not approached as a single, unchanging deity. Additionally, if one focuses on the roles of only female deities in the religions of Southwestern groups, leaving out male roles in fertility and reproduction, one will miss a central point of Pueblo and Navajo religions, that of gender complementarity.

Sam Gill, professor of religion at the University of Colorado, begins his book *Mother Earth, An American Story* (1987) by noting that "there has been uncontested agreement among Indians, scholars, and the general American populace that Mother Earth is a goddess widely known since antiquity, one central especially to the religions of native North American peoples." Yet two things troubled Gill. First, references to Mother Earth appeared to begin in only in the past one hundred years. Second, because virtually every other aspect of Native American life is regionally or tribally specific, Gill reasoned that for all tribes to share any aspect of ideology would be very surprising. He then compared female supernatural beings in the oral traditions of many tribes (including several Southwestern ones) recorded around the turn of the century or earlier and found that the nature and characteristics of female beings vary within and among tribes. No single female being in these records corresponds very well to the present-day view of Mother Earth. Gill concludes that the widely shared view of Mother Earth is, in fact, relatively recent in origin, having emerged over the last century or so during the process of conflicts over land and sovereignty in the American West. The rest of his book focuses on the historic process of developing such a shared imagery.

Navajo and Pueblo traditions provide excellent examples of religions that have several female deities who are more or less identified with the earth and fertility. First Woman, together with First Man, is a central character in many Navajo stories. Although some aspects of her character concern fertility, she has her home beneath the earth and she ends up rather ambiguously associated with witchcraft. The central holy personage in Navajo tradition is Changing Woman, who created humans from her skin and also from cornmeal. She represents the life cycle and the seasons. She lives not underground, but in the western sea; thus, she is not the Mother Earth represented in the popular sandpainting. The horned toad forms of Mother Earth and Father Sky in the paintings recall "the turtle or horned-toad sand-painting called Earth [that] is laid by a shaman at infant-naming" at Acoma pueblo (Parsons 1939:182); this or a similar image from one of the other pueblos is probably the source of the Navajo version of Mother Earth (Navajo and Pueblo people have often intermarried and lived closely intermingled since at least the 1600s). But Acoma does not have a single "Earth Mother" deity any more than Navajos do. The central holy personage in Acoma religion is Iatiku, a female creator who is identified with maize and earth. Parsons notes that she "has the attributes of an earth mother, but Earth is referred to in prayer as a separable supernatural" (Parsons 1939:182). Most of the pueblos (Hopi and others) have other female supernatural characters as well: Corn Maidens, Corn Mothers, Spider Grandmother, Dawn Woman, Dawn Girl, Clay Old Lady, Salt Old Lady. In addition, there is a Lady of Turquoise, Shell and other "hard substances," and a Mother of Game Animals, to name just a few. In contrast, the Sun, Sky, Morning Star, Hero Twins, Coyote, and hunters are invariably male beings. There are also supernatural characters that are variably addressed as male or as female; the moon, for example, is female in some traditions and male in others.

Changes Through Time in Rock Art Depictions

Is the widespread concept of Mother Earth a historic phenomenon, an instance of the converging and conflation of many female holy beings from many Old and New World traditions? Do prehistoric images of women provide any clues to her ancestresses? In this study, I focus on two areas of the Colorado Plateau — the Four Corners, and the Lower Puerco and Little Colorado River drainages. Data come from both published and unpublished sources, as well as original rock art fieldwork and research among extant rock art and artifact collections.

Archaic Period

Rock art that is dated to the Archaic, or pre-agricultural, period in the Southwest is widespread, distinctive, and relatively well recorded. During this time period (about 6500 to 2000 B.C.) rock art is characterized by geometric patterns such as grids and squiggly lines (Table 14.1). In some areas, such as southern Utah, both human and animal figures appear. The Barrier Canyon style emphasizes huge, ghostly humanoid paintings (Schaafsma 1980:61–72). Caves in the Grand Canyon and some sites in Utah yield split-twig figurines of animals, and rarely, humans. Clay figurines appear before agriculture and ceramic containers in some areas of Utah (Coulam and Schroedl 1996). In none of these figures is the subject's sex an obvious attribute. Most rock art scholars, anthropologists included, agree that Archaic rock art is "about" spirit beings that help individual shamans (Cole 1989, Schaafsma 1980); the sex of such spirit beings was evidently not a particularly important or relevant feature.

Basketmaker II

Early agricultural populations of the Basketmaker II period (about 2000 B.C. to A.D. 400) emphasized humans in their rock art, and to a lesser degree, animals and geometric designs. Most of the rock art seems to depict shamans, their helpers, and their visions, but they may also function to mark band territories. Bill Hyder (1994) recorded numerous male-female pairs in the Cedar Mesa area and argues that they represent family ownership of arable lands. Recent research by Michael Robins of Northern Arizona University (personal communication 1996) shows that rows of sexed individuals are frequent in some areas and styles throughout the Basketmaker II period. Groups may consist of males or females only, or mixed groups. Males are indicated by the presence of penises, and females are identified by the triangular string aprons that they apparently wear. Females are rarely identified by their genitalia. While all humans are depicted in a uniform frontal, fairly rigid pose, the details of adornment vary from place to place. Robins argues for a stylistic mosaic at this time, which, together with other data, suggests that seasonally mobile bands of Basketmakers were practicing both farming *and* hunting and gathering. In contrast to the preceding Archaic styles, figures are frequently identifiable as male or female in Basketmaker rock art. Dis-

Table 14.1 Culture Sequence for the Anasazi Culture Area of the Northern U.S. Southwest

Pecos Classification	Date Ranges	Characteristics
Archaic	6500 B.C. to 2000 B.C.	Wild foods; temporary camps; low population density; baskets for gathering food; atlatls and darts for hunting; no pottery; geometric and non-sexed humans in rock art; animal and human figurines.
Basketmaker II	2000 B.C. to A.D. 400	Cultivated maize and squash; small pithouses and storage cists, sometimes in caves; atlatls and darts for hunting; some decorated baskets; no pottery; twined sandals; rock art emphasizes humans, often sexed.
Basketmaker III	A.D. 400 to 700	Cultivated maize, squash, and beans; larger, deeper pithouses, simple great kivas, some surface storage rooms; bow and arrow; pottery, but few decorated vessels; highly varied and often narrative rock art with lobed circles, crooks, staffs, processions, hair whorls, earrings, animals, and geometrics.
Pueblo I	A.D. 700 to 900	Pithouses with above-ground slab structures, simple great kivas; large villages in some areas such as Chaco Canyon; black-on-white pottery; little use of caves — few perishables. Rock art not well understood.
Pueblo II	A.D. 900 to 1150	Small unit pueblos with kivas, large pueblos with multiple kivas and great kivas in some areas; little use of caves — few perishables. Rock art loosely executed, mostly geometric, with lizard/men and animals.
Pueblo III	A.D. 1150 to 1300	Multistoried masonry pueblos, sometimes in caves as at Mesa Verde; polychrome pottery in some areas; elaborate, fine rock art, with frequent depictions of humans (often sexed), ritual paraphernalia and narrative scenes, animals, and pottery/textile designs.
Pueblo IV	A.D. 1300 to Spanish entrada (dates vary)	Large, aggregated communities in multistoried masonry pueblos with plazas; polychrome pottery, depictions of kachinas and other supernaturals frequent in many media.

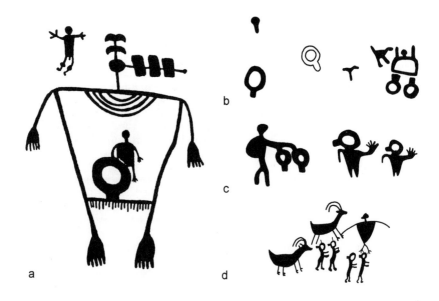

Figure 14.2. The lobed circle in late Basketmaker II-Basketmaker III rock art. (a) Note the lobed circle added later to the abdomen of the large Basketmaker II style figure, from southeastern Utah; (b) Lobed circles from Broken Flute Cave, northeastern Arizona; (c) and (d) are petroglyphs from southeastern Utah (a, c, and d are courtesy of Steven J. Manning; b from Hays 1992).

tinctive male and female clothing styles also appear during this time, which may indicate increasing importance of gender identities.

Basketmaker III

Basketmaker III period (c. A.D. 400 to 700) rock art shows much continuity with its antecedents, but a startling diversity develops over time, beginning perhaps sometime in the fifth century A.D. The size and visibility of human figures are reduced, and in addition to rigidly posed, frontal views of humans, there is a virtual explosion of a wide variety of subjects, including animal figures, geometric designs, and scenes of humans engaged in activities and manipulating a wide range of artifacts. Some of the most striking innovations include the lobed circle (Fig. 14.2), an icon that Steven Manning argues represents a womb (Manning 1992; see also Patterson and Patterson 1993). In rock art, lobed circles appear singly on the abdomens of female figures in fairly early styles, and later, paired on the chests of male figures. They are also found paired in association

Figure 14.3. Petroglyph figure with hair whorls and penis (?) from the Lower Puerco River area, Arizona, undated (drawing by K. Hays-Gilpin).

with representations of great kivas, flute players, plants, and male and female humans. Turquoise-encrusted mosaic pendants have been found on male burials in Canyon de Chelly, and similar items appeared in the fill of pithouses in Broken Flute Cave, also in northeastern Arizona (Hays 1992). Manning (1992) notes that the lobed-circle shape is repeated later in the form of "key-hole shaped" pithouses and kivas, ceremonial structures that contain a symbolic entranceway to the underworld.

Processions become a popular rock art motif probably sometime in the A.D. 600s. Often the figures are phallic. They may depict group ritual activities undertaken primarily by males. I have argued elsewhere (Hays 1992) that men may have developed ritual societies at this time, partly in resistance to the development of matrilocal extended family households. The previous emphasis on individual shamanic activity appears to yield to collective ritual activities that may have helped solidify cooperation among unrelated males.

At this time, a number of icons emerge and proliferate; many of these icons are still important in Pueblo art and ritual today. Items such as flutes, crooks, atlatls, and staffs are depicted frequently; they are wielded by male and nonsexed individuals, but not by females (note that the atlatl or spear-thrower seems to persist as a ritual icon long after it is replaced by a new weapon, the bow and arrow). Some female figures appear with their hair tied in two whorls. Called "wearing a butterfly" in Hopi, these whorls mark a girl who has reached puberty but is not yet married. Some-

times figures with hair whorls have explicitly female genitalia, but sometimes the figures have no particular genitalia shown. Very rarely, a figure
with hair whorls has a possible penis depicted. Figure 14.3, for example,
might represent a male person who has chosen a female gender role in
life (*nadleeh* in Navajo, *llamana* in Zuni [see Roscoe 1991]).

Gender and sex do not always coincide in Pueblo and Navajo cultures.
Zuni has at least three gender categories (male, female, and *llamana*),
and Navajo traditions recognize five (male, female, male *nadleeh* who
assume the role of a woman, female *nadleeh* who assume the role of a
man, and "real" *nadleeh*, who are in fact genitally hermaphroditic). We
do not yet know how long Puebloans have had more than two gender
categories and what gender attributes changed when. Representations in
art may be helpful in resolving this issue, although we do not know which
depictions represent humans and which represent spiritual beings. In
any case, it seems clear that during this time period, conventions for portraying males and females are extended to the representation of cross-
gender individuals as well as to those whose sex corresponds with their
gender identity.

Pueblo I–II

Pueblo I period rock art is difficult to identify in the study areas. It may be
that little rock art was made during this period, or it may have been made
too far from datable habitation sites to be conclusively associated. In the
Pueblo II period (about A.D. 900 to 1150), human figures are few, and
these are rarely sexed. The "lizard/man" figure may be a male human, a
lizard, or deliberately ambiguous. Zuni interpretation of these figures
links them to the mythic story of human emergence, in which people
living in one of the lower worlds had tails and webbed feet, which they
subsequently lost as they moved upward to the next world (Young 1988).
Note also that lizards, like snakes, are creatures that travel between the
earth's surface and the underworld. Therefore, these figures are not
necessarily exclusively male. Depictions of female genitalia are rare or
nonexistent in Pueblo II rock art figures, but depictions of figures with
hair whorls appear occasionally (e.g., Hays 1984:530).

In the late Pueblo II or early Pueblo III period in the Puerco Valley, sets
of carved and painted sandstone figurines usually include female beings,
sometimes together with males, snakes, dogs, sandals, and unsexed humans (Eaton 1991:52; Fane 1991:69; Lanford 1986:35; see also Martin
1961). The females do not appear to represent a single personage, but
one of them appears to be a Hopi deity known as "Child Sticking Out
Woman" (see illustration in Fane [1991:69], third figure from right).
Pottery effigy vessels of seated males appear in Chaco Canyon, New Mex-

ico, during the same era (Pepper 1906, 1920). Sexed beings appear in ritually important portable art more frequently than in rock art. This pattern suggests that depictions of such beings were "private," that is, not meant to be visible to all members of a community. In fact, Hopi elders who were consulted about the most recent find of a set of Puerco Valley figurines asked that they not be made public. They stated that these objects were not traditionally seen by people who were not initiated into one or another religious society. In accordance with these wishes, I will not replicate any of the images here; I am told, however, that the elders are still discussing the meanings and appropriate use of the figurines.

Pueblo III–IV

Sometime after about A.D. 1150, the beginning of the Pueblo III period, human figures in rock art increase in frequency, many of the figures are sexed, and many are shown in active poses. Smaller figures appear to characterize the Pueblo III style, while very large figures appear near many Pueblo IV sites, together with depictions of kachinas, who are spirit beings that still appear in dances and other ceremonies among the Pueblos today. Figures holding staffs, crooks, or bows and arrows usually do not show any indication of their sex, but are sometimes identifiable as males. Female figures rarely hold staffs, but their existence suggests that women sometimes performed ritual roles, much as they do today (McCreery and Malotki 1994:Fig. 9.11). A petroglyph in the Petrified Forest area of Arizona strongly resembles historic photographs of Hopi Marau society initiates (Patricia McCreery, personal communication 1996); Marau is one of three Hopi women's societies that parallel male societies in having kivas, altars, and liturgies presided over by priestesses as well as priests. If men developed ritual societies for themselves in Basketmaker III, as suggested above, when and why did women start their own societies? Further investigation of dated rock art images may someday help answer this question.

During the Pueblo III and IV periods, females are frequently depicted in rock art. Several depictions of females with hair whorls that date to this time period may indicate menstruation. A girl's first menstruation marks the transformation of a girl into a woman with life-giving powers; at this time, a girl first "wears a butterfly." One especially graphic petroglyph in Catron County, New Mexico, (Fig. 14.4a) shows a menstruating maiden with one hand on her belly, her womb indicated by a circle. An ithyphallic flute player serenades her. A similar scene appears in an undated petroglyph on the San Juan River over one hundred miles to the north near the Four Corners region (Fig. 14.4b).

Flute players are apparently never depicted with female genitalia or

Figure 14.4. Maiden serenaded by flute player. (a) Petroglyph from Catron County, New Mexico (copyright J. Louis Argend-Farlow, reprinted by permission); (b) from Bluff, Utah (drawing by K. Hays-Gilpin).

hair whorls. Many are male, and many are ithyphallic. The pueblo of Hopi has a Flute Clan and flute ceremony today, and the flute has traditionally been the young man's instrument of courtship. Pueblo oral traditions contain many references to flute players (Parsons 1939:41), such as the young male solar deity Paiyatamu at the pueblo of Zuni, who courts young women with his beautiful flute playing. The Hopi Locust plays his flute to bring warm weather and help crops grow. As a side note, the Kokopelli kachina is associated with fertility and lewd behavior but rarely carries a flute (when he does, he borrows one from another kachina). Nonetheless, the depictions of flute players in ancient art have captured the public imagination and are now invariably called "Kokopellis."

Women giving birth appear in both rock art and pottery of this era. They do not appear to represent the same personage, a universal Earth Mother, but they do, certainly, suggest a central role for female fertility in Pueblo religion. Pueblo culture makes no distinction between procreation and creation. Creation of anything is like giving birth to a baby. Making a pot, growing corn plants, weaving a blanket, carving a kachina doll, even killing an enemy — all these acts of creation are analogous to giving birth. Ethnographer Alice Schlegel demonstrates that pregnancy and birth are key metaphors in the Pueblo worldview (Schlegel 1977; Young 1988). According to Will Roscoe (1991:140), at Zuni "all forms of making were homologized to the act of birth and the ability of women to create life."

Supernatural Female Figures in Rock Art

Depiction of sexed beings in rock art can be linked with personages mentioned in historic Pueblo oral traditions. This association suggests that similar or identical oral traditions were prevalent in the Pueblo III period, perhaps as early as the 1150s, in the Little Colorado area of Arizona. Supernatural beings that can be tentatively identified in the rock art include the Mother of the Hero Twins, the Mother of Game Animals, and the Corn Maidens. Not all of these characters are benevolent and nurturing, at least not all the time, as befits our contemporary image of Mother Earth.

Maiden Mother of the Hero Twins

Cottonwood Ruin, one of the Homol'ovi pueblos on the middle Little Colorado River in Arizona, was inhabited by Hopi people during the early 1300s. Just below the escarpment of the mesa on which the village perched, a tumble of boulders forms a rectangular chamber with one tunnel entrance and one long corridor entrance from below. The corridor opening is guarded by a large phallic figure executed in the Pueblo IV period style (Fig. 14.5a). His hands and feet have been deeply re-pecked into cupules. Standing on top of the mesa rim and looking into the chamber, one sees a large female figure on her back on the outermost boulder (Fig. 14.5b). Her arms, legs, and vagina are raised to the sky. She is flanked by depictions of frogs and concentric circles, which are probably symbols of water and sun. This female figure recalls Navajo and Pueblo stories about how the Hero Twins or Twin War Gods were conceived. In an Acoma story related by Matthew Stirling, the creator Iatiku's sister, Nautsiti, is lying on her back on a rock in the rain, and "the rain streaming up from the ground enters her. She bears the Twins" (Parsons 1939:245; see also Stirling 1942).

Some Navajo clans trace their origins to Puebloan villages, and some Navajo ceremonial narratives show many similarities to Puebloan ones. Some Navajo traditions, then, may provide additional evidence for interpreting past symbols that are found on the Colorado Plateau. Navajo ceremonial narratives, for example, involve numerous sets of twins. Most are the children of the Sun, an association that is also true at Hopi and Zuni (Parsons 1939:204). In Navajo thought, the sun and water together can cause conception. Water, especially foam and mist, is sometimes considered the semen of the Sun. For example, the Navajo Hero Twins (Monster Slayer and Born for Water) were conceived in this manner. Their mother is Changing Woman, an earth deity who is born in the

Figure 14.5. Petroglyphs near Cottonwood Ruin, Middle Little Colorado River area. (a) male figure; (b) female figure with sun and water symbols (drawing by K. Hays-Gilpin).

spring, matures, and becomes an old lady in the winter. According to the traditional story, "[w]hen Changing Woman first became mature, she had not learned about sexual intercourse, but in trying to satisfy her desire, let the sun shine into her vagina; at noon when the Sun stopped to feed his horse, she went to a spring and let water drip into her" (Reichard 1950:29) and so became pregnant with the twins. They matured rapidly after their birth, underwent an arduous journey to meet their father the Sun, who gave them magic weapons so they could destroy dangerous monsters and make this earth safe for people. Although most published sources refer to the "War Twins" or "Twin War Gods," at Hopi the Twins are not seen as "war gods," but as protectors, and sometimes as tricksters.

A remarkably similar story was told among the Chemehuevi of California, distant linguistic relatives of the Hopi: "A woman was living alone in a cave on Wiyaatuwa, Whipple Mountain. Each morning it was her custom to go outside her cave and lie down with her legs spread wide apart, opening herself toward the rising Sun. On one of these mornings, Tavapitsi, the Sun, by a sudden concentration of his rays, caused her to conceive. She gave birth to twin sons" (Laird 1976:161–162, cited in Gough 1987:58).

At Zuni, the Twin War Gods are said to have been born to their Sun Father from their mother, Laughing Water, at Hantlipinkya. Mathilda Coxe Stevenson (1904:35) records a narrative about how the Sun "caused a heavy rain to fall until the cascade of the mountain side no longer glided placidly over the rocks to the basin below, but danced along; and in her joy, she [the cascade] was caught in the sun's embrace, and bore twin children, who issued from the foam."

The place where the Zuni Twins emerged is a water-washed hollow at the top of a canyon filled with rock art. In the grotto itself, a petroglyph of a rayed circle probably represents the sun (Fig. 14.6a). The sun's rays penetrate this chamber on the summer solstice just as they illuminate the great kiva of Casa Rinconada in Chaco Canyon on this day. The sun thereby impregnates the earth mother on the first day of summer, ushering in a season of warmth and growth. In a rounded chimney-like formation just below the grotto, a petroglyph clearly represents a woman giving birth (Fig. 14.6b). She wears hair whorls, and the U-shaped element beside her probably represents the wooden tool that a young Hopi woman's mother uses today to hold the hair in place as she ties the whorls.

A spectacular petroglyph panel deep in Chevelon Creek near Winslow, Arizona, shows a woman giving birth (Fig. 14.7). Judging by the patina on the rock surface, the style of the rock art, and the ceramic dates of the nearby Homol'ovi pueblos, the scene was probably carved in the A.D. 1300s or early 1400s, during the early Pueblo IV period. Cupules have been pecked all around, and deeply into, this figure; moreover, parts of

Figure 14.6. Petroglyphs at Hantlipinkya, middle Puerco River area. Sun symbol and woman giving birth (drawings by K. Hays-Gilpin).

her hands, torso, and legs have been repeatedly repecked. McCreery and Malotki (1994:Fig. 6.5) suggest this panel may have served as a fertility shrine.

These pecked cupules resemble those described by Stevenson at Zuni fertility shrines where women who wanted to get pregnant would place offerings in natural or pecked rock (Stevenson 1904:294–295 and Plate XII). Jane Young notes that Pueblo women's private pilgrimages to fertility shrines were "a crucial focus of religion" (1987:437), but she does not

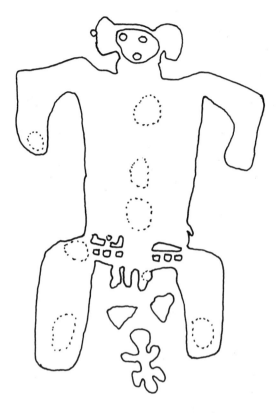

Figure 14.7. Petroglyph depicting a woman giving birth from Baird's Chevelon Steps Site, Middle Little Colorado River area, Arizona, Pueblo IV period. Dotted circles show locations of deeply pecked cupules (drawing by K. Hays-Gilpin).

discuss the form or appearance of such shrines; respecting the wishes of her Zuni hosts, she did not visit shrines that are currently in use (Young 1988:177).

Was the Chevelon Creek figure used to help mortal women cure sterility, ease childbirth, or help offspring survive? Is she simply a depiction of a fertile female? Note that in all accounts of the birth of the Hero Twins, their mother is unmarried. The Chevelon, Cottonwood, and Hantlipinkya figures similarly wear the hair whorls of unmarried women. These are not just any single mothers, however, but may represent the first woman giving birth, or a supernatural being, perhaps an earth deity like the Acoma creator, Iatiku, or the Mother of the Hero Twins.

Figure 14.8. Depictions on pottery of women giving birth. (a) Jeddito black-on-yellow bowl (U.S. National Museum); (b) Jeddito black-on-yellow bowl (Chicago, Field Museum of Natural History, catalog no. 75698; drawing by K. Hays-Gilpin).

In contrast, several depictions of childbirth on Hopi pottery bowls show mothers without hair whorls, indicating that they are married women. The birth of infants is depicted on a Jeddito black-on-yellow bowl found at Chevelon Ruin, another of the Homol'ovi ruins (Fig. 14.8a). One of these infants is clearly female. Two attendants flank the mother, holding branches of some sort of plant, perhaps sage or other herbs that are used today by Hopi midwives. A second bowl (Fig. 14.8b) depicts a mother, attendants, and one or more infants. The draftsmanship on this piece is rather loose, and the images somewhat ambiguous. This image may depict the birth of twins, or the bowls may be simply prayers for a successful marriage that will result in the birth of a certain number of children, including at least one female. Girls are especially desired in the matrilineal pueblos because they inherit the clan house, lands, and important ritual responsibilities.

In summary, whereas the rock art described above may depict supernatural or mythical events and serve as cures for sterility, the pottery depictions of childbirth may represent prayers of or for married women, perhaps even newly wedded women. Today at Hopi, pottery is often exchanged at weddings, and Ruth Bunzel reported that at Zuni some pottery designs were considered to be a special form of prayer just for women (Bunzel 1972:70).

Corn Maidens and Corn Mothers

In addition to identifying the earth as a mother and the sun as a father, Pueblo people say, "corn is life" and "corn is our mother" (Ford 1994). At Hopi, the word *Poshumi* refers both to corn seeds saved for planting and also to the young clan women of childbearing age (Black 1984). Corn plants are called "maidens" until they begin to produce ears. Then they are "women," and the ears of corn are called their children. Some seeds are saved to become next year's "maidens." The rest of the crop becomes "our mother," who will sustain the Hopi people through the year literally as food and metaphorically in the form of perfect ears of corn that are given to infants and initiates (Black 1984; Ford 1994:515; Parsons 1939:319–323).

There are seven Corn Maidens at Zuni, each associated with her own color and direction (including up, down, and center as well as the four cardinal directions) (Young 1987:440; see also Roscoe 1991:140–141). The life cycle of the corn plant is identified with the life cycle of humans. Corn is born with the consent of the earth mother and grows due to the prayers and nurturing of mortal men. Richard Ford argues that when Pueblo people say, "corn is our mother," they mean "that corn creates culture, that it sustains life, and that it is the authority for social action"

Figure 14.9. Corn maidens depicted on pottery and rock art. (a) A Pinedale black-on-white bowl (after Moulard 1984); (b) Fourmile polychrome bowl (Chicago, Field Museum, catalog no. 73447) (drawings by K. Hays-Gilpin); (c) Petroglyph near Springerville, Arizona (copyright J. Louis Argend-Farlow, reprinted by permission).

(1994:513). He suggests that corn has probably been a key metaphor in the Pueblo worldview for at least a thousand years and exhorts archaeologists to look more closely at the contexts of corn in the archaeological record — particularly the perfect ears called "corn mothers" or "corn guardians."

Corn Maidens also appear in prehistoric art. Several pottery bowls (one with explicitly female genitalia, from the Mogollon Rim area, dating to about A.D. 1300 to 1450) depict figures that may represent the Corn Maidens (Fig. 14.9). A nearly identical figure appears in a petroglyph near Springerville in southwestern New Mexico and dates to the same era (Fig. 14.9c; J. Louis Argend-Farlow, personal communication 1995).

Mother of Game Animals

Stories about the mother(s) of game animals abound all over North America. A Hopi earth deity, Sand Altar Woman (also known as Child Sticking Out Woman) bestows infants and also guards game animals. She is the sister of the germination god, Muyingwa, and the wife (sometimes the sister) of the god of death and the earth surface, Maasaw (Stephen 1936:261; Parsons 1939:178, 964). She is not entirely benevolent: one story recounts that she seduced and murdered young men and, when discovered, left Oraibi village to live alone along the Little Colorado River. Hunters who saw her bloody countenance and survived intercourse with her came away covered in blood but were thereafter very lucky in the hunt (Voth 1905:136–141).

The Mother of Game Animals herself appears in petroglyphs in the Little Colorado drainage in Arizona, from the Petrified Forest to Crack-in-Rock Pueblo in Wupatki National Monument (Fig. 14.10; see also McCreery and Malotki 1994:139–142; McCreery and McCreery 1986). A variety of birds and animals accompany her, sometimes striking sexually receptive poses, with tails raised. Parsons notes, however, that not all pueblos share this deity; at Acoma, for example, the female creator Iatiku creates a *Father* of Game Animals.

Pueblo hunters do not rely on luck to find game. Large game such as deer and antelope require respectful treatment and the performance of certain rituals. If the animals are pleased, their spirits will go back to their "mother;" they can then be born again and "give themselves" again to the hunter. Human and animal sexuality and fertility are also related. For example, hunters and their wives must abstain from sexual intercourse during the hunt (Parsons 1939:81). Phallic symbols such as "phallic feet" are also depicted in petroglyphs. Note for example, that the "phallic feet" located beside the female deity in the petroglyph in Figure 14.10 not only have phallic middle toes, but are also accompanied by "penis

Figure 14.10. The "Mother of Game Animals." Lower Puerco River area, Arizona (drawing by Patricia McCreery); note "phallic feet" nearby (drawing by K. Hays-Gilpin).

prints," which appear between each pair of footprints. These are probably meant to be emphatic statements that men made offerings or prayers at this place. Alice Schlegel writes that at Hopi, "There is a subtle relationship between women and game animals, especially antelopes (the major type of hunted game), that crops up in various rituals and even in jokes about extramarital sexual adventures: men talk about hunting for 'two-legged deer'" (1977:259). Such a "two-legged deer," the object of one's desire, may be represented in the depiction of an "antelope maiden" on a polychrome bowl from Sikyatki Pueblo. A similar association of animal as well as human fertility can be seen at Inscription Point, across the Little Colorado River from a Pueblo III site, Crack-in-Rock Pueblo. Here, an extensive but isolated rock art site depicts copulating humans and also copulating animals.

Conclusion

Ancient art of the Puebloan region in the American Southwest shows male and female individuals engaged in a variety of activities, together with a variety of apparently supernatural personages of both sexes. Very often, artists did not indicate sex at all, suggesting it was not always an important attribute of the character depicted. This observation is particularly true for the Archaic period. Imagery such as the lobed circle complex suggests that female fertility was an important metaphor for fertility and reproduction among humans as well as among plants and animals in the natural world. Female fertility may also be associated with some aspects of creation itself as early as the fifth century in the Four Corners area of the northern Southwest.

Female supernatural beings that are known from the historic Pueblo oral traditions are also found in rock art as early as the twelfth century (c. A.D. 1150) in the Little Colorado area of Arizona. These beings include the Mother of the Hero Twins, the Mother of Game Animals, and the Corn Maidens (or Corn Mothers). No single Mother Earth figure is identified in Pueblo oral traditions or in rock art, although female fertility and childbirth provide the central and enduring metaphors for many kinds of creativity, fertility, and well-being in the Puebloan Southwest.

Puebloan ideology of gender complementarity (Schlegel 1977) is expressed in the placement of male and female rock art images relative to each other, and the placement of female images relative to solar events. The central concepts of complementarity and diversity, then, ordered the Pueblo world since at least the twelfth century, long before the recent conflation of many holy beings into a Mother Earth figure to fill contemporary political and spiritual needs. This argument is not simply a rejection of a straw-man hypothesis, but represents an active effort to use archaeological evidence to resist the contemporary misrepresentation of Native American spirituality as an essentialist, unchanging, and unitary phenomenon.

Male figures portrayed in rock art are more difficult to link to specific personages in the oral traditions, but again they are seen in a variety of roles and poses. Priests, hunters, and flute players, although male, are also associated with fertility and increase among the historic pueblos. This association can also be seen in the rock art. The association of male figures with some aspects of fertility and reproduction suggests that, in Pueblo thought, the symbolic job of promoting fertility is not limited to women; the contribution of males is also important. It seems clear, however, that female fertility and childbirth provide the central and enduring metaphors for many kinds of creativity, fertility, and well-being in the Puebloan Southwest.

Acknowledgments

Special thanks to Jerrold Levy for recommending Sam Gill's book and commenting on earlier versions of this research and to Patricia McCreery, Steven Manning, and J. Louis Argend-Farlow for providing illustrations and insights into the rock art record. Claudette Piper and Dennis Gilpin commented on drafts of the chapter, Peter Pilles provided slides of the U.S. National Museum pottery collections, and the Arizona Archaeological and Historical Society sponsored my own studies of the Field Museum of Natural History collections. I would also like to thank the staffs of these two wonderful museums, as well as my colleagues at the Museum of Northern Arizona, for their invaluable assistance with my collections research.

Chapter 15
Father Earth, Mother Sky
Ancient Egyptian Beliefs About Conception and Fertility
Ann Macy Roth

In reconstructing ancient gender relationships, Egyptologists are fortunate. The ancient Egyptians have left not only archaeological remains, but also extensive texts and iconographic evidence, so that one type of data can be checked against and explicated by other types. The analysis presented here would be difficult to duplicate in cultures that are known to us only from their material remains. The value of the approach used here to archaeologists, then, lies less in its methods than in its conclusions, which offer an alternative model of gender relations. Of particular interest is the apparent connection between the views of human conception in ancient Egypt and Egypt's unusual agricultural cycle.

The Egyptian case also suggests a conclusion about the general relationship between views of fertility and women's social roles that many will find counterintuitive. Some scholars would like to locate women's power in their fertility and ability to generate new life. The analysis presented here, however, suggests that women's association with fertility and creative power may actually limit their autonomy. In ancient Egypt, it will be argued, the power of fertility and creation was identified almost exclusively as a male characteristic, yet the women of this culture had far greater autonomy and parity with men than in most other ancient cultures. They could own property, including land, and transmit it by sale or bequest without the intervention of male relatives (Robins 1993:127–131). They could institute legal proceedings (McDowell 1990:152–153), and in rare cases they could rule the country (Robins 1993:50). They also enjoyed a great range of sexual expression (Fox 1985:298–300, 305–307), particularly in comparison to women in most other ancient cultures.

Male and Female Roles in Fertility and Conception

In historic and modern Western culture, the power of procreation is
clearly thought to reside primarily in women. We can see this in the
phrases "Mother Earth" and "Mother Nature," both of which refer to the
female creative principle, and we can see it in the fact that women are
often described as barren (which men never are), and that they have
historically been blamed for a lack of children or for their failure to
produce children of the desired sex. Even European women's dress in
some periods has glorified female fertility by mimicking pregnancy. For
example, in the well-known Arnolfini wedding portrait by van Eyck, the
new bride's dress emphasizes and exaggerates the roundness of her belly.

This assumption that the woman is the principal creator of new life is
so deeply embedded in Western cultural beliefs, that, despite increasingly detailed scientific understanding of the biological process of conception, any female patient in a modern fertility clinic can testify to the
degree to which the medical profession views fertility primarily as a female problem.

The roots of this Western view of women's role in fertility can be traced
to Classical antiquity. Despite the fact that semen is highly visible and the
ovum is not, and despite medical views which held that males were more
fertile, Greek science attributed an important role to the woman. The
Hippocratic view, which was largely followed by Galen and seems to have
been dominant in the medieval European tradition, argued that both
men and women produced "seed," although the male seed was supposed
to have had more intellectual qualities (McLaren 1984:16–17; Musallam
1983:46). On the other hand, Aristotle attributed a much lesser role to
women, arguing that the semen was the sole creative force and that
women were passive in the process of conception, even though men-
strual blood provided the material for the growing child (Zeitlin 1984:
178; Musallam 1983:43–45). This Aristotelian view is also seen in Greek
literature: for example, in the *Eumenides*, Apollo argues that, although
Orestes has killed his mother, he is not guilty of parricide because he is
not in fact related to her, but is the child only of his father (Zeitlin
1984:176–178).

Far stronger and more prevalent than these medical views, however,
was the widespread belief that women were responsible for fertility. These
folk ideas are seen in many ancient myths. The fertility of the earth, for
example, is clearly controlled by a goddess; when Demeter's daughter
Persephone is taken away to the nether world, she mourns and the earth
grows cold and barren. This myth locates both agricultural and human
fertility in the woman, and through her rituals, the goddess Demeter
grants women some control over this fertility (Nixon 1995:91–92).

These Greek folk beliefs in the importance of female fertility are also a common mythological theme. In many myths, male gods try to prevent female fertility (apparently never noticing that they could prevent conception simply by refraining from intercourse); in other myths, male gods attempt to appropriate for themselves women's ability to bear children. An obvious example is the story of Zeus swallowing his wife Metis so that he himself can give birth to their daughter Athena (Zeitlin 1984: 178–179).

This belief that the woman is largely responsible for fertility persisted in European thought even through early modern time. In England, for example, as late as the first years of the nineteenth century, a woman's pregnancy was thought to invalidate a claim of rape, since it was believed that women could not conceive unless intercourse was consensual (McLaren 1984:27). This belief essentially credited women with control over conception and is consistent with the Western assumption that the power to create new life resides in the female.

Egyptologists have tended to assume that this Western model was also held in ancient Egypt. However, if we define fertility specifically as the act of creation itself, it can be argued that in ancient Egypt, women were not credited with creating new life. Instead, the creative role is attached exclusively to the male sex. This association can be seen clearly in the language, where the verb that we translate as "to conceive a child" is the same as the Egyptian verb used for "to receive" or "to take." In the Egyptian view, then, the woman "receives" the child, already fully created, from the man. This view is stated explicitly in Akhenaton's Hymn to the Aton: praising the god as creator of human life, the hymn says he has "placed seed in a woman and made the sperm into a person" (Simpson 1974:291).

The absence of a female role in creation is also seen in Egyptian myths dealing with conception and birth. The sky goddess Nut, for example, swallows the sun, and then gives birth to it, rejuvenated, but otherwise unchanged (Lesko 1991:118). Clearly, Nut has no effect on the sun; it simply passes through her. Likewise, in the "Tale of Two Brothers" (Simpson 1974:92–107), the hero Bata, who has transformed himself into a tree, impregnates his evil wife when a splinter of wood from this tree flies into her mouth. In time, she gives birth to Bata himself. Reborn, Bata is unchanged, inheriting nothing from his evil wife/mother. These two myths describe how women (the sky goddess and also the wife of Bata) simply receive and incubate their children. They conceive by swallowing the man himself (in these cases the mouth is presumably seen as analogous to the opening of the vagina), and he is reborn through them. However, a man can also be impregnated in the same way. In "The Contendings of Horus and Seth," Seth eats lettuce on which the semen of

Horus has been placed, and at the command of the gods, that semen is born as a sun disk on the top of his head (Simpson 1974:120–121).

Only in later periods is there any evidence that the Egyptians granted the female a greater role in forming a child. For example, a fragmentary story implies that bones were contributed by the father and the soft body parts by the mother (Yoyotte 1962:140–146). This text, however, dates to the Greco-Roman period, and its views may indicate Greek influence or the increased role of medical knowledge in structuring belief. However, there is no reason to assume that technically accurate medical knowledge had much impact on general Egyptian cultural assumptions any more than it currently does in Western culture.

Widespread Egyptian beliefs regarding the importance of male fertility are also indicated by the text on a statue that offers to intercede with Hathor on behalf of women who want a "good (probably fertile) husband." Baines argues that this text acknowledges a male role in conception (Baines 1991:182–183, esp. n. 160); it could also be interpreted as viewing fertility as an exclusively male responsibility. Other evidence regarding Egyptian belief includes a letter cited by Robins (1993:77) in which the writer advises a man to adopt a child, saying, "You are not a man, since you cannot make your wives pregnant like other men."

Egyptian belief in the importance of male creativity in fertility may also extend to assigning men responsibility for determining the sex of the child that they create. This view may help explain the lack of evidence of female infanticide in ancient Egypt, which is particularly clear in Greco-Roman Egypt (Pomeroy 1990:136–137). If the sex of a man's children is viewed as the result of his own creative powers, rather than his wife's, he might be less likely to expose his infant daughters.

It is also perhaps worth noting that these ideas of fertility were extended to nonhuman creatures. For example, according to Plutarch (1936:27–29), all scarab beetles were believed by Egyptians to be male. These scarab beetles were closely connected both with the rebirth of people and also the daily rebirth of the sun because they laid their eggs in a ball of dung, from which the newly hatched scarabs would emerge. The Egyptians apparently thought that these beetles reproduced without sexual contact, and, therefore, they concluded that the beetles were all males and that there were no female beetles. Again, this idea shows that ancient Egyptians located fertility and the ability to create new life in the male.

These ideas also affect Egyptian ideas regarding the supernatural world. Egyptian divinities connected with creative fertility are either indisputably male or are androgynous but predominantly male. These gods commonly take three forms: one originating in human fertility, one in animal fertility, and the third in plant fertility. The ithyphallic form

(Fig. 15.1) obviously displays the male sexual potency of human reproduction; but by its mummiform nature, it also alludes to the fertility of human death and burial — the burial of both seeds and human beings in the
earth, from which new life will emerge. The second form associated with
fertility — bulls and rams — is also indisputably male (Quirke 1992:48).
The origin of this form presumably lay in the desire for fertility in these
two animals that were favored for meat (that is, mutton and beef). But
these gods can sometimes also be connected with human fertility, as in
the case of the ram-headed Khnum, who created human children on his
potter's wheel, or the divine king who is called "Strong Bull" to emphasize his ability to conceive his successors.

The third form associated with fertility is the "fecundity figure" or
"Nile god" (Fig. 15.2) (Baines 1985). These figures are predominantly
male and are referred to by male pronouns. But although Baines believes
that they are simply fat, reflecting the richness of the agricultural production brought by the Nile flood (Baines 1985:116, 118–122, 126–127),
Otto (1938:28) has argued that their sagging breasts and protruding
bellies resemble those in the rare depictions of pregnant women and
probably reflect a nature that is at least androgynous. In the later period,
these figures are sometimes shown with nourishing liquid flowing from
their breasts. Baines (1985:118–119) views these examples as a "female
'reinterpretation' " of the figures.

Otto's view, however, makes sense in that fecundity figures are personifications of the agricultural fertility of the annual Nile flood, which was
closely associated with the androgynous primeval waters of the time before creation. The primeval waters lacked any distinctions in sex (Hornung 1982:171), as they did in visibility, form, time, and space. Out of this
undifferentiated pre-existent state came all existing life and, therefore,
the analogs to the primeval waters (the annual Nile flood, the waters of
the womb, the oblivion of death) also held the promise of new life. It
seems entirely consistent with this view to depict the divinities that personified the Nile flood and the resulting produce of the land as essentially male, but with the female characteristics of pregnancy.

Pinch (1993:247) and others have noted the maleness of all these
depictions of fertility, but they have restricted their role to animal and
plant fertility, assigning human fertility to goddesses such as Hathor.
Such a distinction is unlikely, however, because of the blurred boundaries
between the plant and animal depictions of fertility (the fecundity figures and the ram and bull gods) and the depiction of human fertility in
the ithyphallic divinities. The same divinity can occur in several forms,
and all three forms are often shown with black, green, or blue skin. For
example, Atum can be both a ram and a fecundity figure; Amun can be a
ram or ithyphallic; and the symptoms of human fertility are used in the

Figure 15.1. The Egyptian god Amun-Re rendered in ithyphallic form (redrawn by the author from the White Chapel of Senwosret I at Karnak, Egypt).

Figure 15.2. Two gods representing the northern and southern halves of the Nile River depicted as fecundity figures (redrawn by the author from a wall relief at Karnak temple, Egypt).

ithyphallic deities and probably also in fecundity figures. In mythology, the fertility god Bata can be represented as a bull; and the phrase "bull of his mother," implying that a man can impregnate his wife with himself and thus is the "bull" or sexual partner of his own (eventual) mother, clearly applies in a human context, particularly in the case of kings. The major fertility god Osiris, who both represents the ability of the dead to re-engender themselves in the afterlife and of kings to create sons in which they live again, is also closely associated with the planting and sprouting of grain. These overlapping functions and iconography indicate that fertility was seen as the same phenomenon in plants, animals, and humans. Moreover, it was clearly a male phenomenon, with androgynous features deriving from the connection of fertility with the undifferentiated nature of nonexistence.

In Western scholarship, human fertility has traditionally been associated with goddesses, particularly Hathor and Isis. This association is partially justified if one views human fertility as a longer process that includes not only conception, but also the nursing of the child (e.g., Pinch 1993). However, there is no textual or contextual evidence for considering Hathor and Isis to be fertility goddesses in the strictest sense. The evidence suggests that these and other goddesses assisted in fertility, but were not responsible for the actual creation of new life. Like women in general, they played two roles: first, to stimulate fertility in a man; and second, to nurture the results of that fertility, before birth and after. This association explains why such goddesses (and again women in general) are almost always represented as young and sexually enticing, or as nursing a child, rather than as pregnant. According to this interpretation, votives dedicated to Hathor were offered not in the hope that she would grant fertility to women, but that she would stimulate it in men.

One example of this female role in creation can be seen in a puzzling episode in the story about the lawsuit between the gods Horus and Seth. When Re, the sun god, is insulted by a member of his entourage, he lies down on his back, inert and sulking, and thus brings the judicial proceedings to a halt. After a time, his daughter Hathor comes to him and exposes her genitals to him; as a result, he laughs at her and he immediately jumps up and gets back to work (Simpson 1974:112). This incident, I would argue, is a humorous parody of the rebirth of the sun after a night of death. He can be revived because Hathor's gesture has stimulated him sexually and enables him to recreate himself, by himself.

The nature of existence in Egyptian religion, as Hornung (1982:170–185) stressed, is predicated on distinctions and differentiation, the absence of which characterizes nonexistence. Thus the two sexes and their roles in reproduction were clearly differentiated (Hornung 1982:171). These distinct but complementary sexual roles, in which the woman stimulates male creation and nurtures the resulting child, may be at the root of the anomalous social roles of Egyptian women.

For example, Levine (1995:92–110) has noted that a woman's hair, an important symbol of female sexuality in all Mediterranean cultures, was cut at the time of her marriage in both the Classical and Biblical traditions. Egyptian women, by contrast, seem to have cut their hair only at the death of their husbands. According to Plutarch's (1936:31–49) version of the Isis and Osiris myth, the first action of Isis upon hearing of the death of her husband is to cut a lock of her hair; and the word "widow" in

Egyptian is augmented by a sign representing a lock of hair (Erman and Grapow 1971:363, 4–7). In art, women are invariably shown with un-covered heads and long, unbound hair. This convention implies that women's sexual identity (and thus probably also their personal identity) did not disappear with marriage and motherhood. Rather, it was neces-sary that they remain sexually alluring in order to stimulate their hus-bands' fertility.

Earth, Sky, and Fertility in Egyptian Life and Thought

There is an obvious reason for the Egyptians' unusual views of fertility: it lies in the forms and functioning of the Egyptian landscape itself and is rooted in the nature of its resulting agricultural cycle. In most parts of the world, the earth is made fertile by rain from the sky. By analogy with human reproduction, the sky is viewed as an active male deity, from which comes the rain that penetrates the passive and female mother earth and causes her to bring forth new life. The rain is crucial, but the creative power resides in the earth. The sky is thus gendered male and the mother earth, female.

In Egypt, by contrast, the earth was fertilized by the annual flood of the Nile, which at the end of every summer covered the fields with fertile silt as well as water. The water and silt, which renewed the land and made the crops grow, came not from the sky but from the earth. Grammatically, both the earth and the floodwaters were regarded as male, and the deities that personified them (Geb and Hapi) were also male. However, the fact that the earth also received the floodwaters (a female role) and the connection of the floodwaters with the primeval waters of nonexistence (which were sexually undifferentiated) probably explains some of the androgynous characteristics of male fertility deities. The Egyptian sky was also the reverse of the general pattern: it was feminine, grammatically and also in its personification as a goddess, Nut.

Earth and sky clearly act out the relationship between earthly men and women. The typical depiction of the cosmos shows Geb, the earth god, lying down, while the nude, star-spangled body of his sister-wife Nut, the sky goddess, arches above him. In some versions (Fig. 15.3), Geb is de-picted with an erection, clearly creating new life without any physical contact whatsoever with Nut. Her role, however, was essential: her nude body, stretched out above him, is the sexual stimulant that brings about his erection, and, thereby, his creation. Hers was not a passive role.

Egyptian myths dealing with the creation of the cosmos further illus-trate the connection of gender roles with the agricultural cycle. The annual flood was seen as a return of the undifferentiated primeval waters, potentially containing all existence, which had preceded creation and

Figure 15.3. The goddess Nut (the Sky), shown arching herself above her consort Geb (the Earth) (redrawn by the author from a papyrus in the British Museum).

continued to exist as a source of both danger and fertility outside the created cosmos. Floating in these primeval waters, the creator god Atum expelled from his body two distinct substances, air (male: Shu, the son of Atum) and moisture (female: Tefnut, the daughter of Atum). This act could be variously described as spitting or as sneezing, or, significantly, as an ejaculation as a result of masturbation (Lesko 1991:92). Atum refers to this mechanism in the text found on Papyrus Bremner-Rhind, dating to the Ptolemaic period, when he says: "I acted as husband with my fist, I copulated with my hand" (Allen 1988:28). Atum's hand can thus be called the mother of Shu and Tefnut (Blackman 1921:13). The word for hand is feminine, and as such Atum's hand plays the typical feminine role: it stimulates male fertility. This act metaphorically reproduces the self-fertilization of the earth in which the male floodwaters come forth from the male earth itself. Atum's androgynous aspects could be expressed by depicting him as a fecundity figure (Baines [1985:121 Fig. 82] though Baines's interpretation [124] differs from mine).

The androgynous character of male fertility is made clearest by the stories about the gods Osiris and Bata, both emphatically fertile gods, who are both castrated in the course of their myths. In the myth of Isis and Osiris, the ideal king, Osiris, is murdered and cut into pieces; his wife reassembles the pieces and then embraces him so that she is impregnated with Horus, a new ideal king. Osiris then becomes the ruler of the dead, and every dead king (and by extension every dead person) thus becomes "an Osiris," effectively being syncretized, or equated, with the god Osiris himself in order to reconceive himself and be born into the next world. The king's son takes on the role of Horus, taking his father's place on earth. The only full account of this myth is that of the Greek writer Plutarch (1936:31–49), probably dating to the first century C.E. In Plutarch's retelling of the story, Osiris's sexual organ is the only piece of him that is not recovered by Isis; it had been thrown into the river and eaten by three fish before she began her search. This seems a curious deficiency for a fertility god, and Quirke (1992:58) has suggested that this incident was a Greek interpolation. However, the same episode also occurs in another, purely Egyptian, myth.

The Tale of Two Brothers (Simpson 1974:92–107) tells essentially the same story as Isis and Osiris. The main difference is that Bata's evil wife takes on the role of the murderer, and his good brother Anubis takes on the role of the good wife Isis. Although Bata, the hero of the "Tale of Two Brothers," is a fertility god, he castrates himself at one point to demonstrate his chastity; his severed organ is immediately consumed by a catfish. This fish motif is clearly important since it occurs in both stories. Red fish appear as erotic elements in love poems, and fish seem to have been avoided in an ideal diet (Brewer and Friedman 1989:17–9), but their exact significance here is unclear. Like Osiris, Bata is later able to father himself upon his wife after his death, and becomes his own heir—all without benefit of his sexual organ. This accomplishment is presumably a testimony to the creative powers of the now-androgynous fertility god.

A third version of the story, very late in date and badly preserved, is the Papyrus Jumilhac (Vandier 1962; Altenmiller 1973). In this version, the evil role is played by the fertility god as the central character himself, in this case Seth. This text tells us explicitly that Seth's phallus and testicles are cut off though their fate is not recorded and nothing is said about fish. Both Bata and Seth are depicted as bulls in their stories, and both are presumably also reborn as "bulls of their mothers."

While all of these gods represent fertility, the role of Osiris, in particular, is essential in the process of rebirth after death. To re-engender himself as the "bull of his mother," every man is identified with this god after his death, and by sympathetic magic, he is able to reconceive himself just as Osiris did. For this reason, a man named Amenmose, for example, would be referred to in his tomb decorations and in his mortuary literature as Osiris-Amenmose, which represents a species of syncretism with the god.

Women's Role in Death and Rebirth

Egyptian views of fertility and birth are most clearly seen in the realm of tombs and mortuary religion. In recent years, it has been argued that Egyptians of all periods took a very literal view of rebirth after death, so that many of the rituals, artifacts, and representations attested in tombs are taken quite directly from traditions and equipment used to assist in childbirth. This can be seen particularly clearly in the ritual of the "opening of the mouth," which, I have argued, was originally an enactment of birth and childhood developments and was intended to allow the dead person to eat his funerary meal (Roth 1992:113–47; 1993:57–79). Similarly the set of four magical bricks buried in New Kingdom tombs are identical with the four bricks that supported a woman while she was giving birth and played a role in protecting the newborn child (Roth and Roehrig, n.d.).

Dorman, working on the related problem of the birth of the sun (which is often used as an analogy for the rebirth of the dead) has noted that the eastern hills, between which the sun is reborn every morning, are rendered as overlapping red folds and are actually labeled *labia majora*. In addition, a potter's wheel, on which human beings are formed at conception, is sometimes depicted as part of the process (Dorman, in press). Moreover, the coffin or even the entire burial chamber of a tomb could be seen as a womb from which rebirth into the next life took place. It is thus quite clear that what the Egyptians expected after death was a very literal rebirth from a female womb.

The tombs and tomb equipment also make reference to an earlier stage of the process of human rebirth: conception. Like a birth, a rebirth clearly required a conception, and in recent years much attention has been devoted to the metaphorical reconception of the deceased. In burial equipment and in tomb chapel decoration, scholars have seen evidence for the assumption that the dead person was supposed to reconceive himself sexually (Desroches-Noblecourt 1953:15–33; Westendorf 1967:139–150; although Eaton-Krauss and Graefe [1985:29–40] contest Westendorf's interpretation). The nude "concubine figures" and other female "fertility figures" found in tombs, which were once thought to be sex toys for dead men, are now generally believed to be part of this process (Desroches-Noblecourt 1953:15–33); they were meant to stimulate a man to (re)create himself, while the children sometimes shown with them ensured that the surrogate mother could nurture his creation successfully. Images of the tomb owner's wife, often posed in sexually suggestive ways, are similarly thought to have served symbolically as his sexual partner in reconceiving himself, so that he could be reborn in the next world (Robins 1989:109–110).

But a problem arises with this mechanism when the deceased was female. It is clear from both archaeological and textual sources that women were believed to be reborn as well as men. However, the overwhelming maleness of the creative sexual role would seem to make it impossible for a woman to re-engender herself and be reborn into the next world. The burials of women offer no special equipment that could serve as a male surrogate in the process, as the concubine figures are assumed to do in male burials. On the contrary, there seems to be an absolute taboo on the representation of the husband in the tombs of women (Roth 1994; see also Robins [1994] for a related phenomenon). Instead, the burial equipment and mortuary texts provided for women are identical to those provided for men (Fischer 1989:8–9; for examples see D'Auria et al. 1987: 76–77, 98–99, 118–119, 156, 162–163, 164–165, 169–170, 173–175, and 187–189), implying that the mechanisms for rebirth were apparently identical. Thus, while on the surface it seems unlikely that a woman was seen as the "bull of her mother," there is also no evidence that she served as the "cow of her father" in the facilitation of her own rebirth.

The answer must be that a woman, like her husband, was syncretized with Osiris after death, so that a woman named Nofret would become, at her death, "Osiris-Nofret." This syncretism is well attested for women from the time of the earliest religious texts down to the end of Egyptian history (although, puzzlingly, in a few later period burials the woman is syncretized with the goddess Hathor instead [D'Auria et al. 1987:242]). While syncretism and identification with divinities of the same gender are the normal pattern, a woman's syncretism with Osiris was presumably made possible by Osiris's androgynous characteristics: like a woman, he has no phallus. Bata, Osiris's avatar in the Tale of Two Brothers, at one point tells his wife "I am a woman like you" (Simpson 1974:101). Any woman, then, could become Osiris, without abandoning her feminine identity, which was an important characteristic of her existence and needed to be preserved. At the same time, Osiris's role as an androgynous male fertility god allowed her to re-engender herself just as a man would.

But the question remains, who stimulated Osiris-Nofret to reconceive herself? And, even more interesting, who served as her mother in the rebirth process? In a man's tomb, these roles seem to have been played by his wife or, if there is no wife represented, by his mother. In the rare tombs of women, the most prominent woman depicted is the tomb owner herself. It is thus likely that in regenerating herself in the afterlife, Nofret, and other women, played all three roles. She acted as her own husband, her own wife, and her own mother. The depictions of herself in tomb decoration both stimulated her (male) fertility and nurtured her before and after her rebirth.

Conclusion

During life, Egyptian women's sexual roles were distinct from and com-plementary to the roles of men. Death, however, marked a return to the undifferentiated pre-existent state, and in this androgynous environ-ment, dead women could be identified with Osiris. By virtue of that identification they could perform the male role of being "bulls of their mothers," thereby re-conceiving themselves in preparation for a rebirth into the next life. Ancient Egyptian women thus played a variety of sexual roles, although some roles were only accessible to them after death.

These patterns have interesting implications for our understanding not only of Egyptian mortuary religion but also of the way that concep-tions of fertility affect the roles that women play during their lives. The responsibility for fertility and creating new life was *not* laid on the shoul-ders of women in ancient Egypt; instead, they were expected to be sex-ually aggressive, to begin the process of creation by enticing their male partners to create. The Roman perception of Cleopatra as an aggressive seductress (Hughes-Hallett 1990:38–69) may even be based on this per-ceived societal trait among Egyptian women.

This pattern, which is the reverse of the "normal" Western stereotype, deprives women of the one powerful advantage that they seem to have in our own culture: the perceived ability to create new life. However, the location of fertility in the male may, in fact, explain the unusual indepen-dence and autonomy of Egyptian women, who had far greater parity with men than in most other ancient cultures. Perhaps because they were responsible for initiating sexual relations and because they could even take on the male role after death, Egyptian women could more openly show independence in other spheres as well. Furthermore, absolved of any blame for the result of sexual intercourse, women were not seen as the bearers of guilt—there are no Eves or Pandoras in Egyptian my-thology. Viewed from this perspective, the fertility assumed to reside in women by Western tradition may be less about female power and auton-omy than about female passivity and shame.

Acknowledgments

In addition to the participants in the conference upon which this volume is based, I am grateful to the audiences who attended several popular lectures on ancient Egyptian women that I have given for the American Research Center in Egypt (in New York in 1992, in Washington, D.C., in 1993, and in Dallas in 1997), to the Department of Near Eastern Studies at Johns Hopkins University where I pre-sented a similar argument in 1996, to those who attended a presentation of a version of this chapter at the national meetings of the American Research Center in Egypt in 1996, and also to my mythology classes at Howard University. All these groups responded with questions and comments that helped me to refine the ideas in this chapter. In particular, I am grateful to a questioner at the Dallas seminar who suggested the connection between the assumption that men determined their children's gender and the lack of evidence for female infanticide in Egypt. I am especially indebted to Molly Levine and Richard Jasnow for references and to John Baines and two anonymous reviewers from the University of Pennsylvania Press for their bracing criticism.

Chapter 16
Female Figurines in the European Upper Paleolithic
Politics and Bias in Archaeological Interpretation

Margaret Beck

Venus figurines from the Upper Paleolithic of Europe have been interpreted in many different ways: for example, as prehistoric pornography, fertility symbols, images of goddesses, teaching aids, and self-portraits. In this chapter, I consider particularly how the political goals, interpretive bias, and research interests of the investigator have influenced his or her interpretations. Two very different approaches can be seen among feminist scholars alone, and attempting to evaluate the accuracy of either approach raises almost as many questions as it answers. One might think that these depictions of women would be a good way to glean information about women in these prehistoric groups. Depending upon the approach taken, however, this is emphatically not the case.

Venus Figurines: Time, Place, and Context

The term "Venus figurines" refers to the many, presumably female, figurines that are found all across Eurasia (Fig. 16.1) in sites that date to the Upper Paleolithic (Abramova 1967; Bahn and Vertut 1988; Bosinski 1991; Delporte 1993a, b; Duhard 1993; Gvozdover 1989; Hahn 1993; Leroi-Gourhan 1968; Marshack 1991a, b, 1996; Rosenfeld 1977). There are several explanations for the use of the name "Venus" when referring to these artifacts. One author claims that the name is a reference to "the goddess associated with sexual love in Western culture" (Gadon 1989:8); this explanation assumes and implies that these figurines signify female sexuality. Bahn and Vertut (1988:138) emphasize the body shape of the figurines; they state that "[t]he term 'Venus' was first used by the Marquis de Vibraye in the 1860s in connection with his 'Venus impudique' [or "Shameless Venus"] from Laugerie-Basse . . . and was later adopted by Piette for the more corpulent figures from Brassempouy and elsewhere." They suggest that the name is now used to refer primarily to the more obese figures, although this practice is by no means universal. Another explanation refers to the preservation of the images; Rice (1981) proposes that the many of the figurines were missing arms and thus resembled the well-known armless sculpture of the goddess Venus from Greek antiquity.

These Upper Paleolithic figurines are found over an enormous area, from southern Europe to Siberia. In the most comprehensive reference work, Delporte (1993b), lists 75 sites at which human figurines that date to the Upper Paleolithic have been found. He groups these sites into five regions with 20 sites in the Pyreneo-Aquitain region (33 sculptures and 11 half-sculptures), 8 sites in the Mediterranean region (17 sculptures), 31 sites in the Rheno-Danubien region (104 sculptures), 12 sites in the Russian region (63 sculptures), and 4 sites in the Siberian region (35 sculptures).

The name "Venus figurine" suggests that all the sculptures are female, but in fact, while the majority of figurines appear to be female, there are some which appear to be androgynous, and there are a few which are consistently argued to be male. It is therefore difficult to estimate the number of sites with specifically female, rather than human, figurines. Of the 263 relatively complete examples (252 figurines and 11 half-sculptures) discussed by Delporte (1993b), I estimate that 60 percent of them can be conservatively interpreted as female. The sex of the other figurines is more debatable. The estimates above may also include the occasional fraud (for example, the half-sculptures at Abri Pataud [Bahn 1996] or at La Mouthe [White 1996]).

The earliest figurines appear in Aurignacian period sites, with four dated contexts in Central Europe (Vogelherd, Hohlenstein-Stadel, Geissenklosterle, and Stratzing/Krems-Rehberg). The dates at these sites range from roughly 23,000 to 32,000 B.P. (Hahn 1993:230–231). Figurines also occur later, during the Gravettian (or, to the east, the Pavlovian and Kostienkian) period, when dated sites with figurines appear to "cluster around [the time of] one of two interstadials . . . the Tursac Interstadial in the west (23,000 B.P.) and the Briansk Interstadial in Eastern Europe (27,000 to 24,000 B.P.)" (Delporte 1993a:244). Figurines were also made during the Magdalenian period, with most dating to about 15,000 to 9,000 B.P. (Delporte 1993b).

There are numerous figurines, however, that cannot be assigned to a temporal period on the basis of criteria other than style. Many of these

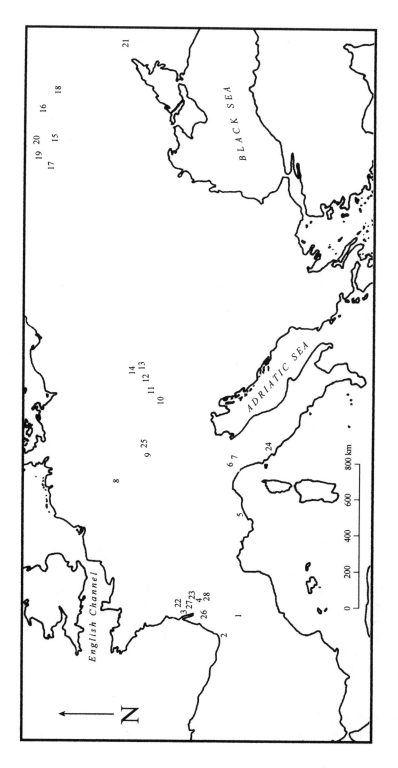

Figure 16.1. The distribution of Venus figurines, c. 25,000–23,000 B.P. Sites marked are (1) Brassempouy; (2) Lespugue; (3) Monpazier; (4) Pechialet; (5) Grimaldi; (6) Chiozza; (7) Savignano; (8) Mainz-Linsenberg; (9) Brillenhöhle VII; (10) Willendorf II/9; (11) Pavlov; (12) Dolni Vestonice; (13) Moravany; (14) Petrkovice; (15) Avdeevo; (16) Gagarino; (17) Khotylevo; (18) Kostienki I/1; (19) Eliseevici; (20) Souponevo; (21) Minevskii Iar; (22) Abri Facteur 10/11; (23) Sireuil; (24) Trasimeno; (25) Mauern; (26) Laussel; (27) Abri Pataud; and (28) Terme Pialat (redrawn, with title and site locations from Gamble 1982:Fig. 2).

figurines were found in early excavations, in which poor stratigraphic data was recorded (such as those at the sites of Pekarna and Brassempouy). Others were found entirely out of context (such as the figurines from Sireuil and Monpazier).

The Upper Paleolithic figurines were sculpted on a wide variety of materials including reindeer antler, bone, ivory, fired clay, jet, hematite, limonite, sandstone, limestone, green and yellow steatite, and horse teeth (Delporte 1993b). The appearance of these figurines ranges from highly stylized (for example, the figurines from Nebra and Gonnersdorf) to more realistic (Moravany-Podovica), from rough and incomplete (Gagarino, Adveevo) to finished and relatively detailed (Willendorf, Lespugue).

It is even difficult to arrive at a total count of known figurines. Documentation is scattered and in several languages, there is debate about the sex and even the humanness of some of the figurines, and many of the figurines are fragmentary. There are also a number of abstract pieces from sites such as Dolni Vestonice and Le Placard that may or may not represent female buttocks, breasts, or genitalia. The well-known "rod with breasts," "breast" pendants, and fork with "vulva" from Dolni Vestonice are examples of sculptures that may represent only portions of the body. In these and other pieces, even the body part represented is debatable. The "rod with breasts," for example, could also be interpreted as stylized male genitalia (Nelson 1990).

Androcentric Interpretation and Feminist Response

Because of the complexity of the entire database, researchers usually focus upon a subset of the figurines. Which figurines are included in (and excluded from) this subset reveals a great deal about the assumptions and biases of each investigator. For example, most researchers generally include the "Venus of Willendorf" in their analyses (see Delporte 1993b: Fig. 128). However, there were in fact two statuettes recovered at Willendorf; the second, which is much more slender and elongated (Delporte 1993b: Fig. 129), is almost never discussed. The second figurine is also apparently more roughly made and possibly incomplete; it is possible that researchers omit this figurine because they assume that it is not "finished" in some way.

This sample bias is also noted by Nelson (1990, 1993) in her study of introductory textbooks. From the discussions of Upper Paleolithic figurines in these texts, "one would suppose that the Willendorf statuette, easily the most familiar, was typical or normal or modal" (Nelson 1990). This impression characterizes not only the twelve anthropology textbooks discussed by Nelson, but also is common in general works about prehistoric art as well (Leroi-Gourhan 1968; Pericot-Garcia et al. 1969;

Torbrugge 1968). This inaccurate generalization is even found in books discussing women's prehistory (Ehrenberg 1989:66–67). For example, Leroi-Gourhan explicitly states: "No matter where found — Brassempouy, Lespugue, Abri Pataud, Willendorf, Dolni Vestonice, Gagarino, Kostienki — [the figures] are practically interchangeable, apart from their proportions. The most complete figures have the same treatment of the head, the same small arms folded over the breasts or pointing toward the belly, the same low breasts drooping like sacks to far below the waist, and the same legs ending in minuscule or nonexistent feet" (1968:96).

Such figurines generally have enlarged breasts and full stomachs and hips, with head, arms, and legs significantly smaller and apparently de-emphasized. As noted by Nelson (1990, 1993), this style of representation has been frequently interpreted as a depiction or glorification of fertility and maternity. This interpretation is clearly linked to the fullness of figure displayed by some of the statuettes, whether they are seen as being pregnant or merely obese. Torbrugge (1968:15), for example, writes, "[t]he ample forms of the Venus of Vestonice and other female figurines which have survived intact unequivocally reveal that these were intended to be images of motherhood."

Rice (1981) and Nelson (1990, 1993) argued that these interpretations represent gender constructs of our own society that are uncritically applied to the Upper Paleolithic. Nelson (1993:51) uses the figurines as an example to "demonstrate that introductory textbooks of archaeology and physical anthropology produce gender metaphors which, by ignoring much of the scholarship on the figurines, reaffirm the folk model of gender preferred by our culture." The teaching of these metaphors actively uses archaeological data to perpetuate our own cultural norms. "Reinforcing present cultural stereotypes by projecting them into the past allows whole generations of students to believe that our present gender constructs are eternal and unchanging" (Nelson 1993:56). Rice argues that an emphasis on fertility has appeared to make sense only because figurines that would contradict that explanation have been ignored. She proposes that the "Venuses represent women throughout their entire adult life, not just when they are pregnant; therefore, it is womanhood rather than motherhood that is symbolically recognized or honored" (Rice 1981:402).

For these authors, the emphasis on fertility is masculinist and androcentric; it narrows or diminishes the role of Upper Paleolithic women to that of simply "mothers or baby makers" (Rice 1981:402), and assumes that females "exist primarily for the use of males, sexually or reproductively" (Nelson 1993:54). Such an interpretation is similar to that of feminist scholars who argue that the identification of women with "nature" and procreation has been the source of their exclusion from "culture"

(Ortner 1974). This approach may be particularly attractive to female scientists, who, like males (to paraphrase Simone de Beauvoir [1953]), also seek to remodel the face of the earth, create new instruments, invent, and shape the future.

These analyses of the Venus figurines stands in sharp contrast to the interpretations of another group of scholars (e.g., Gadon 1989; Gimbutas 1989; Eisler 1987) who interpret these figurines as evidence of worship of the Mother Goddess(es) in Paleolithic times. Similar work has been characterized (Conkey and Gero 1991:4) as "the literature of popular culture . . . which quickly stepped in to do what archaeologists themselves were not doing," that is, providing engendered interpretations of archaeological evidence. While such interpretations may flourish in the absence of alternatives from the archaeological community, they differ fundamentally in approach from the work of archaeologists such as Nelson and Rice.

On one level, it is difficult to distinguish this work from the androcentric presentations criticized by Nelson and Rice. The amount of variability in the figurines is similarly downplayed; the emphasis is again placed on those statuettes with full figures and exaggerated sexual features. The Venus of Willendorf continues to be the most frequently portrayed figurine, referred to in one text as the "Earth Mother of Willendorf" (Gadon 1989:6). The fertility-related functions or meanings of the figurines are not rejected or de-emphasized; they are embraced.

The difference in these interpretations lies in their presentation of "fertility." Rice and Nelson dismiss the "mother goddess" interpretation as simply one of many fertility-related explanations. For Gadon (1989:8), however, the representation of fertility goes beyond the use of such figurines as "cult objects;" rather, the figurines represent "the fecundity of the earth itself in all its abundance, bounty, and creativity." Similarly, Gimbutas (1989:159) states that the "earth mother" (allegedly represented in the Paleolithic by pregnant figures at Laussel, Kostienki I, and La Marche) represents more than "her miraculous womb emitting life energy . . . she is earth fertility incarnate."

Bolen (1992:49) characterizes this type of work as "focused on validating mothering for women." Such a motivation is clear in a passage by Rich (1976:85) that describes why a fertility or Mother Goddess interpretation is so appealing: "The desire for a clearly confirmed past, the search for a tradition of female power . . . springs from an intense need for validation. If women were powerful once, a precedent exists; if female biology was ever once a source of power, it need not remain what it has since become: a root of powerlessness." (See Bamberger [1974] for a very different view on the relationship between tales of matriarchies in the past and advancement of women in the present.)

Both groups discussed above recognize the political implications of archaeological interpretation, and both, I believe, seek to undermine the extent to which androcentric interpretations of these figurines legitimize modern patriarchy and patriarchal views of women. The crucial difference lies in how they seek to move beyond patriarchy. The first group seeks to shift the focus from female fertility to a view of women as people who have a wide range of attributes and skills. The second group emphasizes female reproduction, but seeks to demonstrate that it is a source of power, rather than oppression; they strive to reclaim fertility as a powerful symbol for women.

It should be noted that a focus on Willendorf-style figurines is not a prerequisite for a fertility-related interpretation, in spite of the clear links drawn by Rice (1981) and Nelson (1990, 1993) between the two. Abramova (1967:83), while recognizing several different types of figurines from the then-USSR (including "normal," slender, and obese), claims that "there is a connection between the woman and ideas concerning fertility" and concludes that they represent the Clan Mother, mistress of both "home and hearth" and the elements of nature. Likewise, Marshack (1991a:20) suggests that "all images of the abstracted female trunk or torso," including the fork-shaped piece from Dolni Vestonice and the slender, schematized Magdalenian profiles such as those from Gonnersdorf, "symbolized the potential fertility of the mature female." Guthrie (1984) compared a wide variety of Paleolithic figurine and engraving types to modern erotica, arguing that these works are ancient pornography and suggesting that similar interpretations have used the euphemism "fertility image."

Venus Variability and Sampling Bias

It is apparent that variability among the Venus figurines is treated quite differently in these two general interpretations. Some analysts regard these figurines as essentially similar; however, they de-emphasize the variability in the figurines for very different reasons. Another group is comprised of those who, in the interests of broadening interpretations of women's roles both in the past and the present, focus on the wide range of variability present.

Here I examine how three authors in the anthropological literature (Rice 1981; Gamble 1982, 1986; and McDermott 1996a, 1996b) interpret variability in the figurines by studying the composition of their databases. If figurines in the Willendorf style are truly not representative of Upper Paleolithic figurines, how does recent work justify emphasizing them?

Rice (1981:403) compiled data on 188 Venus figurines; this sample represented "all statuary and engraved female forms from the Eurasian

Upper Paleolithic known to the author . . . [including] full sculptures in the round, half-relief sculptures, and two-dimensional engravings." A panel of five helpers then divided these images into age groups based on five physical attributes of the figurines: breasts, stomachs, hips, buttocks, and faces. Pieces that were judged too stylized, damaged, or ambiguous to rate on these attributes were eliminated from the data set.

Of the remaining 132 Venuses, 23 percent appeared to be of pre-reproductive age, 17 percent were of reproductive age and pregnant, 38 percent were of reproductive age and not pregnant, and 22 percent were of post-reproductive age. These proportions, Rice argues, are consistent with the proportions of these age groups in modern hunter-gatherer societies. She concludes that since "the largest group of Venuses represents nonpregnant adult females, while the smallest group represents pregnant adult females, there is no evidence to support an interpretation focused exclusively on the fertility function" (Rice 1981:409).

While this study is a frequently cited reference for the notion that these statuettes represent a variety of ages of women (Delporte 1993a, 1993b; McDermott 1996a; Duhard 1993; Nelson 1990, 1993), Rice's approach has also met with some criticism. Duhard (1993), for example, disagrees with the selection of the sample and, as a gynecologist, with the classification of some of the Venuses on physiological grounds. The estimated percentage of pregnant images is one point of contention. As noted above, Rice argued that only 17 percent of the assemblage as a whole appeared pregnant. Duhard (1993:88), looking only at French Venuses, finds that 68 percent of images from the Gravettian, and 36 percent from the Magdalenian, appear to be pregnant. This disparity suggests, as Duhard observes, that chronology and geography are important factors to consider when discussing any overall interpretation. The importance of chronological and geographical variation is also emphasized by Delporte (1993a). Rice (1981) groups all of the images together and does not include chronological and geographical information in her analysis.

Nevertheless, Rice's main premise — that there is considerable variability in morphology and age — is accepted by Duhard (1993) and other authors (Nelson 1990, 1993; Bahn and Vertut 1988). Morphological variation in particular has been demonstrated for Russian figurines by Gvozdover (1989).

Gamble (1982, 1986) is one author who downplays this variability, citing Leroi-Gourhan's (1968) remarks about the "stability of the [Venus] design" (Gamble 1982:93). He relies heavily on Leroi-Gourhan's description of the so-called lozenge design: "The leading convention that characterizes these statuettes is the way breast, abdomen, and pelvic region are grouped approximately within a circle. The rest of the body — toward the head and the feet — tapers gradually, even dwindling away along the vertical poles of the circle. As a result, most of the figurines can be in-scribed within a lozenge" (Leroi-Gourhan 1968:90). There has been some disagreement about the use of the lozenge framework, citing the possibility that any human figure would share this basic shape due to general anatomy (Dobres 1992a:10; Bahn and Vertut 1988:138), or that it was also a function of "the difficulty of carving the human body in ivory, 'bone,' and stone" (Marshack 1991b:259).

Gamble divides figurines from twenty-eight sites into three groups (groups A, B, and C) based on variations of this basic lozenge design. Ironically, three of the sites included (Petrkovice, Eliseevici, and Sireul) have figurines used by Nelson (1993:53) to challenge the idea that all Venuses conformed to the basic type of Willendorf. Gamble argues that the lozenge-shaped figurines all date to a relatively narrow window of time and presents a map of the geographic distribution of these artifacts stretching across Europe. This distribution, he proposes, is the result of the need for open social networks and "visual methods of information exchange" to support these networks, in an increasingly deteriorating environment after 30,000 B.P., as the last glacial maximum drew closer.

It is important to note which figurines Gamble excludes from his data-base. "The figurines from Enval (Pales 1979) and Farincourt (Delporte 1979) . . . show several affinities with [group B] but their clear association with late glacial Magdalenian assemblages prevents their inclusion here" (Gamble 1982:94). Other female images are explicitly excluded on the basis of stylistic incompatibility (from the sites of Trou Magrite, Pred-most, Brno) as well as age (Mal'ta and Buret) (Gamble 1982:94–95).

The associated radiocarbon dates for these images are initially given as ranging from 29,000 to 23,000 B.P. (Gamble 1982). Some of the figurines from Eliseevici and Mauern that have older dates are then also elimi-nated from the sample. "If these [older figurines] are discounted then it is possible to see a time horizon for these figurines of between 25,000 and 23,000 B.P. The date of 14,020 B.P. from Kostienki I/I is still problematic" (Gamble 1982:97).

In other words, Gamble admits to eliminating figurines from his sam-ple on the basis of age and stylistic differences; he finds reasons to dismiss outliers in his radiocarbon dates, and then — not surprisingly — he ends up with a set of Venus figurines that show stylistic similarities and date to a fairly narrow window of time (that is, when they have an associated date; pieces from six of the sites in his database are not dated, and as Gamble [1982:94] himself observed, stylistically similar pieces may in fact date to different time periods). Gamble is admirably explicit about his process of sample selection, a factor which should be taken into consideration when evaluating his conclusions.

Not surprisingly, some archaeologists have criticized Gamble's exclusion of certain dates for the female images as well as his presentation of these images as similar. Soffer (1987:335–336), for example, cites the work of Gvozdover (1985), who identified four distinct types of figurines in the Russian Plain and found evidence for further typological division in Siberia and Central and Western Europe (see Gvozdover 1989 for a discussion of this work in English). Bisson and others (1996), while recognizing that Gamble has restricted his discussion of the images to a particular style, present dates that show that this style occurs well outside of Gamble's 26,000 to 23,000 time window.

There is nothing wrong with restricting one's study to a particular style, but Gamble (1982, 1986) is not careful about specifying that he is using a subset of the female images. His remarks have been interpreted as referring to the entire spectrum of images by at least one specialist (Soffer 1987) and one general author (Ehrenberg 1989). His interpretation of this subset as a stylistic horizon is also contradicted by data he himself acknowledges (the presence of similar figurines dating to the Magdalenian). This contradiction is reinforced by Bisson and others (1996). While these problems do not invalidate his interesting and worthwhile discussion of social mechanisms that may account for these stylistic similarities, it does suggest that perhaps cause other than simply the approach of the last glacial maximum may be responsible.

This environmental explanation seems even more unlikely when the distribution of another style of Paleolithic female figurine is considered. These figurines are called the Gonnersdorf type (Bosinski 1991); they are sometimes also called the "buttocks" style (Marshack 1991a:19). This style of figurine dates to the Magdalenian period, after the last glacial maximum (Fig. 16.2). The widespread distribution of these figurines is markedly similar to that of the lozenge-style figurine, suggesting the presence of social networks that may have functioned to reduce subsistence risk in general, but certainly not any particular risk such as the advance of the glaciers.

McDermott (1996a; see also McCoid and McDermott 1996) is a second recent author who focuses on a subset of the Venus figurines—those of the so-called "PKG" style. McDermott, like Gamble, is not careful about specifying that he is using a subset of figurines within a given time period. Certain "distortions" of the female figure characterize this style, including the presence of enlarged breasts, fragmented arms with only the forearm clearly outlined, and shortened legs with small feet. He argues that these "distortions" are due to foreshortening and that the figures represent a woman's view of her own body as she looks down at herself. These statuettes are interpreted, therefore, as the work of women creating self-portraits, "executed millennia before the invention of mirrors" (McDermott 1996a:245). "When properly viewed, stylistic or structural

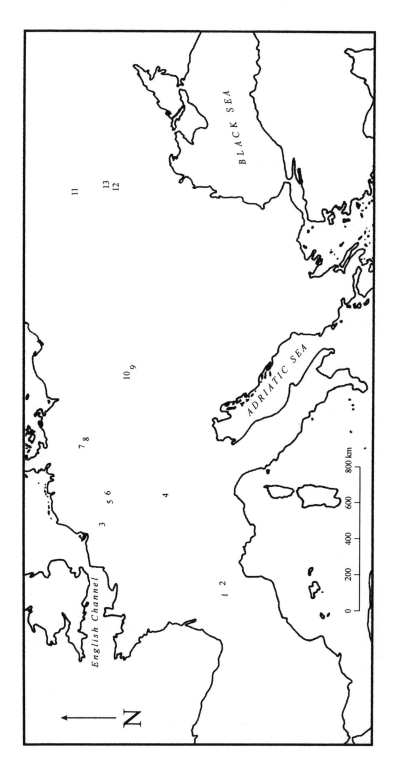

Figure 16.2. Distribution of female figurines of the Gonnersdorf type. Sites marked are (1) Fontales; (2) Courbet; (3) Abri de Megarnie; (4) Petersfels; (5) Andernach; (6) Gonnersdorf; (7) Nebra; (8) Oelknitz; (9) Pekarna; (10) Mezin; (11) Byci-Skala; (12) Mezhirich; and (13) Dobranicevka (redrawn, with title and site locations from Bosinski 1991:Fig. 24).

regularities such as the generalized atrophy of the upper and lower body of the 'lozenge composition' emerge as the function of a common creative process determined by the fixed position of the eye" (McDermott 1996a:245).

Gamble and McDermott are two examples of authors who, in their attempts to find meaningful patterns in the data, deliberately restrict their sample of figurines to those that are relatively similar to Willendorf. The fact that they do not acknowledge or discuss the wider variability in form may or may not affect the credibility of their papers, but it does reinforce the notion that this style is the most common or typical. That this particular subset of data continues to be the most popular may be revealing of what our own culture finds most interesting or compelling about these ancient figurines.

Conclusion

This discussion has provided some idea of the inherent problems of this database. The assessment of humanness as well as gender is problematic for a number of examples. There are numerous fragmentary figurines in addition to the more complete specimens. To add to the confusion, many of the figurines from Western Europe do not come from dated contexts (Bahn and Vertut 1988; Delporte 1993b). Last, authors — myself included — may overlook work on certain figurines published in languages they cannot read. All of these factors combine to make sampling a nightmare. Under these conditions, how can one assess the relative proportions of different figurine styles in a way that cannot be immediately contradicted by different examples and different interpretations of the figurines in one's own sample? Duhard's (1993) critique of Rice's (1981) study lists a number of differences in both the chosen sample and the interpretation. With such an inherently problematic database, authors may choose a sample of figurines with respect to their research interests, without clearly articulating its relationship to the body of known figurines.

In the first half of this chapter, I demonstrated that two groups of feminist researchers had very different assessments of the overall assemblage. Some see the full-figured Willendorf Venus as typical of all figurines; some focus on the wide range of variation found in the assemblage. Associated with these different assessments is a differential emphasis on fertility-related interpretations.

The second half of the chapter shows that authors compile a more- or less-variable database depending upon their research goals. For example, Gamble (1982) explored the notion of widespread social interaction through the analysis of what he decided was one style of figurine. McDermott (1996a), using a similar group of figurines, attempted to find one mechanism which explained similarities in style. By way of contrast, Gvoz-dover (1989), in examining the variation within a geographically defined set of figurines, proposed that different types may have had different functions.

In light of these problems, it seems unlikely that the figurines could be used to say anything about the real status or role of women during the Upper Paleolithic. Contextless depictions of women are, not surprisingly, a poor way to study women, a point made by Dobres (1992a, b).

One provocative observation is that the proportion of figurines depicting pregnancy changes over time (Duhard 1993; McDermott 1996a, b). Unfortunately, pregnancy and obesity are surprisingly difficult to distinguish, as shown by the debate about whether the Willendorf Venus is or is not pregnant (Bahn and Vertut 1988; Gadon 1989; McDermott 1996a, b). There are clear examples of figurines with full stomachs who do not appear to be pregnant, such as the statuette from Chiozza di Scandiano (Delporte 1993b: Fig. 99).

One can debate, therefore, how literally the physiology of these figurines should be interpreted given the difficulties of working with the raw material (Bahn and Vertut 1988:87; Marshack 1996:259) and the factor of artistic license. Guthrie (1984:64), for example, suggests that the vulvar slit is misplaced on these representations of women, stating that "instead of being between the legs, it is brought to the front where male genitalia are located," and where, presumably, it would also be more visible to the observer.

In sum, the known assemblage of Upper Paleolithic figurines constitutes an inherently difficult database which, perhaps more than others, is affected by the theoretical biases of the investigators. Female figurines and other depictions of women divorced from their context (archaeological or otherwise) seem particularly defenseless against the imposition of our own cultural norms and biases. Given the myriad of difficulties — practical and theoretical — with the database of figurines as a whole, I must applaud the work of those (Delporte 1993a; Gvozdover 1989; Dobres 1992a, 1992b) who keep these statuettes in their regional and site-specific contexts.

References

Abercrombie, Nicholas, Stephen Hill, and Dryan Turner
    1980   *The Dominant Ideology Thesis*. George Allen and Unwin, London.
Abramova, Zoya A.
    1967   Palaeolithic Art in the U.S.S.R. *Arctic Anthropology* 4 (2):1–179.
Adams, Barbara
    1987   *The Fort Cemetery at Hierakonpolis*. Kegan Paul, London.
Adams, Robert McCormick
    1981   *Heartland of Cities*. University of Chicago Press, Chicago.
Adler, K., and M. Pointon, eds.
    1993   *The Body Imaged*. Cambridge University Press, Cambridge, U.K.
Adovasio, James M., Olga Soffer, and Bohuslav Klima
    1996   Upper Paleolithic Fibre Technology: Interlaced Woven Finds from
              Pavlov I, Czech Republic, c. 26,000 Years Ago. *Antiquity* 70:526–534.
Ajootian, Aileen
    1997   The Only Happy Couple: Hermaphrodites and Gender. In *Naked
              Truths: Women, Sexuality, and Gender in Classical Art and Archaeology*,
              edited by Ann Olga Koloski-Ostrow and Claire L. Lyons, pp. 220–
              242. Routledge, New York.
Alfieri, Nereo, and Paolo Arias
    1958   Spina. *Die neuentdeckte Etruskerstadt*. Hirmer Verlag, Munich, Ger-
              many.
Algaze, Guillermo
    1993   *The Uruk World System*. University of Chicago Press, Chicago.
Allen, James P.
    1988   *Genesis in Egypt: The Philosophy of Ancient Egyptian Creation Accounts*.
              Yale University Press, New Haven, Conn.
Altenmiller, H.
    1973   Bemerkungen zum Hirtenlied des Alten Reiches. *Chronique
              d'Égypte* 48:211–231.
Amiet, Pierre
    1980   *La Glyptique Mésopotamienne Archaïque*. Éditions du Centre National
              de la Recherche Scientifique, Paris, France.
Amiran, Ruth
    1970   *Ancient Pottery of the Holy Land*. Rutgers University Press, New
              Brunswick, N.J.

Anderson, Ian
1995 Bodies, Disease, and the Problem of Foucault. *Social Analysis: Journal of Social and Cultural Practice* 37:67–81.
Anderson, Marilyn
1978 *Guatemalan Textiles Today.* Watson-Guptill, New York.
Angelino, Henry, and Charles L. Shedd
1955 A Note on Berache. *American Anthropologist* 57:121–126.
Anyon, Roger, Patricia A. Gilman, and Steven A. LeBlanc
1981 A Re-evaluation of the Mogollon-Mimbres Archaeological Sequence. *The Kiva* 46 (3):209–225.
Anyon, Roger, and Steven A. LeBlanc
1980 The Architectural Evolution of Mogollon-Mimbres Communal Structures. *The Kiva* 45 (4):253–277.
Archer, Leonie J.
1994 Notions of Community and the Exclusion of the Female in Jewish History and Historiography. In *Women in Ancient Societies: An Illusion of the Night,* edited by Leonie J. Archer, Susan Fischler, and Maria Wyke, pp. 53–69. Routledge, New York.
Aristotle
1972 *Politics.* Translated by H. Rackham. Harvard University Press, Cambridge, Mass.
Arnold, Bettina
1991 The Deposed Princess of Vix: The Need for an Engendered Prehistory. In *The Archaeology of Gender: Proceedings of the Twenty-second Annual Conference of the Archaeological Association of the University of Calgary,* edited by Dale Walde and Noreen D. Willows, pp. 366–374. The Archaeological Association of the University of Calgary, Alberta, Canada.
1996 Are You a Boy or Are You a Girl? Archaeological Correlates of Sex and Gender Disjunction in Mortuary Ritual. Paper presented at the Fourth Gender and Archaeology Conference, Michigan State University, East Lansing, Mich.
Arutiunov, Sergei A., and Dorian A. Sergeyev
1969 *Drevnie kul'tury Aziatskikh Eskimosov* (Uelenskii Mogil'nik). [Ancient Cultures of the Asiatic Eskimo]. Nauka, Moscow.
1975 *Problemy etnicheskoi istorii Beringo mor'ia. Ekvenskii Mogil'nik.* [Problems of the Ethnic History of the Bering Sea: The Ekven Cemetery]. Nauka, Moscow.
Ashmole, Bernard, and Nicholas Yalouris
1967 *Olympia: The Sculptures of the Temple of Zeus.* Phaidon, London.
Athearn, Robert G.
1967 *Forts of the Upper Missouri.* Prentice-Hall, Englewood Cliffs, N.J.
Atwater, Mary Meigs
1928 *The Shuttle-Craft Book of American Hand-Weaving.* Macmillan, New York.
Babcock, Barbara E., ed.
1991 *Pueblo Mothers and Children: Essays by Elsie Clews Parsons, 1915–1924.* Ancient City Press, Sante Fe, N.M.
Badre, Leila
1986 Machoire (no. 349). *Les Phéniciens et Le Monde Mediterranéen,* exh. cat., edited by Eric Gubel. C. Coessens, Brussels, Belgium.

Bahn, Paul G.
1996   Comment. *Current Anthropology* 37 (2):248–249.
Bahn, Paul G., and Jean Vertut
1988   Images of the Ice Age. *Facts on File.* New York.
Bailey, Douglass W.
1994   Reading Prehistoric Figurines as Individuals. *World Archaeology*
            25:321–331.
Baines, John
1985   *Fecundity Figures: Egyptian Personification and the Iconology of a Genre.*
            Aris and Phillips, Warminster, U.K.
1991   Society, Morality, and Religious Practice. In *Religion in Ancient
            Egypt*, edited by B. E. Shafer, pp. 123–200. Cornell University
            Press, Ithaca, N.Y.
Bamberger, Joan
1974   The Myth of Matriarchy: Why Men Rule in Primitive Society. In
            Women, Culture, and Society, edited by Michelle Zimbalist Rosaldo
            and Louise Lamphere, pp. 263–280. Stanford University Press,
            Stanford, Calif.
Bandi, Hans-Georg
1984   *St. Lorenz Insel-Studien. Berner Beiträge zur archäologischen und eth-
            nologischen Erforschung des Beringstrassengebietes. Band I. Allgemeine
            Einführung und Gräberfunde bei Gambell am Nordwestkap der St. Lorenz
            Insel, Alaska.* Verlag Paul Haupt, Bern and Stuttgart, Germany.
Banning, Edward B., and Brian F. Byrd
1987   Houses and the Changing Residential Unit: Domestic Architec-
            ture at PPNB 'Ain Ghazal, Jordan. *Proceedings of the Prehistoric Society*
            53:309–325.
1989   Alternative Approaches for Exploring Levantine Neolithic Archi-
            tecture. *PaleoOrient* 15:154–160.
Barber, Elizabeth J. W.
1991   *Prehistoric Textiles: The Development of Cloth in the Neolithic and Bronze
            Ages, with Special Reference to the Aegean.* Princeton University Press,
            Princeton, N.J.
Bard, Kathryn A.
1992   Toward an Interpretation of the Role of Ideology in the Evolution
            of Complex Society in Egypt. *Journal of Anthropological Archaeology*
            11 (1):1–24.
Bard, Kathryn, and Robert Carneiro
1989   Society Urbaines en Egypte et au Soudan. *Cahiers de Recherches de
            l'Institut de Papyrologie et d'Égyptologie de Lille* 11:15–23.
Barker, Robin
1995   Seeing Wisely, Crying Wolf: A Cautionary Tale on the Euro-Yup'ik
            Border. In *When Our Words Return: Writing, Hearing, and Remember-
            ing Oral Traditions of Alaska and the Yukon*, edited by Phyllis Mor-
            row and William Sneider, pp. 79–98. Utah State University Press,
            Logan.
Barrett, John C.
1994   *Fragments from Antiquity: An Archaeology of Social Life in Britain,
            2900–1200 B.C.* Blackwell, Oxford, U.K.
Barrett, M. J.
1977   Masticatory and Non-Masticatory Uses of Teeth. In *Stone Tools as*

Markers, edited by R. V. S. Wright, pp. 18–23. Australian Institute of Aboriginal Studies, Canberra, Australia.

Bass, William M., D. R. Evans, and Richard L. Jantz
1971   The Leavenworth Site Cemetery: Archaeology and Physical Anthropology. *University of Kansas Publications in Anthropology,* no. 2. Lawrence.

Bazant, Jan
1987   Les vases athéniens et les réformes démocratiques. In *Images et Société en Grèce Ancienne,* edited by C. Bérard, C. Bron, and A. Pomari, pp. 33–40. Université de Lausanne, Switzerland.

Beaglehole, Earnest
1936   Hopi Hunting and Hunting Ritual. In *Yale University Publications in Anthropology,* no. 4. Yale University Press, New Haven, Conn.
1937   Notes on Hopi Economic Life. In *Yale University Publications in Anthropology,* no. 15. Yale University Press, New Haven, Conn.

Beals, Ralph L.
1933   Ethnology of the Nisenan. *University of California Publications in American Archaeology and Ethnography* 31 (6):335–414.

Beazley, John D.
1956   *Attic Black-Figure Vase-Painters.* Oxford University Press, Oxford, U.K.
1963   *Attic Red-Figure Vase-Painters.* Oxford University Press, Oxford, U.K.

Beck, Lois
1978   Women among Qashaq'i Nomadic Pastoralists in Iran. In *Women in the Muslim World,* edited by Lois Beck and N. Keddie, pp. 351–373. Harvard University Press, Cambridge, Mass.

Becker, Marshall Joseph
1990   Etruscan Social Classes in the Sixth Century B.C.E.: Evidence from Recently Excavated Cremations and Inhumations in the Area of Tarquinia. In *Die Welt der Etrusker Internationales Kolloquium* (October 1988), edited by Huberta Heres and Max Kunze, pp. 23–35. Berlin Akademie-Verlag, Berlin, Germany.
1992a   An Etruscan Gold Dental Appliance in the Collections of the Danish National Museum: Evidence for the History of Dentistry. *Tandlaegebladet* (Danish Dental Journal) 18 (96): Cover, 599–609.
1992b   Cultural Uniformity During the Italian Iron Age: Sardinian Nuraghi as Regional Markers. In *Sardinia in the Mediterranean: A Footprint in the Sea,* edited by Robert H. Tykot and T. K. Andrews, pp. 204–209. Sheffield Academic Press, Sheffield, U.K.
1993   Human Skeletons from Tarquinia: A Preliminary Analysis of the 1989 Cimitero Site Excavations with Implications for the Evolution of Etruscan Social Classes. *Studi Etruschi* 58 (1992):211–248.
1994a   Etruscan Gold Dental Appliances Origins and Functions as Indicated by an Example from Valsiarosa, Italy. *Journal of Paleopathology* 6 (2):69–92.
1994b   Etruscan Gold Dental Appliances Origins and Functions as Indicated by an Example from Orvieto, Italy, in the Danish National Museum. *Dental Anthropology Newsletter* 8 (3):2–8.
1994c   Spurious "Examples" of Ancient Dental Implants or Appliances. *Dental Anthropology Newsletter* 9 (1):5–10.

1994d   An Analysis of the Cremated Human Remains from Tomb XVII of
             the 1896 Excavations at Satricum, Italy. In *The Northwest Necropolis
             of Satricum: An Iron Age Cemetery in Latium Vetus*, by Demetrius
             Joannes Waarsenburg (Appendix 3.3 [pp. 147–148]). Ph.D. disser-
             tation, Faculty of Letters, University of Amsterdam, Netherlands.
1995a   Female Vanity Among the Etruscans: The Copenhagen Gold Den-
             tal Appliance. In *Actas del I Congreso Internacional de Estudios sobre
             Momias, 1992*, vol. 2, edited by Arthur C. Aufderheide, pp. 651–
             658. Santa Cruz de Tenerife Museo Arqueolo'gico y Etnolo'gico
             de Tenerife.
1995b   Tooth Evulsion Among the Ancient Etruscans: Recycling in Antiq-
             uity. *Dental Anthropology Newsletter* 9 (3):8–9.
1995/6   Early Dental Appliances in the Eastern Mediterranean. *Berytus*
             42:71–102.
1996   An Unusual Etruscan Gold Dental Appliance from Poggio Gaiella,
             Italy. Fourth in a Series. *Dental Anthropology Newsletter* 10 (1):10–16.
In press a   The Valsiarosa Gold Dental Appliance: Etruscan Origins for Den-
             tal Prostheses. *Etruscan Studies* 4 (1997).
In press b   Skulls and Teeth Associated with Etruscan Dental Appliances: An
             Evaluation of the Poggio Gaiella Example. Fifth in a series. *Dental
             Anthropology Newsletter*.
In press c   Dentistry in Ancient Rome: Direct Evidence Based on an Analysis
             of the Teeth from the Excavations at the Temple of Castor and
             Pollux in the Roman Forum. In *The Temple of Castor and Pollux*, vol.
             2, edited by S. Sande and Jan Zahle, pp. 218–231. Lavori e Studi di
             Archeologia. Roma Edizione De Luca, Rome, Italy.
In press d   Early Appliances in the Eastern Mediterranean. *Berytus* 42 (1997).
Ms. a   Two Dental Appliances in the Liverpool Museum and Two in the
             Villa Giulia Museum, Rome (field notes, May–June 1988).
Ms. b   Ancient Dental Appliances: A Corpus and Typology. (Manuscript
             in review by G. Maetzke for *Studi Etruschi*).
Ms. c   An Analysis of Human Skeletal Remains from Recent Excavations
             at Tarquinia, Italy. Manuscript on file, Soprintendenza Archeo-
             logica per l'Etruria Meridionale.
Becker, Marshall Joseph, and Loretana Salvadei
1992   Analysis of the Human Skeletal Remains from the Cemetery of
             Osteria dell'Osa. In *Osteria dell'Osa*, edited by Anna Maria Bietti
             Sestieri, pp. 53–292. Quasar, Rome, Italy.
Ms. a   Correlation Between Maxillary Central Incisor M-D Length and
             Sex at the Iron Age Site of Osteria dell'Osa, Italy. Manuscript on
             file, Department of Anthropology, West Chester University of
             Pennsylvania, and at the Pigorini Museum, Rome, Italy.
Bender, Barbara
1978   Gatherer-Hunter to Farmer: A Social Perspective. *World Archaeology*
             10:204–222.
1985   *Farming in Prehistory: From Hunter-Gatherer to Food Producer*. St. Mar-
             tin's Press, New York.
Benjamin, Oslynn
1993   *Enthesites and Osteoarthritis in Sadlermuit Eskimo: A Correlative Os-
             teological Study of the Upper Limb*. Master's thesis, Arizona State Uni-
             versity, Tempe.

Bérard, Claude, Christiane Bron, Jean-Louis Durand, Françoise Frontisi-Ducroux, Fançois Lissarague, Alain Schnapp and Jean-Pierre Vernant
1989   *A City of Images: Iconography and Society in Ancient Greece*, translated by Deborah Lyons. Princeton University Press, Princeton, N.J.

Berget, K. A., and Steve A. Churchill
1994   Subsistence Activity and Humeral Hypertrophy Among Western Aleutian Islanders (abstract). *American Journal of Physical Anthropology* Supplement 18:55.

Berlo, Janet Catherine
1991   Beyond *Bricolage*: Women and Aesthetic Strategies in Latin American Textiles. In *Textile Traditions of Mesoamerica and the Andes: An Anthology*, edited by Margot Blum Schevill, Janet Catherine Berlo, and Edward B. Dwyer, pp. 437–479. Garland, New York.

Bernbeck, Reinhard
1995   Die Uruk-Zeit: Perspektiven einer komplexen Gesellschaft. In *Zwischen Euphrat und Indus: Aktuelle Forschungsprobleme in der Vorderasiatischen Archäologie*, edited by K. Bartl, R. Bernbeck, and M. Heinz, pp. 57–67. Georg Olms, Hildesheim, Germany.

Berthelot, J. M.
1991   Sociological Discourse and the Body. In *The Body: Social Process and Cultural Theory*, edited by M. Featherstone, M. Hepworth, and B. S. Turner, pp. 390–404. Sage, London.

Bilby, Julian William
1923   *Among Unknown Eskimo: An Account of Twelve Years Intimate Relations with the Primitive Eskimo of Ice-Bound Baffin Land, with a Description of Their Ways of Living, Hunting Customs, and Beliefs*. J. B. Lippincott, Philadelphia.

Binford, Lewis R.
1971   Mortuary Practices: Their Study and Potential. In *Approaches to the Social Dimensions of Mortuary Practice*, edited by James A. Brown. Society for American Archaeology Memoirs 25:6–29.

Birket-Smith, Kaj
1928   *Five Hundred Eskimo Words: A Complete Vocabulary from Greenland and Central Eskimo Dialects*. Gyldendalske Boghandel, Nordisk Forlag, Copenhagen, Denmark.

Bisson, Michael S., Nadine Tisnerat, and Randall White
1996   Radiocarbon Dates from the Upper Paleolithic of the Barma Grande. *Current Anthropology* 37 (1):156–162.

Bittencourt, Luciana Aguiar
1996   *Spinning Lives*. University Press of America, Lanham, Md.

Black, Joel
1998   Taking the Sex Out of Sexuality: Foucault's Failed History. In *Rethinking Sexuality: Foucault and Classical Antiquity*, edited by D. H. J. Larmour, P. A. Miller, and C. Platter, pp. 42–60. Princeton University Press, Princeton, N.J.

Black, Mary
1984   Maidens and Mothers: An Analysis of Hopi Corn Metaphors. *Ethnology* 23:279–288.

Blacking, John, ed.
1977   *The Anthropology of the Body*. Academic Press, New York.

Blackman, Alward M.
1921   On the Position of Women in the Ancient Egyptian Hierarchy. *Journal of Egyptian Archaeology* 7:8–30.
Blakeslee, Donald
1975   The Plains Interband Trade System: An Ethnohistorical and Archaeological Investigation. Ph.D. dissertation, Department of Anthropology, University of Wisconsin, Milwaukee. University Microfilms, Ann Arbor, Mich.
Bliquez, Lawrence J.
1996   Prosthetics in Classical Antiquity Greek, Etruscan, and Roman Prosthetics. In *Aufstieg und Niedergang der Römischen Welt*, edited by Wolfgang Haase and Hildegard Temporini (Part 2 Principate), vol. 37 (3):2640–2676.
Blumler, M. A., and R. Byrne
1990   The Ecological Genetics of Domestication and the Origins of Agriculture. *Current Anthropology* 32:23–54.
Boardman, John
1974   *Athenian Black Figure Vases*. Oxford University Press, New York.
1975   *Athenian Red Figure Vases: The Archaic Period*. Thames and Hudson, London.
Bodenhorn, Barbara
1990   "I'm Not the Great Hunter, My Wife Is": Iñupiat and Anthropological Models of Gender. *Inuit Studies* 14 (1–2):55–74.
Bolen, Kathleen
1992   Prehistoric Construction of Mothering. In *Exploring Gender Through Archaeology: Selected Papers from the 1991 Boone Conference*, edited by Cheryl Claassen, pp. 49–62. Monographs in World Archaeology, no. 11. Prehistory Press, Madison, Wis.
Bolin, Anna
1992   Coming of Age among Transexuals. In *Gender Constructs and Social Issues*, edited by Tony L. Whitehead and Barbara V. Reid, pp. 13–39. University of Illinois Press, Urbana.
Boller, Henry M.
1959   *Among the Indians Eight Years in the Far West, 1858–1866*. Lakeside Press, Chicago.
Bosinski, Gerhard
1991   The Representation of Female Figures in the Rhineland Magdalenian. *Proceedings of the Prehistoric Society* 57 (Pt. 1):51–64.
Bothmer, Dietrich von
1957   *Amazons in Greek Art*. Oxford University Press, Oxford, U.K.
Böttiger, Karl August
1797   *Griechische Vasengemälde, Mit Archäologischen und Artistischen Erläuterungen der Originalkupfer*, vol. 1. Weimar Industrie-comptoir, Germany.
Bourdieu, Pierre
1977   *Outline of a Theory of Practice*. Cambridge University Press, Cambridge, U.K.
1998   *Practical Reason: On the Theory of Action*. Polity, Cambridge, U.K.
Bourke, John G.
1984   *Snake-Dance of the Moquis of Arizona*. Scribner, New York. University
[1884]   of Arizona Press, Tucson.

Bowers, Alfred W.
1965   *Hidatsa Social and Ceremonial Organization*. Smithsonian Institution,
            Bureau of American Ethnology Bulletin 194. U.S. Government
            Printing Office, Washington D.C.
Brackenridge, H. M.
1904   Journal of a Voyage Up the Missouri Performed in Eighteen Hun-
            dred and Eleven. In *Early Western Travels, 1748–1848*, vol. 5, edited
            by Reuben G. Thwaites. Arthur H. Clark, Cleveland, Ohio.
Brandes, Mark
1979   *Siegelabrollungen aus den archaischen Bauschichten in Uruk-Warka*.
            Freiburger Altorientalisch Studien Band 3. Franz Steiner, Wies-
            baden, Germany.
Braun, David P.
1981   A Critique of Some Recent North American Mortuary Studies.
            American Antiquity 46 (2):398–416.
Bremmer, Jan
1992   Walking, Standing, and Sitting in Ancient Greek Culture. In *A
            Cultural History of Gesture*, edited by Jan Bremmer and Herman
            Roodenburg. Cornell University Press, Ithaca, N.Y.
Brewer, Douglas, and Rene Friedman
1989   *Fish and Fishing in Ancient Egypt*. American University Press, Cairo,
            Egypt.
Bridges, Patricia S.
1991   Skeletal Evidence of Changes in Subsistence Activities between
            Archaic and Mississippian Time Periods in Northwestern Ala-
            bama. In *What Mean These Bones*, edited by Mary L. Powell, Patri-
            cia S. Bridges, and A. W. Mires, pp. 102–113. University of Ala-
            bama Press, Tuscaloosa.
Brody, J. J.
1977   *Mimbres Painted Pottery*. University of New Mexico Press, Albuquer-
            que.
1983   Mimbres Painting. In *Mimbres Pottery: Ancient Art of the American
            Southwest*, edited by J. J. Brody, Catherine J. Scott, and Steven A.
            LeBlanc, pp. 69–125. Hudson Hills Press, N.Y.
Brody, J. J., and Rina Swentzell
1996   *To Touch the Past: The Painted Pottery of the Mimbres People*. Hudson
            Hills Press, N.Y.
Brown, James A.
1971   *Approaches to the Social Dimensions of Mortuary Practices*. Society for
            American Archaeology, Memoirs 25.
1981   The Search for Rank in Prehistoric Burials. In *The Archaeology of
            Death*, edited by R. Chapman, I. Kinnes and K. Randsborg, pp. 25–
            38. Cambridge University Press, Cambridge, U.K.
1996   *The Spiro Ceremonial Center*. University of Michigan Museum of An-
            thropology Memoirs 29. Ann Arbor, Mich.
Brown, Lawrence Parmly
1936   Appellations of the Dental Practitioner. *Dental Cosmos* 78:246–258,
            378–389, 481–495.
Brumfiel, Elizabeth M.
1991   Weaving and Cooking: Women's Production in Aztec Mexico. In
            Engendering Archaeology: Women and Prehistory, edited by Joan M.

Gero and Margaret W. Conkey, pp. 224–251. Basil Blackwell, Oxford, U.K.

1992   Distinguished Lecture in Archaeology: Breaking and Entering the Eco-System: Gender, Class, and Faction Steal the Show. *American Anthropologist* 94:551–567.

1996a   Figurines and the Aztec State: Testing the Effectiveness of Ideological Domination. In *Gender and Archaeology*, edited by Rita P. Wright, pp. 143–166. University of Pennsylvania Press, Philadelphia.

1996b   The Quality of Tribute Cloth: The Place of Evidence in Archaeological Argument. *American Antiquity* 61:453–462.

Brunton, Guy, and Gertrude Caton-Thompson
1928   *The Badarian Civilisation and Predynastic Remains near Badari.* British School of Archaeology in Egypt and Egyptian Research Account, Bernard Quaritch, London.

Buchner, Giorgia, and David Ridgway
1993   *Pithekoussai I.* La Necropoli: Tombe 1–723 scavate dal 1952 al 1961. Giorgio Bretschneider Editore, Rome, Italy.

Budge, E. A. Wallis
1972   *The Book of Opening the Mouth* [1909], vols. 1 and 2 (published as one volume). Benjamin Blom, New York.

Buitron, Diana
1972   *Attic Vase Painting in New England Collections.* Harvard University Press, Cambridge, Mass.

Bunzel, Ruth
1972   *The Pueblo Potter: A Study of Creative Imagination in Primitive Art.*
[1929]   Dover, New York.

Burch, Ernest S., Jr.
1988   *The Eskimos.* University of Oklahoma Press, Norman.

Butler, Judith
1990a   *Gender Trouble: Feminism and the Subversion of Identity.* Routledge, New York.

1990b   Gender Trouble, Feminist Theory, and Psychoanalytic Discourse. In *Feminism/Postmodernism*, edited by L. J. Nicholson, pp. 324–340. Routledge, New York.

1990c   Performative Acts and Gender Constitution: An Essay in Phenomenology and Feminist Theory. In *Performing Feminism*, edited by S. Case. Johns Hopkins University Press, Baltimore, Md.

1993   *Bodies that Matter: On the Discursive Limits of "Sex."* Routledge, New York.

Butzer, Karl W.
1976   *Early Hydraulic Civilization in Egypt: A Study in Cultural Ecology.* University of Chicago Press, Chicago.

Burton, Michael L., Lilyan A. Brudner, and Douglas R. White
1977   A Model of the Sexual Division of Labor. *American Ethnologist* 4:227–251.

Burton, Michael L., and Douglas R. White
1984   Sexual Divisions of Labor in Agriculture. *American Anthropologist* 86:568–583.

Bynum, Caroline Walker
1995   Why All The Fuss About The Body? A Medievalist's Perspective. *Critical Inquiry* 22:1–33.

Byrd, Brian F.
1994   Public and Private, Domestic and Corporate: The Emergence of the Southwest Asian Village. *American Antiquity* 59:639–666.

Carabelli, Edlen von Lunkaszprie, Georg
1831   Systematisches Handbuch de Zahnheilkunde (Vol. 1). A. Dolls Universitätsbuchhandlung, Vienna, Austria.

Carneiro, Robert
1970   A Theory for the Origin of the State. *Science* 69:733–778.

Carr, Pat
1979   Mimbres Mythology. *Southwestern Studies Monograph*, no. 56. University of Texas, El Paso.

Casotti, Luigi
1947   L'odontotecnica degli Etruschi. *Rivista Italiana di Stomatologia* 2:661–678.

Chapman, Robert, and Klavs Randsborg
1981   Approaches to the Archaeology of Death. In *The Archaeology of Death*, edited by R. Chapman, I. Kinnes, and K. Randsborg, pp. 1–24. Cambridge University Press, Cambridge, U.K.

Chardon, Francis A.
1932   *Chardon's Journal at Fort Clark, 1834–1838*, edited by Annie H. Abel. Department of History, Pierre, S.D.

Charles, M.
1984   Present-Day Field Practices in Near Eastern Agriculture: Possible Parallels for Ancient Sumer. *Bulletin for Sumerian Agriculture* 1.

Chester, Hillary
1996   Nineteenth-Century American Archaeology: No Place for a Lady. Paper presented at the Fourth Gender and Archaeology Conference, Michigan State University, East Lansing, Mich.

Cixous, Hélène, and C. Clément
1986   *The Newly Born Woman*. University of Minnesota Press, Minneapolis.

Claassen, Cheryl
1992   Questioning Gender: An Introduction. In *Exploring Gender Through Archaeology*, edited by Cheryl Claassen, pp. 1–9. Prehistory Press, Madison, Wis.

Clark, R. T. Rundle
1991   *Myth and Symbol in Ancient Egypt* [1959]. Thames and Hudson, London.

Clawson, Don
1934   Phoenician Dental Art. *Berytus* 1:23–31.

Cohen, A. P.
1994   *Self-Consciousness: An Alternative Anthropology of Identity*. Routledge, London.

Cohen, Ada
1996   Portrayals of Abduction in Greek Art: Rape or Metaphor? In *Sexuality in Ancient Art*, edited by Natalie Kampen, pp. 117–135. Cambridge University Press, Cambridge, U.K.

Cohen, Beth
1997   Divesting the Female Breast of Clothes in Classical Sculpture. In *Naked Truths: Women, Sexuality, and Gender in Classical Art and Archaeology*, edited by Ann Olga Koloski-Ostrow and Claire L. Lyons, pp. 66–92. Routledge, New York.

Cohen, D., and R. Saller
1994   Foucault on Sexuality in Greco-Roman Antiquty. In *Foucault and the Writing of History*, edited by J. Goldstein, pp. 35–59. Blackwell, Oxford, U.K.

Cohodas, Marvin
1996   Ideologies of Gender in Late Classic Maya Ceramic Imagery. Paper presented at the Fourth Gender and Archaeology Conference, Michigan State University, East Lansing, Mich.

Cole, Sally
1989   Iconography and Symbolism in Basketmaker Rock Art. In *Rock Art of the Western Canyons*. Colorado Archaeological Society Memoir 3: 59–85. Denver Museum of Natural History, Denver.

Cole, Theodore M., III
1994   Size and Shape of the Femur and Tibia in Northern Plains Indians. In *Skeletal Biology in the Great Plains: Migration, Warfare, Health and Subsistence*, edited by Douglas W. Owsley and Richard L. Jantz, pp. 219–233. Smithsonian Institution Press, Washington, D.C.

Collins, Henry B., Jr.
1955   *Field Notes, Native Point, Southampton Island, 1954 and 1955.* Manuscript on file (MS no. 1974). Document Collection, Information Management Services, Canadian Museum of Civilization, Quebec, Canada.

Collins, Henry B., Jr., and J. N. Emerson
1954   *Tunirmiut I Site, Native Point.* Manuscript on file (MS no. 1523, Book 1). Document Collection Information Management Services, Canadian Museum of Civilization, Quebec, Canada.

Collon, Dominique
1987   *First Impressions: Cylinder Seals in the Ancient Near East.* British Museum Publications, London.

Conkey, Margaret W., and Joan M. Gero
1991   Tensions, Pluralities, and Engendering Archaeology: An Introduction to Women and Prehistory. In *Engendering Archaeology: Women and Prehistory*, edited by Joan M. Gero and Margaret W. Conkey, pp. 3–30. Basil Blackwell, Oxford, U.K.

Conkey, Margaret, and Janet Spector
1984   Archaeology and the Study of Gender. *Advances in Archaeological Method and Theory*, edited by Michael J. Schiffer, pp. 1–38. Academic Press, New York.

Cornwall, Andrea, and Nancy Lindisfarne, eds.
1994   *Dislocating Masculinity: Comparative Ethnographies.* Routledge, New York.

Cordell, Linda S.
1979   Prehistory: Eastern Anasazi. In *Handbook of North American Indians: Southwest*, vol. 9, edited by Alfonso Ortiz, pp. 131–151. Smithsonian Institution Press, Washington, D.C.
1984   *Prehistory of the Southwest.* Academic Press, New York.

Corruccini, Robert S., and Elsa Pacciani
1989   "Orthodontistry" and Dental Occlusion in Etruscans. *Angle Orthodontist* 59 (1):61–64.

Cosar, Fatma M.
1978   Women in Turkish Society. In *Women in the Muslim World*, edited by

Lois Beck and N. Keddie, pp. 124–140. Harvard University Press, Cambridge, Mass.

Coues, Elliott, ed.
1893   *History of the Expedition Under the Command of Captains Lewis and Clark*, vols. 1–4. F. P. Harper, New York.

Coulam, Nancy J., and Alan R. Schroedl
1996   Early Archaic Clay Figurines from Cowboy and Walters Caves in Southeastern Utah. *The Kiva* 61:401–412.

Cowgill, George L.
1975   On the Causes and Consequences of Ancient and Modern Population Changes. *American Anthropologist* 77:505–525.

Cozza, Adolfo, and Angela Pasqui
1981   *Carta Archeologica D'Italia (1881–1897): Materiali per Agro Falisco*. Forma Italiae, Serie II, Documenti 2. Leo S. Olschki for Unione Accademica Nazionale, Firenze, Italy.

Crabtree, Pam J.
1991   Gender Hierarchies and the Sexual Division of Labor in the Natufian Culture of the Southern Levant. In *The Archaeology of Gender: Proceedings of the Twenty-second Annual Conference of the Archaeological Association of the University of Calgary*, edited by Dale Walde and Noreen D. Willows, pp. 384–391. Archaeological Association of the University of Calgary, Alberta, Canada.

Cribb, R.
1991   *Nomads in Archaeology*. Cambridge University Press, Cambridge, U.K.

Cullen, Tracey, and Lauren E. Talalay
1994   Recovering Gender in the Greek Neolithic: A Viable Goal? Paper presented at the Ninety-fifth Annual Meeting of the Archaeological Institute of America, Atlanta, Ga.

Curtis, Edwin S.
1970   *The North American Indians*, vol. 5. Johnson Reprint Company, London.

Cushing, Frank Hamilton
1896   *Outlines of Zuñi Creation Myths*. Bureau of American Ethnology, Thirteenth Annual Report, 1891–1892, Washington, D.C.
1920   *Zuñi Breadstuff*. Indian Notes and Monographs, vol. 8, Museum of the American Indian, Heye Foundation, New York.

D'Auria, Sue, Peter Lacovar, and Catharine Roehrig, eds.
1987   *Mummies and Magic: The Funerary Arts of Ancient Egypt*. Museum of Fine Arts, Boston, Mass.

Davidson, A. I.
1987   Sex and the Emergence of Sexuality. *Critical Inquiry* 14:16–48.

Davis, Ellen N.
1987   The Knossos Miniature Frescoes and the Function of the Central Courts. In *The Function of the Minoan Palaces: Proceedings of the Fourth International Symposium of the Swedish Institute in Athens, 10–16 June, 1984*, edited by R. Hägg and N. Marinatos, pp. 157–161. Paul Åströms Förlag, Göteborg, Sweden.
1986   Youth and Age in the Thera Frescoes. *American Journal of Archaeology* 90:399–406.

Davis, Fred
1992   *Fashion, Culture, and Identity*. University of Chicago Press, Chicago.

Davis, Whitney
　1989　　　Representation, Legitimation, and the Emergence of the Early
　　　　　　Egyptian State. In *The Emergence of Complex Society in Africa*, edited
　　　　　　by Robert McIntosh and S. McIntosh. School of American Re-
　　　　　　search Advanced Seminar, Santa Fe, N.M.
de Beauvoir, Simone
　1953　　　*The Second Sex*. Knopf, New York.
Debono, Fernand, and Bodil Mortensen
　1988　　　*The Predynastic Cemetery at Heliopolis, Season March–September 1950*.
　　　　　　Philipp von Zabern, Mainz am Rhein, Germany.
DeLand, Edmund, ed.
　1918　　　Fort Tecumseh and Fort Pierre Journal and Letter Books. South
　　　　　　Dakota State Historical Society, Historical Collections 9:69–239.
Delougaz, Pinhas, and Helene Kantor
　1996　　　*Chogha Mish: The First Five Seasons of Excavation, 1961–1971*, edited
　　　　　　by Abbas Alizadeh. Oriental Institute Publications 101. Oriental
　　　　　　Institute, Chicago.
Delporte, Henri
　1993a　　　Gravettian Female Figurines: A Regional Survey. In *Before Lascaux:
　　　　　　The Complex Record of the Early Upper Paleolithic*, edited by Heidi
　　　　　　Knecht, Anne Pike-Tay, and Randall White, pp. 243–257. CRC
　　　　　　Press, Boca Raton, Fla.
　1993b　　　*L'image de la femme dans l'art préhistorique*. Picard, Paris, France.
Demargne, Pierre
　1949　　　La robe de la déesse minoenne sur un cachet de Mallia. (*Mélanges
　　　　　　d'archéologie et d'histoire offerts à Charles Picard à l'occasion de son
　　　　　　65ième anniversaire*), *Revue Archéologique* 6 (29):280–288.
Deneffe, Victor
　1899　　　*La prothèse dentaire dans l'Antiquité*. H. Caals, Firenze, Italy.
Denig, Edwin T.
　1961　　　*Five Tribes of the Upper Missouri: Sioux, Arikaras, Assiniboines, Crees,
　　　　　　Crows*, edited by John C. Ewers. University of Oklahoma Press,
　　　　　　Norman.
Dennis, Wayne
　1940　　　*The Hopi Child*. D. Appleton-Century Company, New York.
DePratter, Chester B.
　1991　　　*Late Prehistoric and Early Historic Chiefdoms in the Southeastern United
　　　　　　States*. Garland, New York.
Desroches-Noblecourt, Christiane
　1953　　　Concubines du Mort. *Bulletin d'Institut Français d'Archéologie Orien-
　　　　　　tale* 53:7–47.
Diamond, E.
　1996　　　*Performance and Cultural Politics*. Routledge, London.
Diamond, Irene, and Lee Quinby, eds.
　1988　　　*Feminism and Foucault: Reflections on Resistance*. Northeastern Uni-
　　　　　　versity Press, Boston, Mass.
Dickinson, Oliver
　1994　　　*The Aegean Bronze Age*. Cambridge University Press, Cambridge, U.K.
Diogenes Laertius
　1966　　　*Lives of the Eminent Philosophers*. Trans. by R. D. Hicks. Harvard
　　　　　　University Press, Cambridge, Mass.

Ditch, L. E., and J. C. Rose
1972   A Multivariate Dental Sexing Technique. *American Journal of Physical Anthropology* 37:61–64.

Dobres, Marcia-Anne
1992a   Re-Presentations of Palaeolithic Visual Imagery: Simulacra and their Alternatives. *Kroeber Anthropological Society Papers* 73–74:1–23.
1992b   Re-Considering Venus Figurines: A Feminist-Inspired Re-Analysis. In *Ancient Images, Ancient Thought: The Archaeology of Ideology*, edited by A. Sean Goldsmith, Sandra Garvie, David Selin, and Jeannette Smith, pp. 245–262. Archaeological Association of the University of Calgary, Alberta, Canada.
1995   Gender and Prehistoric Technology: On the Social Agency of Technical Strategies. *World Archaeology* 27 (1):25–49.

Dollfus, Genevieve, and Zeidan Kafafi
1986   Preliminary Results of the First Season of the Joint Jordano-French Project at Abu Hamid. *Annual of the Department of Antiquities of Jordan* 30:353–379.

Dorman, Peter.
In press   Creation on the Potter's Wheel at the Eastern Horizon of Heaven. In *Gold of Praise: Studies in Honor of Edward F. Wente*, edited by E. Teeter and J. Larson. Studies in Ancient Oriental Civilizations. Oriental Institute, Chicago.

Dorsey, George A.
1904   *Traditions of the Arikara*. Carnegie Institution Publication 17. Washington, D.C.

Dover, Kenneth
1985   *Greek Homosexuality*. Harvard University Press, Cambridge, Mass.

Drooker, Penelope Ballard
1989   Textile Impressions on Mississippian Pottery at the Wickliffe Mounds Site (15Ba10), Ballard County, Kentucky. Master's thesis, Harvard University Extension School. University Microfilms, Ann Arbor, Mich.
1992   *Mississippian Village Textiles at Wickliffe*. University of Alabama Press, Tuscaloosa.

Du Bois, Cora
1935   *Wintu Ethnography*. University of California Publications in American Archaeology and Ethnography 36:1–148.

duBois, Page
1988   *Sowing the Body: Psychoanalysis and Ancient Reprsentations of Women*. University of Chicago Press, Chicago.

Duhard, Jean-Pierre
1993   Upper Palaeolithic Figures as a Reflection of Human Morphology and Social Organization. *Antiquity* 67:83–91.

Dumond, Don
1987   *The Eskimos and Aleuts*. Thames and Hudson, London.

Dunham, Sean
1996   Fruits of the Earth: Discerning Gender in the Archaeological Record. Paper presented at the Fourth Gender and Archaeology Conference, Michigan State University, East Lansing, Mich.

Dutour, O.
1986   Enthesopathies (Lesions of Muscular Insertions) as Indicators of

the Activities of Neolithic Saharan Populations. *American Journal of Physical Anthropology* 71:221–224.

Eaton, Linda
1991 The Heart of the Region: The Anthropology Collections of the Museum of Northern Arizona. *American Indian Art* 16 (3):46–53.

Eaton-Krauss, Marianne, and Erhart Graefe
1985 *The Small Golden Shrine from the Tomb of Tutankhamun.* Griffith Institute, Oxford, U.K.

Edwards, Philip C.
1989 Revising the Broad Spectrum Revolution. *Antiquity* 63:225–246.

Ehrenberg, Margaret R.
1989 *Women in Prehistory.* University of Oklahoma Press, Norman.

Eisler, Riane
1987 *The Chalice and the Blade: Our History, Our Future.* Harper and Row, San Francisco.

Ember, Carol R.
1983 The Relative Decline in Women's Contribution to Agriculture with Intensification. *American Anthropologist* 85:285–304.

Emerson, J. N.
1954 *Field Notes, Tunirmiut 1 (T1) Burial 2, Southampton Island, 1954.* Manuscript on file (MS no. 1973). Document Collection, Information Management Services, Canadian Museum of Civilization, Quebec, Canada.

Emerson, Thomas E.
1982 Mississippian Stone Images in Illinois. Illinois Archaeological Survey, Circular no. 6.
1989 Water, Serpents, and the Underworld: An Exploration into Cahokian Symbolism. In *The Southeastern Ceremonial Complex: Artifacts and Analysis*, edited by Patricia Galloway, pp. 45–92. University of Nebraska Press, Lincoln.

Emerson, Thomas E., and Douglas K. Jackson
1987 *The Marcus Site.* American Bottom Archaeology, FAI-270 Site Reports, vol. 17 (Pt. 2). University of Illinois Press, Urbana.

Emerson, Thomas E., and R. Barry Lewis, eds.
1991 *Cahokia and the Hinterlands.* University of Illinois Press, Urbana.

Emptoz, François
1987 La prothèse dentaire dans la Civilisation étrusque. *Archéologie et Médecine*: VII Rencontre Internationale d'Archéologie et d'Histoire (Antibes 1986), pp. 545–560. Editions APDCA: Juan-les-Pins, France.

Engels, Frederick
1972 *Origin of the Family, Private Property, and the State* [1884], edited by E. Leacock. International, New York.

Englund, Robert, and Hans Nissen, with Peter Damerow
1993 *Die Lexikalischen Listen der Archaischen Texte aus Uruk.* Archaische Texte aus Uruk 3. Gebr. Mann, Berlin, Germany.

Enninger, Werner
1985 The Design Features of Clothing Codes: The Functions of Clothing Displays in Interaction. *Kodikas/Code* 8 (1–2):81–110.
1984 Inferencing Social Structure and Social Processes from Nonverbal Behavior. *American Journal of Semiotics* 3 (2):77–96.

Epstein, Julia, and Kristina Straub, eds.
1991   *Body Guards: The Cultural Politics of Gender Ambiguity.* Routledge, New York.
Erman, Adolph, and Hermann Grapow
1971   *Wörterbuch der Ägyptischen Sprache*, vol. 3. Akademie-Verlag, Berlin, Germany.
Euripides
1979   *Bacchanals, Madness of Hercules, Children of Hercules, Phoenician Maidens, Suppliants.* Translated by Arthur Way. Harvard University Press, Cambridge, Mass.
Evans, Arthur J.
1902–3   The Palace of Knossos. *Annual of the British School at Athens* 9:1–153.
1921   *The Palace of Minos*, vol. 1. Macmillan, London.
Ewers, John C.
1968   *Indian Life on the Upper Missouri.* University of Oklahoma Press, Norman.
1994   Women's Roles in Plains Indian Warfare. In *Skeletal Biology in the Great Plains: Migration, Warfare, Health and Subsistence*, edited by Douglas W. Owsley and Richard L. Jantz, pp. 325–332. Smithsonian Institution Press, Washington, D.C.
Falkner, Thomas
1989   *Epi geraos oudo*: Homeric Heroism, Old Age and the End of the Odyssey. In *Old Age in Greek and Latin Literature*, edited by Thomas Falkner and Judith de Luce, pp. 27–28, 34. State University of New York Press, Albany.
Fane, Diana
1991   The Southwest. In *Objects of Myth and Memory: American Indian Art at the Brooklyn Museum*, edited by D. Fane, I. Jacknis, and L. M. Breen, pp. 45–159. The Brooklyn Museum in Association with the University of Washington Press, Brooklyn, N.Y.
Fantham, Elaine, Helene P. Foley, Natalie B. Kampen, Sarah B. Pomeroy, and Harry A. Shapiro, eds.
1995   *Women in the Classical World: Image and Text.* Giorgio Bretschneider, Rome, Italy.
Farquharson-Roberts, M. A., and P. C. Fulford
1980   Stress Fracture of the Radius. *Journal of Bone Joint Surgery* 62:194–195.
Fausto-Sterling, Anne
1992   *Myths of Gender: Biological Theories About Women and Men.* Basic Books, New York.
1993   The Five Sexes: Why Male and Female Are Not Enough. *The Sciences*, March–April, pp. 20–25.
Feher, Michel, ed., with Ramona Naddaff and Nadia Tazi
1989   *Fragments for a History of the Human Body.* Zone Books, Cambridge, Mass.
Fewkes, Jesse Walter
1989a   *The Mimbres Art and Archaeology.* Smithsonian Miscellaneous Collections, vol. 63, no. 10. 1989 reprint, Avanyu Publishing, Albuquerque, N.M.
[1914]
1989b   *Designs on Prehistoric Pottery from the Mimbres Valley, New Mexico.* Smithsonian Miscellaneous Collections, vol. 74, no. 6. 1989 reprint, Avanyu Publishing, Albuquerque, N.M.
[1923]

1989c   *Additional Designs on Prehistoric Mimbres Pottery.* Smithsonian Mis-
[1924]   cellaneous Collections, vol. 76, no. 8. 1989 reprint, Avanyu Pub-
            lishing, Albuquerque, N.M.

Fischer, Henry G.
1989   *Egyptian Women of the Old Kingdom and of the Heracleopolitan Period.*
            Metropolitan Museum of Art, New York.

Fischler, Susan
1994   Social Stereotypes and Historic Analysis: The Case of the Imperial
            Women at Rome. In *Women in Ancient Societies: An Illusion of the
            Night*, edited by Leonie J. Archer, Susan Fischler, and Maria Wyke,
            pp. 115–133. Routledge, New York.

Flannery, Kent V.
1972   The Origins of the Village as a Settlement Type in Mesoamerica
            and the Near East: A Comparative Study. In *Man, Settlement, and
            Urbanism*, edited by Peter J. Ucko, Ruth Tringham, and G. W. Dim-
            bleby, pp. 23–53. Duckworth, London.
1973   Origins of Agriculture. *Annual Review of Anthropology* 2:271–301.

Ford, Richard I.
1994   Corn Is Our Mother. In *Corn and Culture in the Prehistoric New World*,
            edited by Sissel Johannesson and Christine A. Hastorf, pp. 513–
            525. Westview Press, Boulder, Colo.

Fortescue, Michael
1984   *West Greenlandic.* Croom Helm, London.

Fortier, Andrew C.
1992   Stone Figurines. In *The Sponemann Site: The Formative Emergent Mis-
            sissippian Sponemann Phase Occupations*, edited by Andrew C. For-
            tier, Thomas O. Maher, and Joyce A. Williams, pp. 277–303. Ameri-
            can Bottom Archaeology, FAI-170 Site Reports, vol. 23. University
            of Illinois Press, Urbana.

Foucault, Michel
1972   *The Archaeology of Knowledge.* Routledge, London.
1977   *Discipline and Punish: The Birth of the Prison.* Penguin, London.
1989a   *The Birth of the Clinic: An Archaeology of Medical Perception.* Rout-
            ledge, London.
1989b   *Madness and Civilization: A History in the Age of Reason.* Routledge,
            London.

Fox, Michael V.
1985   *The Song of Songs and the Ancient Egyptian Love Songs.* University of
            Wisconsin Press, Madison.

Foxhall, Lyn
1997   Pandora Unbound: A Feminist Critique of Foucault's *History of
            Sexuality*. In *Naked Truths: Women, Sexuality, and Gender in Classical
            Art and Archaeology*, edited by Ann Olga Koloski-Ostrow and Claire
            L. Lyons, pp. 133–146. Routledge, New York.

Frank, A. W.
1991   For a Sociology of the Body: An Analytical Review. In *The Body:
            Social Process and Cultural Theory*, edited by M. Featherstone, M.
            Hepworth, and B. S. Turner, pp. 36–102. Sage, London.

Frankfort, Henri
1955   *Stratified Cylinder Seals from the Diyala Region.* Oriental Institute Pub-
            lication 72. University of Chicago Press, Chicago.

Friedman, Reneé
1981   Spatial Distribution in a Predynastic Cemetery: Naga-ed-Dêr
           N7000. Master's thesis, department of Near Eastern studies, Uni-
           versity of California, Berkeley.
Frink, Lisa M., Brian Hoffman, and Debra Corbett
1996   Gender, Space, and the Division of Labor: Women's Activities
           in Eastern Aleut Prehistory. Paper presented at the Fourth Gen-
           der and Archaeology Conference, Michigan State University, East
           Lansing.
Frolich, Bruno, and Donald J. Ortner
1982   Excavations of the Early Bronze Age Cemetery at Bab edh-Dhra,
           Jordan 1981, a Preliminary Report. *Annual of the Department of An-
           tiquities of Jordan* 26:247–269.
Frontisi-Ducroux, Françoise
1996   Eros, Desire, and the Gaze. In *Sexuality in Ancient Art*, edited by
           Natalie Kampen, pp. 81–100. Cambridge University Press, Cam-
           bridge, U.K.
Gadon, Elinor
1989   *The Once and Future Goddess: A Symbol for Our Time.* Harper and Row,
           San Francisco.
Gallinger, Osma Couch
1950   *The Joy of Hand Weaving.* International Textbook Company, Scran-
           ton, Pa.
Galloway, Patricia, ed.
1989   *The Southeastern Ceremonial Complex: Artifacts and Analysis.* Univer-
           sity of Nebraska Press, Lincoln.
Gamble, Clive
1982   Interaction and Alliance in Paleolithic Society. *Man* 17:92–107.
1986   *The Paleolithic Settlement of Europe.* Cambridge University Press,
           Cambridge, U.K.
Gatens, M.
1996   *The Imaginary Body.* Routledge, London.
Gero, Joan
1991   Genderlithics: Women's Roles in Stone Tool Production. In *Engen-
           dering Archaeology: Women and Prehistory*, edited by Joan M. Gero and
           Margaret W. Conkey, pp. 163–193. Basil Blackwell, Oxford, U.K.
Gero, Joan M., and Margaret W. Conkey
1991   *Engendering Archaeology: Women and Prehistory.* Basil Blackwell, Ox-
           ford, U.K.
Giddens, Anthony
1984   *The Constitution of Society: Outline of a Theory of Structuration.* Polity
           Press, Cambridge, U.K.
1991   *Modernity and Self-Identity: Self and Society in the Late Modern Age.*
           Polity Press, Cambridge, U.K.
Giffen, Naomi M.
1930   *The Rôles of Men and Women in Eskimo Culture.* University of Chicago
           Press, Chicago.
Gilbert, B. Miles, and T. Dale Stewart
1973   A Method for Aging the Females Os Pubis. *American Journal of
           Physical Anthropology* 38 (1):31–38.

Gilead, Issac
1988   The Chalcolithic Period in the Levant. *Journal of World Prehistory* 2:397–443.
Gill, Sam
1987   *Mother Earth, An American Story.* University of Chicago Press, Chicago.
Gilman, Patricia A.
1987   Architecture as Artifact: Pit Structures and Pueblos in the American Southwest. *American Antiquity* 52:538–564.
Gilmore, David
1990   *Manhood in the Making: Cultural Concepts of Masculinity.* Yale University Press, New Haven, Conn.
Gilmore, Melvin R.
1926a   Arikara Genesis and Its Teachings. *Indian Notes* 3:188–193.
1926b   Arikara Commerce. *Indian Notes* 3:13–18.
1928   The Making of a New Head Chief by the Arikara. *Indian Notes* 5:411–418.
1930   Notes on the Gynecology and Obstetrics of the Arikara Tribe of Indians. *Papers of the Michigan Academy of Science, Arts and Letters* 14:71–81.
Gimbutas, Marija
1989   *The Language of the Goddess.* Harper and Row, San Francisco.
Ginsburg, Faye, and Anne Lowenhaupt Tsing, eds.
1990   *Uncertain Terms: Negotiating Gender in American Culture.* Beacon Press, Boston.
Godelier, Maurice
1981   The Origins of Male Domination. *New Left Review* 127:3–17.
Golden, Mark
1990   *Children and Childhood in Classical Athens.* Johns Hopkins University, Baltimore.
Goldhill, Simon
1995   *Foucault's Virginity: Ancient Erotic Fiction and the History of Sexuality.* Cambridge University Press, Cambridge, U.K.
Goldstein, Lynne
1976   Spatial Structure and Social Organization: Regional Manifestations of Mississippian Society. Ph.D. dissertation, Northwestern University. University Microfilms, Ann Arbor, Mich.
1981   One-Dimensional Archaeology and Multi-Dimensional People: Spatial Organisation and Mortuary Analysis. In *The Archaeology of Death,* edited by R. Chapman, I. Kinnes, and K. Randsborg, pp. 53–70. Cambridge University Press, Cambridge, U.K.
Goodenough, Ward H.
1965   Rethinking "Status" and "Role:" Toward a General Model of the Cultural Organization of Social Relationships. In *The Relevance of Models for Social Anthropology,* edited by M. Gluckman and F. Eggan, Monograph 1:1–24. Association of Social Anthropologists of the Commonwealth.
Goose, D. H.
1963   Dental Measurement: An Assessment of Its Value in Anthropological Studies. In *Dental Anthropology,* edited by Don R. Brothwell, pp. 125–148. Pergamon, New York.

Gottdeiner, Mark
1986   Fashion. In *Encyclopedic Dictionary of Semiotics*, Approaches to Semi-
            otics, vol. 73, edited by T. A. Sebeok, pp. 252–255. Mouton de
            Gruyter, New York.
Gough, Galal R.
1987   The Indian Hill Ceremonial Fertility Site Complex. In *Rock Art
            Papers*, vol. 5, edited by Ken Hedges, pp. 55–60. San Diego Mu-
            seum Papers 23, San Diego, Calif.
Grosz, E.
1994   *Volatile Bodies: Toward a Corporeal Feminism*. Indiana University
            Press, Bloomington.
1995   *Space, Time and Perversion*. Routledge, London.
Guerini, Francesco
1909   *A History of Dentistry*. Lea and Febiger, Philadelphia, Pa.
Guldager, Pia
1990   En tandklinik og sko/nhedssalon i Rom. *Tandlaegebladet* (Danish
            Dental Journal) 94 (10):422–426.
Guldager, Pia, and Karen Slej
1986   Il Tempio di Castore e Polluce. *Archeologia Viva* 5 (4):24–37.
Gullberg, Elsa, and Paul Åström
1970   *The Thread of Ariadne: A Study of Ancient Greek Dress*. Studies in Medi-
            terranean Archaeology, vol. 21. Paul Åströms Förlag, Göteborg,
            Sweden.
Guthrie, R. Dale
1984   Ethological Observations from Palaeolithic Art. In *La Contribution
            de la Zoologie et de L'Ethologie a l'Interpretation de l'Art de Peuples Chas-
            seurs Prehistoriques*, edited by H.-G. Bandi, W. Huber, M. R. Sauter,
            and B. Sitter, pp. 35–74. Editions Universitaires Fribourg Suisse,
            Saint-Paul Fribourg, Switzerland.
Guyer, Jane
1988   The Multiplication of Labor. *Current Anthropology* 29:247–272.
1991   Female Farming in Anthropology and African History. In *Gender at
            the Crossroads of Knowledge*, edited by M. diLeonardo, pp. 257–277.
            University of California Press, Berkeley.
Gvozdover, Mariana D.
1985   Tipologiya Zhenskikh Statuetok Kostenkovskoi Paleoliticheskoi
            Kul'tury. *Voprosy Antropologii* 75:27–66.
1989   The Typology of Female Figurines of the Kostenki Paleolithic Cul-
            ture. *Soviet Anthropology and Archeology* 27 (4):32–94.
Habermas, Jürgen
1971   *Knowledge and Human Interests*. Translated by J. Shapiro. Beacon
            Press, Boston.
Hägg, Robin
1983   Epiphany in Minoan Ritual. *Institute of Classical Studies Bulletin*
            30:184–85.
1986   Die Göttliche Epiphanie im Minoischen Ritual. *Mitteilungen des
            Deutschen Archäologischen Instituts. Athenische Abteilung* 101:41–62.
Hahn, Joachim
1993   Aurignacian Art in Central Europe. In *Before Lascaux: The Complex
            Record of the Early Upper Paleolithic*, edited by Heidi Knecht, Anne Pike
            Tay, and Randall White, pp. 229–241. CRC Press, Boca Raton, Fla.

Hall, Edith
  1989   *Inventing the Barbarian, Greek Self-Definition through Tragedy.* Oxford University Press, Oxford, U.K.
Hall, Robert L.
  1975   Chronology and Phases at Cahokia. In *Perspectives in Cahokia Archaeology.* Illinois Archaeological Survey Bulletin 10:15–31.
  1991   Cahokia Identity and Interaction: Models of Cahokia Mississippian. In *Cahokia and the Hinterlands,* edited by Thomas E. Emerson and R. Barry Lewis, pp. 3–34. University of Illinois Press, Urbana.
Hall, Stuart
  1986   Gramsci's Relevance for the Study of Race and Ethnicity. *Journal of Communication Inquiry* 10:5–27.
Hallager, Erik
  1988   The Roundel in the Minoan Administrative System. In *Studies in Ancient History and Numismatics, Papers Presented to Rudi Thomsen,* pp. 11–21, Århus.
  1995   *The Minoan Roundel and Other Sealed Documents in the Neopalatial Linear A Administration.* Universite de Liege, Liege, Belgium.
Hallo, W. W.
  1987   The Birth of Kings. In *Love and Death in the Ancient Near East: Essays in Honor of Marvin H. Pope,* edited by John Marks and Robert Good, pp. 45–52. Four Quarters Publishing, Guilford, Conn.
Hamann, Byron
  1997   Weaving and the Iconography of Prestige: The Royal Gender Symbolism of Lord 5 Flower's /Lady 4 Rabbit's Family. In *Women in Prehistory: North America and Mesoamerica,* edited by Cheryl Claassen and Rosemary A. Joyce, pp. 152–172. University of Pennsylvania Press, Philadelphia.
Hamilton, Naomi
  In press Ungendering Archaeology: Concepts of Sex and Gender in Figurine Studies in Prehistory. In *Gender and Material Culture 2: Representations of Gender from Prehistory to the Present* (Proceedings of the 1994 Conference on Gender), edited by Moira Donald and Linda M. Hurcombe. Macmillan, London.
  1994   A Fresh Look at the "Seated Gentleman" in the Pierides Foundation Museum, Republic of Cyprus. *Cambridge Archaeological Journal* 4:302–312.
Hanbury-Tenison, J. W.
  1986   *The Late Chalcolithic to Early Bronze I in Palestine and TransJordan.* BAR International Series 311, Oxford, U.K.
Harper, Prudence, Joan Aruz, and Francoise Tallon, eds.
  1992   *The Royal City of Susa: Ancient Near Eastern Treasures in the Louvre.* Metropolitan Museum of Art, New York.
Harris, David R.
  1986   Plant and Animal Domestication and the Origins of Agriculture: The Contribution of Radiocarbon Accelerator Dating. In *Archaeological Results from Accelerator Dating,* edited by J. A. J. Gowlett and R. E. M. Hedges, Monograph 11: 5–12. Oxford Committee for Archaeology, Oxford, U.K.
Hassan, Fekri A.
  1988   The Predynastic of Egypt. *Journal of World Prehistory* 2:135–185.

Hawkes, Jacquetta
1968   *Dawn of the Gods.* Random House, New York.
Hawkey, Diane E.
1988   *Use of Upper Arm Extremity Enthesopathies to Indicate Habitual Activity Patterns.* Master's thesis, Arizona State University, Tempe.
Hawkey, Diane E., and Charles F. Merbs
1995   Activity-Induced Musculoskeletal Stress Markers (MSM) and Subsistence Strategy Changes among Ancient Hudson Bay Eskimos. *International Journal of Osteoarchaeology* 5:324–338.
Hays, Kelley A.
1984   Rock Art of Northern Black Mesa. In *Excavations on Black Mesa, 1982: A Descriptive Report,* edited by Deborah L. Nichols and F. E. Smiley, pp. 517–540, Research Paper 39. Southern Illinois University at Carbondale Center for Archaeological Investigations, Carbondale.
1992   Anasazi Ceramics as Text and Tool: Toward a Theory of Ceramic Design "Messaging." Ph.D. dissertation, University of Arizona. University Microfilms, Ann Arbor, Mich.
Hayter, Holly Martelle
1996   In Search of the Huron Potter: Reviewing Disciplinary and Historical Constructions of Women's Work. Paper presented at the Fourth Gender and Archaeology Conference, Michigan State University, East Lansing.
Hecht, Ann
1989   *The Art of the Loom.* British Museum Publications, London.
Heffron, Roderick
1939   *Pneumonia.* The Commonwealth Fund, New York.
Hekman, Susan
1990   *Gender and Knowledge: Elements of a Postmodern Feminism.* Polity Press, Cambridge, U.K.
Hengen, O. P.
1971   Cribra Orbitalia: Pathogenesis and Probable Etiology. *Homo* 22: 57–75.
Herdt, Gilbert, ed.
1994   *Third Sex, Third Gender: Beyond Sexual Dimorphism in Culture and History.* Zone Books, New York.
Heyne, Rudolf
1924   Zähne und Zahnärzliches in der schönen Literatur der Römer. Ph.D. dissertation. Leipzig, Germany.
Hillman, Gordon C.
1984   Traditional Husbandry and Processing of Archaic Cereals in Recent Times: The Operations, Products, and Tools Which Might Feature in Sumerian Tests. *Bulletin for Sumerian Agriculture* 1.
Hippocrates
1923/31   *Hippocrates: Ancient Medicine,* vols. 1, 2, and 4, translated by William H. S. Jones. William Heinemann, London.
1928   *Hippocrates: Ancient Medicine,* vol. 3, translated by E. T. Withington. William Heinemann, London.
Hitchcock, Louise
In press   Engendering Ambiguity in Minoan Crete: It's a Drag To Be a King. In *Gender and Material Culture: Representations of Gender from Prehistory*

to the Present (Proceedings of the 1994 Conference on Gender), edited by Moira Donald and Linda M. Hurcombe. Macmillan, London.

Hodder, Ian
1982   *Symbols in Action: Ethnoarchaeological Studies of Material Culture.* Cambridge University Press, Cambridge, U.K.
1984   Burials, Houses, Women, and Men in the European Neolithic. In
Ideology, Power and Prehistory, edited by Daniel Miller and Christopher Tilley, pp. 51–68. Cambridge University Press, Cambridge,
U.K.

Hoffmann-Axthelm, Walter
1985   *Die Geschichte der Zahnheilkunde.* 2nd ed. Quintessenz Verlags-
GmbH, Berlin, Germany.

Hofmann-Wyss, Anna Barbara
1987   *St. Lorenz Insel-Studien. Berner Beiträge zur archäologischen und ethno-
logischen Erforschung des Beringstrassengebietes. Band II. Prähistorische
Eskimogräber an der Dovelavik Bay und bei Kitnepaluk im Westen der
St. Lorenz Insel, Alaska.* Verlag Paul Haupt, Bern und Stuttgart,
Germany.

Holder, A. B.
1889   The Bote: Description of a Peculiar Sexual Perversion Found
among North American Indians. *New York Medical Journal* 50
(23):623–625.

Holder, Preston
1970   *The Hoe and the Horse on the Plains: A Study of Cultural Development
Among North American Indians.* University of Nebraska Press,
Lincoln.

Hollimon, Sandra E.
1992   Health Consequences of Sexual Division of Labor Among Native
Americans: The Chumash of California and the Arikara of the
Northern Plains. In *Exploring Gender Through Archaeology*, edited by
Cheryl Claassen, pp. 81–88. Monographs in World Archaeology,
no. 11, Prehistory Press, Madison, Wis.
1996   Sex, Gender and Health among the Chumash: An Archaeological
Examination of Prehistoric Gender Roles. *Proceedings of the Society
for California Archaeology* 9:205–208.
1997   The Third Gender in Native American Society: Two-Spirit Under-
takers Among the Chumash and Their Neighbors. In *Women in
Prehistory: North America and Mesoamerica* edited by Cheryl Claassen
and Rosemary Joyce, pp. 173–188. University of Pennsylvania
Press, Philadelphia.

Hollimon, Sandra E., and Douglas W. Owsley
1994   Osteology of the Fay Tolton Site: Implications for Warfare During
the Middle Missouri Variant. In *Skeletal Biology in the Great Plains:
Migration, Warfare, Health and Subsistence*, edited by Douglas W.
Owsley and Richard L. Jantz, pp. 345–353. Smithsonian Institution
Press, Washington, D.C.

Hornung, Erik
1982   *Conceptions of God in Ancient Egypt: The One and the Many*, translated
by John Baines. [Original German edition published in 1971].
Cornell University Press, Ithaca, N.Y.
1992   *Idea into Image.* Timken, New York.

Hudson, Charles
1976   *The Southeastern Indians.* University of Tennessee Press, Knoxville.
Hughes-Hallett, Lucy
1990   *Cleopatra: Histories, Dreams, and Distortions.* Harper and Row, New York.
Huntington, Richard, and Peter Metcalf
1979   *Celebrations of Death.* Cambridge University Press, Cambridge, U.K.
Hurt, Wesley R.
1969   Seasonal Economic and Settlement Patterns of the Arikara. *Plains Anthropologist* 14 (43):32–37.
Hyder, William D.
1994   Basketmaker Social Identity: Rock Art as Culture and Praxis. Paper presented at the 1994 International Rock Art Conference, American Rock Art Research Association, Flagstaff, Ariz.
Ions, Veronica
1982   *Egyptian Mythology.* Peter Bedrick Books, New York.
Jackson, Michael
1989   *Paths toward a Clearing: Radical Empiricism and Ethnographic Inquiry.* Indiana University Press, Bloomington.
Jackson, Ralph
1988   *Doctors and Diseases in the Roman Empire.* British Museum Publications, London.
1990   Roman Doctors and Their Instruments: Recent Research into Ancient Practice. *Journal of Roman Archaeology* 3:5–27.
Jacobs, Linda
1979   Tell-i-Nun: Archaeological Implications of a Village in Transition. In *Ethnoarchaeology: Implications of Ethnography for Archaeology,* edited by Carole Kramer, pp. 175–191. Columbia University Press, New York.
Jacobsen, Thorkild
1976   *Treasures of Darkness: A History of Mesopotamian Religion.* Yale University Press, New Haven, Conn.
James, T. G. H.
1979   *An Introduction to Ancient Egypt.* Harper and Row, New York.
Jantz, Richard L., and Douglas W. Owsley
1984   Long Bone Growth Variation Among Arikara Skeletal Populations. *American Journal of Physical Anthropology* 63:13–20.
Jenkins, Ian
1983   Is There Life After Marriage? A Study of the Abduction Motif in Vase Paintings of the Athenian Wedding Ceremony. *Bulletin of the Institute of Classical Studies, University of London* 30:137–145.
Jenness, Diamond
1957   *Dawn in Arctic Alaska.* University of Chicago Press, Chicago.
Jett, Stephen C., and Peter B. Moyle
1986   The Exotic Origins of Fishes Depicted on Prehistoric Mimbres Pottery from New Mexico. *American Antiquity* 51:688–720.
Johnson, Gregory A.
1989   Dynamics of Southwestern Prehistory: Far Outside—Looking In. In *Dynamics of Southwestern Prehistory,* edited by Linda S. Cordell and George J. Gumerman, pp. 371–389. Smithsonian Institution Press, Washington, D.C.

Johnstone, Mary A.

1932a   The Etruscan Collection in the Free Public Museums of Liverpool. *Annals of Archaeology and Anthropology* 19:121–137, Plates 93–94.

1932b   The Etruscan Collection in the Public Museum of Liverpool. *Studi Etruschi* 6:443–452.

Johnson, Matthew H.

1989   Conceptions of Agency in Archaeological Interpretation. *Journal of Anthropological Archaeology* 8:189–211.

Jones, William Henry Samuel

1946   *Philosophy and Medicine in Ancient Greece.* Johns Hopkins Press, Baltimore.

1953   Ancient Documents and Contemporary Life, with Special Reference to the Hippocratic Corpus, Celsus and Pliny. In *Science, Medicine and History*, edited by E. Ashworth Underwood, pp. 100–110. Oxford University Press, London.

Joyce, Rosemary A.

1992   Images of Gender and Labor Organization in Classic Maya Society. In *Exploring Gender Through Archaeology*, edited by Cheryl Claassen, pp. 63–70. Prehistory Press, Madison, Wis.

1993   Women's Work: Images of Production and Reproduction in Prehispanic Southern Central America. *Current Anthropology* 34:255–274.

1998   Beauty, Sexuality, Body Ornamentation, and Gender in Ancient Mesoamerica. Paper presented at the conference "World Wide Perspectives on Women and Gender in Archaeology," Villa Serbelloni Conference Center of the Rockefeller Foundation, Bellagio, Italy.

Joyce, Rosemary A., and Cheryl Claassen

1997   Women in the Ancient Americas: Archaeologists, Gender, and the Making of Prehistory. In *Women in Prehistory: North America and Mesoamerica*, edited by Cheryl Claassen and Rosemary A. Joyce, pp. 1–16. University of Pennsylvania Press, Philadelphia.

Kabotie, Fred

1982   *Designs from the Ancient Mimbrenos with Hopi Interpretation.* Northland Press, Flagstaff, Ariz.

Kaempf-Dimitriadou, Sophia

1979   *Die Liebe der Götter in der attischen Kunst des 5. Jahrhunderts v. Chr.* Francke Verlag, Bern, Switzerland.

Kaiser, Susan B.

1990   *The Social Psychology of Clothing: Symbolic Appearances in Context.* 2nd ed. Macmillan, New York.

1983–84   Towards a Contextual Social Psychology of Clothing: A Synthesis of Symbolic Interactionist and Cognitive Theoretical Perspectives. *Clothing and Textiles Research Journal* 2:1–9.

Kamp, Kathryn A.

1987   Affluence and Image: Ethnoarchaeology in a Syrian Village. *Journal of Field Archaeology* 14:283–296.

Kampen, Natalie B., ed.

1996   *Sexuality in Ancient Art: Near East, Egypt, Greece and Italy.* Cambridge University Press, Cambridge, U.K.

Kantor, Helene J.
1992   The Relative Chronology of Egypt and Its Foreign Correlations before the First Intermediate Period. In *Chronologies in Old World Archaeology*. 3rd ed., edited by R. W. Ehrich, pp. 3–21. University of Chicago Press, Chicago.

Kawagley, A. Oscar
1995   *A Yupik Worldview: A Pathway to Ecology and Spirit.* Waveland Press, Prospect Heights, Ill.

Kehoe, Alice B.
1970   The Function of Ceremonial Intercourse Among the Northern Plains Indians. *Plains Anthropologist* 15:99–103.
1983   The Shackles of Tradition. In *The Hidden Half: Studies of Plains Indian Women*, edited by P. Albers and B. Medicine, pp. 53–73. University Press of America, Lanham, Md.
1990   Points and Lines. In *Powers of Observation: Alternate Views in Archaeology*, edited by Sarah M. Nelson and Alice B. Kehoe, pp. 23–37. Archaeological Papers of the American Anthropological Association 2, Washington D.C.
1991a   The Weaver's Wraith. In *The Archaeology of Gender*, edited by Dale Walde and Noreen Willows, pp. 430–435. University of Calgary Archaeological Association, Calgary, Alberta, Canada.
1991b   No Possible, Probable Shadow of Doubt. *Antiquity* 65:129–131.

Kelley, Marc A., Sean P. Murphy, Dianne R. Levesque, and Paul S. Sledzik
1994   Respiratory Disease Among Protohistoric and Early Historic Plains Indians. In *Skeletal Biology in the Great Plains: Migration, Warfare, Health, and Subsistence*, edited by Douglas W. Owsley and Richard L. Jantz, pp. 345–353. Smithsonian Institution Press, Washington, D.C.

Kemp, Barry J.
1983   Old Kingdom, Middle Kingdom, and Second Intermediate Period, c. 2686–1552 B.C. In *Ancient Egypt: A Social History*, contributions by Bruce G. Trigger, Barry J. Kemp, D. O'Connor, and Alan B. Lloyd, pp. 71–182. Cambridge University Press, Cambridge, U.K.
1989   *Ancient Egypt: Anatomy of a Civilization.* Routledge, London.

Kennedy, Kenneth A. R.
1983   Morphological Variations in Ulnar Supinator Crests and Fossae as Identification Markers of Occupational Stress. *Journal of Forensic Science* 28:871–876.
1989   Skeletal Markers of Occupational Stress. In *Reconstruction of Life from the Skeleton*, edited by M. Y. Iscan and K. A. R. Kennedy, pp. 129–160. Alan R. Liss, New York.

Keuls, Eva
1985   *Reign of the Phallus: Sexual Politics in Ancient Athens.* Harper and Row, New York.

Kieser, Julius A.
1990   *Human Adult Odontometrics: The Study of Variation in Adult Tooth Size.* Cambridge University Press, Cambridge, U.K.

King, Helen
1994   Producing Women: Hippocratic Gynaecology. In *Women in Ancient Societies: An Illusion of the Night*, edited by Leonie J. Archer, Susan Fischler, and Maria Wyke, pp. 102–114. Routledge, New York.

Kintigh, Keith W.
1994   *Tools for Quantitative Archaeology.* Software and operator's manual. Manuscript on file at the Department of Anthropology, Arizona State University, Tempe.

Knapp, A. Bernard, and Lynn Meskell
1997   Bodies of Evidence on Prehistoric Cyprus. *Cambridge Archaeological Journal* 7 (2):183–204.

Knight, Vernon James, Jr.
1986   The Institutional Organization of Mississippian Religion. *American Antiquity* 51:675–687.

Koehl, Robert
1986   The Chieftain Cup and a Minoan Rite of Passage. *Journal of Hellenic Studies* 106:99–110.

Koloski-Ostrow, Ann Olga
1997   Violent Stages in Two Pompeian Houses: Imperial Taste, Aristo-cratic Response, and Messages of Male Control. In *Naked Truths: Women, Sexuality, and Gender in Classical Art and Archaeology*, edited by Ann Olga Koloski-Ostrow and Claire L. Lyons, pp. 243–266. Routledge, New York.

Koloski-Ostrow, Ann Olga, and Claire L. Lyons, eds.
1997   *Naked Truths: Women, Sexuality, and Gender in Classical Art and Archaeology.* Routledge, New York.

Kramer, Carole
1979   An Archaeological View of a Contemporary Kurdish Village: Do-mestic Architecture, Household Size, and Wealth. In *Ethnoarchaeology: Implications of Ethnography for Archaeology*, edited by Carole Kramer, pp. 139–163. Columbia University Press, New York.
1982   *Village Ethnoarchaeology: Rural Iran in Archaeological Perspective.* Academic Press, New York.

Krieger, Xenia
1973   *Das Kampf zwischen Peleus und Thetis in der griechischen Vasenmalerei.* Westfälisches Wilhelms-Universität, Münster, Germany.

Kroeper, Karla
1988   Excavations of the Munich East-Delta Expedition in Minshat in Abu Omar. In *The Archaeology of the Nile Delta, Egypt: Problems and Priorities*, edited by E. C. M. van den Brink, pp. 11–33. Netherlands Foundation for Archaeological Research in Egypt, Netherlands.

Kulick, Don
1997   The Gender of Brazilian Transgendered Prostitutes. *American Anthropologist* 99:574–585.

Kus, Susan
1982   Matters Material and Ideal. In *Symbolic and Structural Archaeology*, edited by Ian Hodder, pp. 47–62. Cambridge University Press, Cambridge, U.K.

Lai, Ping, and Nancy C. Lovell
1992   Skeletal Markers of Occupational Stress in the Fur Trade: A Case Study from a Hudson's Bay Company Fur Trade Post. *International Journal of Osteoarchaeology* 2:221–234.

Lallo, John, George Armelagos, and Robert Mensforth
1978   The Role of Diet, Disease, and Physiology in the Origin of Porotic Hyperostosis. *Human Biology* 49:471–483.

Lanciani, Rodolfo
1892   *Pagan and Christian Rome* [Reissued in 1967]. Benjamin Blom, New
            York.
Lanford, Benson L.
1986   The Southwest Museum. *American Indian Art* 12:30–37.
Lange, Charles H.
1959   *Cochiti: A New Mexico Pueblo, Past and Present.* University of Texas
            Press, Austin.
Laqueur, Thomas
1990   *Making Sex: Body and Gender from the Greeks to Freud.* Cambridge
            University Press, Cambridge, U.K.
Larmour, David H. J., et al.
1998   Introduction: Situating *The History of Sexuality.* In *Rethinking Sex-
            uality: Foucault and Classical Antiquity,* edited by D. H. J. Larmour,
            P. A. Miller, and C. Platter, pp. 3–41. Princeton University Press,
            Princeton, N.J.
Larsen, Clark S.
1985   Dental Modifications and Tool-Use in the Western Great Basin.
            American Journal of Physical Anthropology 67:393–402.
Larsen, Clark S., and C. B. Ruff
1991   Biomechanical Adaptation and Behavior on the Prehistoric Geor-
            gia Coast. In *What Mean These Bones,* edited by Mary L. Powell,
            Patricia S. Bridges, and A. W. Mires, pp. 102–113. University of
            Alabama Press, Tuscaloosa.
La Verendrye, Le Chevalier De
1914   Journal of La Verendrye. *South Dakota Historical Collections* 7:323–
            348.
Layton, Robert, Robert Foley, and Elizabeth Williams
1991   The Transition between Hunting-Gathering and the Specialized
            Husbandry of Resources. *Current Anthropology* 32:255–274.
Leach, Edmund R.
1954   *Political Systems of Highland Burma.* G. Bell and Son, London.
Leacock, Eleanor
1981   History, Development, and the Division of Labor by Sex. *Signs*
            7:474–491.
LeBlanc, Steven A.
1983a   *The Mimbres People.* Thames and Hudson, London.
1983b   The Mimbres Culture. In *Mimbres Pottery: Ancient Art of the American
            Southwest,* by J. J. Brody, Catherine J. Scott, and Steven A. LeBlanc,
            pp. 23–38. Hudson Hills Press, N.Y.
LeBreton, Louis
1957   The Early Periods at Susa. *Iraq* 19:79–124.
LeBrun, Alain, and François Vallat
1978   L'origine de l'écriture à Suse. *Cahiers de la Délégation Archéologique
            Française en Iran* 8:11–59.
Lee, Mireille M.
1994   Semiotic Approaches to the Iconography of Gender in Minoan
            Neopalatial Bronze Votive Figurines. Master's thesis, Bryn Mawr
            College, Bryn Mawr, Pa.
1996   The Iconography of Gender in Minoan Neopalatial Bronze Votive
            Figurines (abstract). *American Journal of Archaeology* 100:336.

Lefkowitz, Mary
1993   Seduction and Rape in Greek Myth. In *Consent and Coercion to Sex and Marriage in Ancient and Mediaeval Societies*, edited by Angeliki Laiou, pp. 17–37. Dumbarton Oaks, Washington, D.C.
Lefkowitz, Mary R., and Maureen B. Fant
1982   *Women's Life in Greece and Rome*. Duckworth, London.
Lehmer, Donald J.
1971   Middle Missouri Archaeology. *National Park Service Papers* 1.
1977   Epidemics among the Indians of the Upper Missouri. *Reprints in Anthropology* 8:105–111.
Lehmer, Donald J., and David T. Jones
1968   Arikara Archaeology: The Bad River Phase. *Smithsonian Institution River Basin Surveys Publications in Salvage Archaeology* 7.
Lerner, Gerda
1986   *The Creation of Patriarchy*. Oxford University Press, New York.
Leroi-Gourhan, Andre
1968   *The Art of Prehistoric Man in Western Europe*. Thames and Hudson, London.
Lesko, Leonard
1991   Ancient Egyptian Cosmogonies and Cosmology. In *Religion in Ancient Egypt*, edited by B. E. Shafer, pp. 88–122. Cornell University Press, Ithaca, N.Y.
Levi, Doro
1926   Le Cretule di Zakro. *Annuario della Scuola archeologica di Atene e delle Missioni in Oriente* 8–9:157–201.
Levine, Molly M.
1995   The Gendered Grammar of Ancient Mediterranean Hair. In *Off with Her Head: The Denial of Women's Identity in Myth, Religion, and Culture*, edited by Howard Eilberg-Schwartz and Wendy Doniger, pp. 76–130. University of California Press, Berkeley.
Levy, L. F.
1968   Porter's Neck. *British Medical Journal* 2:16–19.
Levy, Thomas E.
1983   The Emergence of Specialized Pastoralism in the Southern Levant. *World Archaeology* 15:15–36.
1986   The Chalcolithic Period. *Biblical Archaeologist* 49:82–108.
1993   Tuleilat el-Ghassul. In *The New Encyclopedia of Excavations in the Holy Land*, edited by E. Stern, pp. 506–511. Simon and Schuster, New York.
Lincoln, Charles E.
1985   Cahokia and the American Bottom: Evolutionary Sequence or Social Hierarchy. Seminar paper for Anthropology 208, Harvard University. Manuscript on file with Alice Kehoe, Marquette University, Milwaukee, Wis.
Lissarague, François
1990   The Sexual Life of Satyrs. In *Before Sexuality*, edited by David Halperin, John Winkler, and Froma Zeitlin, pp. 53–81. Princeton University Press, Princeton, N.J.
Little, Kitty
1973   *Bone Behavior*. Academic Press, New York.

Lloyd, Alan B.
    1983   The Late Period, 664–323 B.C. In *Ancient Egypt: A Social History*, contributions by Bruce G. Trigger, Barry J. Kemp, David O'Connor, and Alan B. Lloyd, pp. 279–348. Cambridge University Press, Cambridge, U.K.
    1989   Psychology and Society in the Ancient Egyptian Cult of the Dead. In *Religion and Philosophy in Ancient Egypt*, edited by W. K. Simpson, pp. 117–133. Yale Egyptological Studies, New Haven, Conn.

Loraux, Nichole
    1995   *The Experiences of Tiresias: The Feminine and the Greek Man*, translated by Paula Wissing. Princeton University Press, Princeton, N.J.

Lyon, George Francis
    1825   *The Private Journal of Captain G. F. Lyon, of H. M. S. Hecla, During the Recent Voyage of Discovery under Captain Parry*. 2nd ed. J. Murray, London.

Lythgoe, Albert M., and Dows Dunham
    1965   *The Predynastic Cemetery, N 7000. Naga-ed-Dêr, Part IV*. University of California Press, Berkeley and Los Angeles.

MacNeish, Richard S.
    1992   *The Origins of Agriculture and Settled Life*. University of Oklahoma Press, Norman.

Maekawa, Kazuya
    1980   Female Weavers and Their Children in Lagash — Pre-Sargonic and Ur III. *Acta Sumerologica* 2:81–125.

Manning, Steven James
    1992   The Lobed-Circle Image in the Basketmaker Petroglyphs of Southwestern Utah. *Utah Archaeology* 1992:1–37.

Marcus, Michelle
    1993   Incorporating the Body: Adornment, Gender, and Social Identity in Ancient Iran. *Cambridge Archaeological Journal* 3 (2):157–178.
    1994   Dressed to Kill: Women and Pins in Early Iran. *Oxford Art Journal* 17:3–15.
    1995   Art and Ideology in Ancient Western Asia. In *Civilizations of the Ancient Near East*, vol. 4, edited by J. Sasson, J. Baines, G. Beckman, and K. Rubinson, pp. 2487–2505. Scribner, New York.
    1996   Sex and the Politics of Female Adornment in Pre-Achaemenid Iran. In *Sexuality in Ancient Art*, edited by Natalie Kampen. Cambridge University Press, Cambridge, U.K.

Marinatos, N.
    1995   *Minoan Religion: Ritual, Image and Symbol*. University of North Carolina Press, Chapel Hill.

Marshack, Alexander
    1991a   The Female Image: A "Time-Factored" Symbol. A Study in Style and Aspects of Image Use in the Upper Palaeolithic. *Proceedings of the Prehistoric Society* 57 (Pt. 1):17–31.
    1991b   *The Roots of Civilization: The Cognitive Beginnings of Man's First Art, Symbol, and Notation*. McGraw-Hill, New York.
    1996   Comments. *Current Anthropology* 37 (2):259–262.

Martin, M. K., and Barbara Voorhies
    1975   *Female of the Species*. Columbia University Press, New York.

Martin, Paul S.
 1961   A Human Effigy of Stone from a Great Kiva near Springerville, Arizona. *The Kiva* 26:1–5.
Marx, Karl, and Friedrich Engels
 1939   *German Ideology*. International Publishers, New York.
 [1845–46]
Masali, L., and A. Peluso
 1985   L'odontoiatria nell'antico Egitto. In *Storia della Odontoiatria*, edited by G. Vogel and G. Gambacorta, pp. 51–66. Ars Medica Antiqua, Milan, Italy.
Mata, Leonardo, Richard A. Kronmal, and Hugo Villegas
 1980   Diarrheal Diseases: A Leading World Health Problem. In *Cholera and Related Diarrheas: Molecular Aspects of a Global Health Problem*, edited by Orjan Ouchterlony and Jan Homgren, pp. 1–14. Forty-third Nobel Symposium, Karger, Basel, Switzerland.
Maximilian, Prince of Wied-Neuwied
 1906   Travels in the Interior of North America. In *Early Western Travels*, vols. 21–23, edited by R. G. Thwaites. Arthur H. Clark, Cleveland, Ohio.
McCafferty, Sharisse D., and Geoffrey G. McCafferty
 1991   Spinning and Weaving as Female Gender Identity in Post-Classic Mexico. In *Textile Traditions of Mesoamerica and the Andes: An Anthology*, edited by Margot Blum Schevill, Janet Catherine Berlo, and Edward B. Dwyer, pp. 19–44. Garland, New York.
McCartney, Allen P.
 1971   Thule Eskimo Prehistory Along Northwestern Hudson Bay. Ph.D. dissertation, University of Wisconsin — Madison. University Microfilms, Ann Arbor, Mich.
McCoid, Catherine Hodge, and LeRoy D. McDermott
 1996   Toward Decolonizing Gender: Female Vision in the Upper Paleolithic. *American Anthropologist* 98:319–326
McCorriston, Jill, and Frank Hole
 1991   The Ecology of Seasonal Stress and the Origins of Agriculture in the Near East. *American Anthropologist* 93:46–69.
McCracken, Grant
 1987   Clothing as Language: An Object Lesson in the Study of the Expressive Properties of Material Culture. In *Material Anthropology: Contemporary Approaches to Material Culture*, edited by B. Reynolds and M. A. Stott, pp. 103–128. University Press of America, Lanham, Md.
McCreery, David W.
 1981   Flotation of the Bab edh-Dhra and Numeira Plant Remains. In *The Southeastern Dead Sea Plain Expedition*, edited by Walter E. Rast and R. Thomas Schaub, pp. 165–169. Annual of the American Schools of Oriental Research 46. American Schools of Oriental Research, Cambridge, Mass.
McCreery, Patricia, and Jack McCreery
 1986   A Petroglyph Site with Possible Hopi Ceremonial Association. *American Indian Rock Art II*, edited by Ernest Snyder, pp. 1–7. American Rock Art Research Association, El Toro, Calif.
McCreery, Patricia, and Ekkehart Malotki
 1994   *Tapamveni: The Rock Art Galleries of Petrified Forest and Beyond*. Petrified Forest Museum Association, Petrified Forest, Ariz.

McDermott, LeRoy
  1996a   Self-Representation in Upper Paleolithic Female Figurines. *Current Anthropology* 37 (2):227–275.
  1996b   Comments. *Current Anthropology* 37 (2):259–262.
McDowell, Andrea
  1990   *Jurisdiction in the Workmen's Community of Deir el-Medna*. Nederlands Instituut voor het Nabije Oosten, Leiden, Netherlands.
McGhee, Robert
  1977   Ivory for the Sea Woman: The Symbolic Attributes of a Prehistoric Technology. *Canadian Journal of Archaeology* 1:141–149.
McKern, Thomas W., and T. Dale Stewart
  1957   Skeletal Age Changes in Young American Males. Headquarters, Quartermaster Research and Development Command, Technical Report EP-45. Natick, Mass.
McLaren, Angus
  1984   *Reproductive Rituals: The Perception of Fertility in England from the Sixteenth Century to the Nineteenth Century*. Methuen, New York.
McNally, Sheila
  1978   The Maenad in Early Greek Art. *Arethusa* 11:101–135.
McNay, Lois
  1992   *Foucault and Feminism*. Polity Press, Cambridge, U.K.
McNiven, Timothy
  1982   *Gestures in Attic Vase Painting*. University Microfilms, Ann Arbor, Mich.
  1996   The Construction of Gender-Specific Behavior in Attic Vase Painting. *American Journal of Archaeology* 100:388.
Meiklejohn, A.
  1957   *The Life, Work, and Times of Charles Turner Thackrah, Surgeon and Apothecary of Leeds (1795–1833)*. E. and S. Livingston, London.
Mensforth, Robert, C. Owen Lovejoy, John Lallo, and George Armelagos
  1978   The Role of Constitutional Factors, Diet, and Infectious Disease in the Etiology of Porotic Hyperostosis and Periosteal Reactions in Prehistoric Infants and Children. *Medical Anthropology* 2 (Pt. 1).
Merbs, Charles F.
  1964   *Summary of Field Work*. Manuscript on file (MS no. 603), Document Collection, Information Management Services, Canadian Museum of Civilization, Quebec, Canada.
  1967   *Human Burials of Silumiut, A Thule Culture Site North of Chesterfield Inlet, Northwest Territories, Preliminary Report*. Manuscript on file (MS no. 605), Document Collection, Information Management Services, Canadian Museum of Civilization, Quebec, Canada.
  1968   *Eskimo Burial Studies: The Kamarvik and Silumiut Sites, Preliminary Report*. Manuscript on file (MS no. 607), Document Collection, Information Management Services, Canadian Museum of Civilization, Quebec, Canada.
  1983   *Patterns of Activity-Induced Pathology in a Canadian Inuit Population*. Archaeological Survey of Canada, Paper no. 119, National Museum of Canada, Ottawa.
  1996   Thule Concepts of Gender and the Souls of the Dead. Paper presented at the Sixty-first Annual Meeting of the Society for American Archaeology, New Orleans.

Merkur, Daniel
1991   *Powers Which We Do Not Know: The Gods and Spirits of the Inuit.* University of Idaho Press, Moscow.
Merleau-Ponty, Maurice
1980   *The Phenomenology of Perception.* Routledge and Kegan Paul, London.
Masali, L., and A. Peluso
1985   L'odontoiatria nell'antico Egitto. In *Storia della odontoiatria,* edited by G. Vogel and G. Gambacorta, pp. 51–66. Ars Medica Antiqua, Milan, Italy.
Meskell, Lynn M.
1994a   Desperately Seeking Gender: A Review Article. *Archaeological Review from Cambridge* 13:105–111.
1994b   Dying Young: The Experience of Death at Deir el Medina. *Archaeological Review from Cambridge* 13:35–45.
1996   The Somatisation of Archaeology: Institutions, Discourses, Corporeality. *Norwegian Archaeological Review* 29 (1):1–16.
1997a   The Irresistible Body and the Seduction of Archaeology. In *The Body in Transition: Antiquity,* edited by D. Monsterrat. Routledge, London.
1997b   Egyptial Social Dynamics: The Evidence of Age, Sex, and Class in Domestic and Mortuary Contexts. Ph.D. dissertation, Archaeology Department, Cambridge University, Cambridge, U.K.
1998a   The Irresistible Body and the Seduction of Archaeology. In *Changing Bodies, Changing Meanings: Studies of the Body in Antiquity,* edited by D. Monsterrat. Routledge, London.
1998b   Intimate Archaeologies: The Case of Kha and Merit. *World Archaeology* 29 (3):363–379.
1999   *Archaeologies of Social Life: Age, Sex, and Class in Ancient Egypt.* Basil Blackwell, Oxford, U.K. Forthcoming.
In press   Embodying Archaeology: Theory and Praxis, In *Materials for a History of the Human Body in the Ancient Near East,* edited by T. G. Wilfong and C. E. Jones. Styx, Groeningen, Netherlands.
Messing, Simon D.
1978   The Non-Verbal Language of the Ethiopian Toga. *Social Aspects of the Human Body,* edited by T. Polhemus, pp. 251–57. Penguin, Harmondsworth, England.
Meyer, Roy W.
1977   *The Village Indians of the Upper Missouri: The Mandans, Hidatsas, and Arikaras.* University of Nebraska Press, Lincoln.
Michalowski, Piotr
1990   Early Mesopotamian Communicative Systems: Art, Literature, and Writing. In *Investigating Artistic Environments in the Ancient Near East,* edited by Ann Gunter, pp. 53–69. Smithsonian Institution Press, Washington, D.C.
Milde, H.
1988   "Going Out into the Day:" Ancient Egyptian Beliefs and Practices Concerning Death. In *Hidden Futures: Death and Immortality in Ancient Egypt, Anatolia, the Classical, Biblical, and Arabic-Islamic World,* edited by J. M. Bremer, Theo. P. van den Hout, and R. Peters. University of Amsterdam Press, Amsterdam, Netherlands.

Miller, Alfred J.
1968   *The West of Alfred Jacob Miller from the Notes and Water Colors in the Walters Art Gallery with an Account of the Artist by Marvin C. Ross.* University of Oklahoma Press, Norman.

Miller, Margaret
1995   Priam, King of Troy. In *The Ages of Homer*, edited by Jane Carter and Sarah Morris, pp. 449–465. University of Texas Press, Austin.

Molleson, Theya
1989   Seed Preparation in the Mesolithic: the Osteological Evidence. *Antiquity* 63:356–362.

1994   The Eloquent Bones of Abu Hurerya. *Scientific American*, August: 70–75.

Mond, Sir Oliver, and Robert H. Meyers
1937   *Cemeteries of Armant I.* Egyptian Exploration Society, London.

Moore, Henrietta L.
1986   *Space, Text, and Gender: An Anthropological Study of the Marakwet of Kenya.* Cambridge University Press, Cambridge, U.K.

1994   *A Passion for Difference: Essays in Anthropology and Gender.* Indiana University Press, Bloomington.

Moore, Jenny, and Eleanor Scott, eds.
1997   *Invisible People and Processes: Writing Gender and Childhood into European Archaeology.* Leicester University Press, New York.

Moorrees, Coenraad F. A., Elizabeth A. Fanning, and Edward E. Hunt, Jr.
1963a   Formation and Resorption of Three Deciduous Teeth in Children. *American Journal of Physical Anthropology* 21:205–213.

1963b   Age Variation of Formation Stages for Ten Permanent Teeth. *Journal of Dental Research* 42 (6):1490–1502.

Morgan, Livia
1988   *The Miniature Wall Paintings of Thera: A Study in Aegean Culture and Iconography.* Cambridge University Press, Cambridge, U.K.

Morris, Ian
1987   *Burial and Ancient Society: The Rise of the Greek City-State.* Cambridge University Press, Cambridge, U.K.

1992   *Death Ritual and Social Structure in Classical Antiquity.* Cambridge University Press, Cambridge, U.K.

Moss, Madonna L.
1996   Gender, Social Inequality, and Cultural Complexity: Northwest Coast Women in Prehistory. In *Debating Complexity*, edited by Daniel A. Meyer, Peter C. Dawson, and Donald T. Hanna, pp. 81–88. Archaeological Association of the University of Calgary, Alberta, Canada.

In press   George Catlin Among the Nayas: Understanding the Practice of Labret Wearing on the Northwest Coast. *Ethnohistory.*

Moulard, Barbara L.
1984   *Within the Underworld Sky: Mimbres Ceramic Art in Context.* Twelvetrees Press, Pasadena, Calif.

Murdock, George P., and Caterina Provost
1973   Factors in the Division of Labor by Sex: A Cross-Cultural Analysis. *Ethnology* 12:203–225.

Murra, John V.
1989   Cloth and Its Function in the Inca State. In *Cloth and Human Experi-*

ence, edited by Annette B. Weiner and Jane Schneider, pp. 275–302. Smithsonian Institution Press, Washington, D.C.

Musallam, Basim F.
1983   *Sex and Society in Islam*. Cambridge University Press, Cambridge, U.K.

Nelson, Sarah M.
1990   Diversity of the Upper Paleolithic "Venus" Figurines and Archaeological Mythology. In *Powers of Observation: Alternative Views in Archaeology*, edited by Sarah M. Nelson and Alice B. Kehoe, pp. 11–22. Archaeological Papers of the American Anthropological Association 2. Washington, D.C.
1993   Diversity of the Upper Paleolithic "Venus" Figurines and Archeological Mythology. In *Gender in Cross-Cultural Perspective*, edited by Caroline B. Brettell and Carolyn F. Sargent, pp. 51–58. Prentice-Hall, Englewood Cliffs, N.J.
1997   *Gender in Archaeology: Analyzing Power and Prestige*. Alta Mira Press, Walnut Creek, Ill.

Nicholson, Linda J., ed.
1990   *Feminism/Postmodernism*. Routledge, New York.

Nielsen, Inge
1992   The Metellan Temple. In *The Temple of Castor and Pollux I*, edited by Inge Nielsen and Birte Poulsen, pp. 87–117. De Luca for the Soprintendenza Archeological di Roma, Rome, Italy.

Nielsen, Inge, and Jan Zahle
1987   The Temple of Castor and Pollux on the Forum Romanum. Preliminary Report on the Scandinavian Excavations 1983–1985. *Acta Archaeologica* 56 (1985):1–30.

Niemeier, Wolf-Dietrich
1986   Zur Deutung des Thronraumes im Palast von Knossos. *Mitteilungen des Deutschen archäologischen Instituts. Athenische Abteilung* 101:63–95.
1987   On the Function of the "Throne Room" in the Palace at Knossos. In *The Function of the Minoan Palaces: Proceedings of the Fourth International Symposium of the Swedish Institute in Athens, 10–16 June, 1984*, edited by R. Hägg and N. Marinatos, pp. 163–168. Paul Åströms Förlag, Göteborg, Sweden.

Nissen, Hans
1977   Aspects of the Development of Early Cylinder Seals. In *Seals and Sealing in the Ancient Near East*, edited by McGuire Gibson and Robert Biggs, pp. 15–23. Bibliotheca Mesopotamica 6. Undena, Malibu.
1988   *The Early History of the Ancient Near East, 9000–2000 B.C.* University of Chicago Press, Chicago.

Nixon, Lucia
1995   The Cults of Demeter and Kore. In *Women in Antiquity: New Assessments*, edited by Richard Hawley and Barbara Levick, pp. 75–96. Routledge, New York.

Nobles, Connie
1996   Barred from Public Knowledge: Women in the Old Baton Rouge Penitentiary. Paper presented at the Fourth Gender and Archaeology Conference, Michigan State University, East Lansing.

250 **References**

North, Helen
1966   *Sophrosune: Self-Knowledge and Self-Restraint in Greek Literature.* Cornell University Press, Ithaca, N.Y.

Oakley, John
1995   Nuptial Nuances: Wedding Images in Non-Wedding Scenes of Myth. In *Pandora*, edited by Ellen Reeder, pp. 63–73. Princeton University Press, Princeton, N.J.

O'Connor, David
1983   New Kingdom and Third Intermediate Period, 1152–664 B.C. In *Ancient Egypt: A Social History*, contributions by Bruce G. Trigger, Barry J. Kemp, David O'Connor, and Alan B. Lloyd, pp. 183–278. Cambridge University Press, Cambridge, U.K.

O'Kane, Walter Collins
1950   *Sun in the Sky.* University of Oklahoma Press, Norman.

Olin, M. S., H. A. Young, D. Seligson, and H. H. Schmidek
1982   An Unusual Cervical Injury Occurring During Cow Milking. *Spine* 7:514–515.

Olsen, Sandra L., and Pat Shipman
1994   Cutmarks and Perimortem Treatment of Skeletal Remains on the Northern Plains. In *Skeletal Biology in the Great Plains: Migration, Warfare, Subsistence, and Health*, edited by Douglas W. Owsley and Richard L. Jantz, pp. 377–387. Smithsonian Institution Press, Washington, D.C.

O'Neale, Lila M.
1945   *Textile of Highland Guatemala.* Carnegie Institution of Washington, Publication 567. Washington, D.C.

Orser, Charles E., Jr.
1980   Toward a Partial Understanding of Complexity in Arikara Mortuary Practice. *Plains Anthropologist* 25:113–120.
1984   Trade Good Flow in Arikara Villages: Expanding Ray's "Middleman Hypothesis." *Plains Anthropologist* 29:1–12.

Orser, Charles E., Jr., and Larry Zimmerman
1984   A Computer Simulation of Euro-American Trade Good Flow to the Arikara. *Plains Anthropologist* 29:199–210.

Ortner, Donald J.
1979   Disease and Mortality in the Early Bronze Age People of Bab edh-Dhra, Jordan. *American Journal of Physical Anthropology* 51:589–598.
1981   A Preliminary Report on the Human Remains from the Bab edh-Dhra Cemetery. In *The Southeastern Dead Sea Plain Expedition*, edited by Walter E. Rast and R. Thomas Schaub, pp. 119–132. Annual of the American Schools of Oriental Research 46, American Schools of Oriental Research, Cambridge, Mass.
1982   The Skeletal Biology of an Early Bronze IB Charnel House at Bab edh-Dhra, Jordan. *Studies in the History and Archaeology of Jordan*, edited by A. Hadidi, pp. 93–95. Department of Antiquities, Amman, Jordan.

Ortner, Donald J., and Walter G. J. Putschar
1985   *Identification of Pathological Conditions In Human Skeletal Remains.* Smithsonian Institution Press, Washington, D.C.

Ortner, Sherry B.
1974   Is Female to Male as Nature Is to Culture? In *Women, Culture, and*

Society, edited by Michelle Zimbalist Rosaldo and Louise Lamphere, pp. 67–87. Stanford University Press, Stanford, Calif.

Ortner, Sherry B., and Harriet Whitehead
1981   Introduction: Accounting for Sexual Meanings. In *Sexual Meanings: The Cultural Construction of Gender and Sexuality*, edited by Sherry B. Ortner and Harriet Whitehead, pp. 1–27. Cambridge University Press, Cambridge, U.K.

Osborne, Robin
1996   Desiring Women on Athenian Pottery. In *Sexuality in Ancient Art*, edited by Natalie Kampen, pp. 65–80. Cambridge University Press, Cambridge, U.K.

O'Shea, John
1981   Social Configurations and the Archaeological Study of Mortuary Practices. In *The Archaeology of Death*, edited by R. Chapman, I. Kinnes, and K. Randsborg, pp. 39–52. Cambridge University Press, Cambridge, U.K.
1984   *Mortuary Variability: An Archaeological Investigation*. Academic Press, New York.

Otto, Eberhard
1938   Beitrage zur Geschichte der Stierkulte in Aegypten. *Untersuchung zur Geschichte und Altertumskunde Aegyptens* 13. Leipzig.

Owsley, Douglas W.
1992   Demography of Prehistoric and Early Historic Northern Plains Populations. In *Disease and Demography in the Americas*, edited by John W. Verano and Douglas H. Ubelaker, pp. 75–86. Smithsonian Institution Press, Washington, D.C.
1994   Warfare in Coalescent Tradition Populations of the Northern Plains. In *Skeletal Biology in the Great Plains: Migration, Warfare, Health, and Subsistence*, edited by Douglas W. Owsley and Richard L. Jantz, pp. 333–343. Smithsonian Institution Press, Washington, D.C.

Owsley, Douglas W., and William M. Bass
1979   A Demographic Analysis of Skeletons from the Larson Site (39WW2) Walworth County, South Dakota: Vital Statistics. *American Journal of Physical Anthropology* 51 (2):145–154.

Owsley, Douglas W., and Bruce Bradtmiller
1983   Mortality of Pregnant Females in Arikara Villages: Osteological Evidence. *American Journal of Physical Anthropology* 61:331–336.

Owsley, Douglas W., Hugh E. Berryman, and William M. Bass
1977   Demographic and Osteological Evidence for Warfare at the Larson Site, South Dakota. *Plains Anthropologist* 22 (78): 119–131.

Owsley, Douglas W., and Richard L. Jantz
1994   An Integrative Approach to Great Plains Skeletal Biology. In *Skeletal Biology in the Great Plains: Migration, Warfare, Health, and Subsistence*, edited by Douglas W. Owsley and Richard L. Jantz, pp. 3–8. Smithsonian Institution Press, Washington, D.C.

Pader, Ellen-Jane
1982   *Symbolism, Social Relations, and the Interpretation of Mortuary Remains*. British Archaeological Reports, International Series 130, Oxford, U.K.

Padgug, R. A.
1979   Sexual Matters: On Conceptualizing Sexuality in History. *Radical History Review* 20:3–23.

Palkovich, Ann M.
1981   Demography and Disease Patterns in a Protohistoric Plains Group: A Study of the Mobridge Site (39WW1). *Plains Anthropologist Memoir* 17:71–84.

Panofsky, Erwin
1955   *Meaning in the Visual Arts: Papers in Art and Art History*. Doubleday, Garden City, N.Y.

Parezo, Nancy J.
1983   *Navajo Sandpainting: From Religious Act to Commercial Art*. University of Arizona Press, Tucson.

Parken, D., L. Caplan, and H. Fisher, eds.
1996   *The Politics of Cultural Performance*. Berghahn Books, Providence, R.I.

Parmalee, Paul W.
1979   Inferred Arikara Subsistence Patterns Based on a Selected Faunal Assemblage from the Mobridge Site, South Dakota. *The Kiva* 44 (2–3):191–218.

Parsons, Elsie Clewes
1939   *Pueblo Indian Religion*. University of Chicago Press, Chicago.

Patterson, Alex, and Mary Patterson
1993   The Rock Art of Bluff, Utah, and the Pendant Circle Complex. In *Utah Rock Art*, vol. 12, edited by Frankie Harris, pp. 187–211. Utah Rock Art Research Association, John Wesley Powell Museum, Green River, Utah.

Pauketat, Timothy, and Thomas Emerson
1991   The Ideology of Authority and the Power of the Pot. *American Anthropologist* 93:919–941.

Peebles, Christopher
1971   Moundville and Surrounding Sites: Some Structural Considerations of Mortuary Practices II. In *Approaches to the Social Dimensions of Mortuary Practices*, edited by James A. Brown. Society for American Archaeology Memoirs 25:68–91.

Pepper, George H.
1906   Human Effigy Vases from Chaco Canyon, New Mexico. In *Boas Anniversary Volume*, pp. 320–34, American Museum of Natural History, New York.
1920   *Pueblo Bonito*. Anthropological Papers of the American Museum of Natural History 27, New York.

Pericot-García, Luis, John Galloway, and Andreas Lommel
1969   *Prehistoric and Primitive Art*. Thames and Hudson, London.

Pericot-García, Luis, John Galloway, and Leon Pales
1979   L'Abri Durif à Enval (Vic-le-Comte, Puy-de-Dome) II, Gravures et sculptures sur pierre. *Galla Prehist*. 22:113–142.

Perrin du Lac, François Marie
1817   *Travels Through the Two Louisianas, and Among the Savage Nations of the Missouri; Also, in the United States, along the Ohio, and the Adjacent Provinces, in 1801, 1802, and 1803*. R. Phillips, London.

Perrot, Jean
1984   Structures d'habitat, mode de vie, et environment. Les villages
              souterrains des pasteurs de Beersheba dans le sud d'Israël au IV
              millennium avant l'ère chrétien. *PaleoOrient* 10:75–96.
Peters, Emrys L.
1978   The Status of Women in Four Middle East Communities. In *Women
              in the Muslim World*, edited by Lois Beck and N. Keddie, pp. 311–
              350. Harvard University Press, Cambridge, Mass.
Peterson, Jane
1994   Changes in the Sexual Division of Labor in the Prehistory of the
              Southern Levant. Ph.D. dissertation, Department of Anthropol-
              ogy, Arizona State University. University Microfilms, Ann Arbor,
              Mich.
1997   Tracking Activity Patterns through Skeletal Remains: A Case Study
              from Jordan and Palestine. In *The Prehistory of Jordan II*, edited by
              H. G. Gebel, Z. Kafafi, and G. O. Rollefson. Berlin, Germany.
Petrie, W. M. Flinders
1900   *The Royal Tombs of the First Dynasty, Part I*. Egyptian Exploration
              Society. Kegan Paul, Trench, Trubner and Company, London.
1901a   *Diospolis Parva: The Cemeteries of Abadiyeh and Hu*. Egyptian Explora-
              tion Society. Kegan Paul, Trench, Trubner and Company, London.
1901b   *The Royal Tombs of the Earliest Dynasties, Part II*. Egyptian Exploration
              Society. Kegan Paul, Trench, Trubner and Company, London.
1902   *Abydos, Part I*. Egyptian Exploration Society. Kegan Paul, Trench,
              Trubner and Company, London.
1903   *Abydos, Part II*. Egyptian Exploration Society. Kegan Paul, Trench,
              Trubner and Company, London.
Petrie, W. M. Flinders, and J. E. Quibell
1896   *Naqada and Ballas*. Quaritch, London.
Phillips, Philip, and James A. Brown
1978   *Pre-Columbian Shell Engravings from the Craig Mount at Spiro, Okla-
              homa*. Peabody Museum of Archaeology and Ethnology, vols. 1–3,
              Cambridge, Mass.
Pinch, Geraldine
1993   *Votive Offerings to Hathor*. Griffith Institute, Ashmolean Museum,
              Oxford, U.K.
Pittman, Holly
1994   Towards an Understanding of the Role of Glyptic Imagery in the
              Administrative Systems of Proto-Literate Greater Mesopotamia. In
              Archives Before Writing, edited by Piera Ferioli, Enrica Fiandra, Gian
              Fissore, and Marcella Frangipane, pp. 177–203. Scriptorium,
              Turin, Italy.
Platon, N.
1971   *Zakros: The Discovery of a Lost Palace*. Charles Scribner's Sons, New
              York.
Plutarch
1936   *Moralia V*. Loeb Classical Library. Harvard University Press, Cam-
              bridge, Mass.
Podzorski, Patricia
1990   *Their Bones Shall Not Perish: An Examination of Predynastic Human*

Skeletal Remains from Naga-ed-Dêr in Egypt. SIA Publishing, Surrey, Kent, U.K.

Pollock, Susan
1983   The Symbolism of Prestige: An Archaeological Example from the Royal Cemetery of Ur. Ph.D. dissertation, Department of Anthropology, University of Michigan. University Microfilms, Ann Arbor, Mich.
1991   Women in a Men's World: Images of Sumerian Women. In *Engendering Archaeology: Women and Prehistory,* edited by Joan M. Gero and Margaret W. Conkey, pp. 366–387. Basil Blackwell, Oxford, U.K.
1999   *Mesopotamia: The Eden that Never Was.* Cambridge University Press, Cambridge, U.K. Forthcoming.

Pomeroy, Sarah B.
1990   *Women in Hellenistic Egypt from Alexander to Cleopatra.* Wayne State University Press, Detroit, Mich.

Popham, Mervyn R., and Margaret A. V. Gill
1995   *The Latest Sealings from the Palace and Houses at Knossos.* British School at Athens, Studies 1. Alden Press, Oxford, U.K.

Potts, A.
1990   Beautiful Bodies and Dying Heroes: Images of Heroic Manhood in the French Revolution. *History Workshop Journal* 30:1–21.

Poulsen, Birte
1992   The Written Sources. In *The Temple of Castor and Pollux I,* edited by Inge Nielsen and Birte Poulsen, pp. 54–60. De Luca for the Soprintendenza Archeological di Roma, Rome, Italy.

Powell, J. W.
1972   *The Hopi Villages: The Ancient Province of Tusayan.* Filter Press, Palmer Lake, Colo.

Price, Mary F.
1996   Community Begins at Home: Rethinking the Place of the Household in Archaeological Interpretive Models. Paper presented at the Fourth Gender and Archaeology Conference, Michigan State University, East Lansing, Mich.

Quirke, Stephen
1992   *Ancient Egyptian Religion.* British Museum, Avon, U.K.

Ramenofsky, Ann
1987   *Vectors of Death: The Archaeology of European Contact.* University of New Mexico Press, Albuquerque.

Rast, Walter E.
1981   Patterns of Settlement at Bab edh-Dhra. In *The Southeastern Dead Sea Plain Expedition,* edited by Walter E. Rast and R. Thomas Schaub, pp. 7–34. Annual of the American Schools of Oriental Research 46, American Schools of Oriental Research, Cambridge, Mass.

Rathbun, Ted A.
1984   Skeletal Pathology from the Paleolithic through the Metal Ages in Iran and Iraq. In *Pathology at the Origins of Agriculture,* edited by Richard Cohen and George Armelagos, pp. 137–167. Academic Press, New York.

Ray, Lt. Patrick H.
1988   Ethnographic Sketch of the Natives of Point Barrow in Murdoch,

John. *Ethnological Results of the Point Barrow Expedition.* Smithsonian Institution Press, Washington, D.C.

Redding, Richard
1989   A General Explanation of Subsistence Change: From Hunting and Gathering to Food Production. *Journal of Anthropological Archaeology* 7:56–97.

Redman, Charles L.
1978   *The Rise of Civilization: Early Farmers to Urban Society in the Ancient Near East.* Freeman, San Francisco.

Reeder, Ellen, ed.
1995   *Pandora.* Princeton University Press, Princeton, N.J.

Rehak, Paul
1995   Enthroned Figures in Aegean Art and the Function of the Mycenaean Megaron. In *The Role of the Ruler in the Prehistoric Aegean*, edited by Paul Rehak, pp. 95–118. Proceedings of a panel discussion presented at the annual meeting of the Archaeological Institute of America, New Orleans, Louisiana, 28 December 1992. University of Texas at Austin, Program in Aegean Scripts and Prehistory.
1996a   The Construction of Gender in Late Bronze Age Aegean Art: A Prolegomenon. Paper presented at the Third Australian Women in Archaeology Conference, Sydney, Australia.
1996b   Aegean Breechcloths, Kilts, and the Keftiu Paintings. *American Journal of Archaeology* 100:35–51.

Reichard, Gladys A.
1950   *Navajo Religion: A Study in Symbolism.* Princeton University Press, Princeton, N.J.

Reinhard, Karl J., Larry Tieszen, Karin L. Sandness, Lynae M. Beiningen, Elizabeth Miller, A. Mohammad Ghazi, Christiana E. Miewald, and Sandra V. Barnum
1994   Trade, Contact, and Female Health in Northeast Nebraska. In *In the Wake of Contact: Biological Responses to Conquest*, edited by Clark S. Larsen and George R. Milner, pp. 63–74. Wiley-Liss, New York.

Rice, Patricia C.
1981   Prehistoric Venuses: Symbols of Motherhood or Womanhood? *Journal of Anthropological Research* 7 (4):402–416.

Rich, Adrienne C.
1976   *Of Woman Born: Motherhood as Experience and Institution.* Norton, New York.

Riches, David
1982   *Northern Nomadic Hunter-Gatherers: A Humanistic Approach.* Academic Press, New York.

Richlin, Amy
1998   Foucault's History of Sexuality: A Useful Theory for Women? In *Rethinking Sexuality: Foucault and Classical Antiquity*, edited by D. H. J. Larmour, P. A. Miller, and C. Platter, pp. 138–170. Princeton University Press, Princeton, N.J.

Rindos, David
1980   Symbiosis, Instability, and the Origins and Spread of Agriculture: A New Model. *Current Anthropology* 21:751–772.

Roach-Higgins, Mary Ellen, and Joanne B. Eicher
1992   Dress and Identity. *Clothing and Textiles Research Journal* 10 (4):1–8.

Robarchek, Clayton A.
1994   Plains Warfare and the Anthropology of War. In *Skeletal Biology in the Great Plains: Migration, Warfare, Health, and Subsistence,* edited by Douglas W. Owsley and Richard L. Jantz, pp. 307–316. Smithsonian Institution Press, Washington, D.C.

Robb, John
1994   Issues in the Skeletal Interpretation of Muscle Attachments. Paper presented at the Annual Meeting of the Paleoanthropology Society, Anaheim, Calif.
1997   Violence and Gender in Early Italy. In *Troubled Times: Osteological and Archaeological Evidence of Violence,* edited by Anne Olga Kosloski-Ostrow and Claire L. Lyons, pp. 43–65. Routledge, New York.

Robins, Gay
1989   Some Images of Women in New Kingdom Art. In *Women's Earliest Records from Ancient Egypt and Western Asia,* edited by Barbara Lesko, pp. 109–110. Scholars Press, Atlanta, Ga.
1993   *Women in Ancient Egypt.* Harvard University Press, Cambridge, Mass.
1994   Some Principles of Compositional Dominance and Gender Hierarchy in Ancient Egypt. *Journal of the American Research Center in Egypt* 31:33–40.
1996   Dress, Undress, and the Representation of Fertility and Potency in New Kingdom Egyptian Art. In *Sexuality and Ancient Art,* edited by Natalie Boymel Kampen. Cambridge University Press, New York.

Rogers, J. Daniel
1990   *Objects of Change: The Archaeology and History of Arikara Contact with Europeans.* Smithsonian Institution Press, Washington, D.C.

Roscoe, Will
1991   *The Zuni Man-Woman.* University of New Mexico Press, Albuquerque.

Rosenfeld, Andrée
1977   Profile Figures: Schematization of the Human Figure in the Magdalenian Culture of Europe. In *Form in Indigenous Art,* edited by Peter J. Ucko. Humanities Press, Atlantic Highlands, N.J.

Roth, Ann Macy
1992   The *Ps-kf* and the Opening of the Mouth Ceremony: A Ritual of Birth and Rebirth. *Journal of Egyptian Archaeology* 78:113–147.
1993   Fingers, Stars, and the Opening of the Mouth: The Nature and Function of the *Ntrwj* Blades. *Journal of Egyptian Archaeology* 79:57–79.
1994   The Absent Spouse: Patterns and Taboos in Egyptian Tomb Decoration. Paper presented at the Annual Meeting of the American Research Center in Egypt (Toronto, Canada).

Roth, Ann Macy, and Catharine Roehrig
n.d.   Magical Bricks and Bricks of Birth. Unpublished manuscript in possession of the authors (1998).

Roth, H. Ling
1974   *Studies in Primitive Looms.* Burt Franklin Reprints, New York. (Origi-

nal publication 1918, Journal of the Royal Anthropological Institute, vols. 46–48.)

Rowe, Ann Pollard
1981   *A Century of Change in Guatemalan Textiles.* Center for Inter-American Relations, New York.

Ruff, Christopher
1994   Biomechanical Analysis of Northern and Southern Plains Femora: Behavioral Implications. In *Skeletal Biology in the Great Plains: Migration, Warfare, Health and Subsistence,* edited by Douglas W. Owsley and Richard L. Jantz, pp. 235–245. Smithsonian Institution Press, Washington, D.C.

Ruscheinsky, Lynn
1996   Display of Gender Identity and Social Reproduction in Mayan Figurines. Paper presented at the Fourth Gender and Archaeology Conference, Michigan State University, East Lansing, Mich.

Rutkowski, Bogden
1986   *Cult Places of the Aegean.* Yale University Press, New Haven, Conn.

Sacks, Karen
1974   Engels Revisited: Women, the Organization of Production, and Private Property. In *Woman, Culture, and Society,* edited by Michelle Rosaldo and Louise Lamphere, pp. 207–222. Stanford University Press, Stanford, Calif.

Salter, Elizabeth Mary
1984   Skeletal Biology of Cumberland Sound, Baffin Island, NWT. Ph.D. dissertation, Department of Anthropology, University of Toronto, Ontario, Canada.

Sampson, Edward
1993   *Celebrating the Other: A Dialogic Account of Human Nature.* Harvester Wheatsheaf, New York.

Saunders, J. B. de C. M.
1963   *The Transitions from Ancient Egyptian to Greek Medicine.* University of Kansas Press, Lawrence.

Savage, Stephen H.
1995   Descent, Power, and Competition in Predynastic Egypt: Mortuary Evidence from Cemetery N7000 at Naga-ed-Dêr. Ph.D. dissertation, Arizona State University. University Microfilms, Ann Arbor, Mich.
In press a   Descent Group Competition and Economic Strategies in Predynastic Egypt. *Journal of Anthropological Archaeology* 23.
In press b   AMS 14 Carbon Dates from the Predynastic Egyptian Cemetery, N7000, at Naga-ed-Der. *Journal of Archaeological Science.* Forthcoming.

Sawicki, Jana
1991   *Disciplining Foucault: Feminism, Power and the Body.* Routledge, New York.

Saxe, Arthur A.
1970   Social Dimensions of Mortuary Practices. Ph.D. dissertation, University of Michigan. University Microfilms, Ann Arbor, Mich.

Schaafsma, Polly
1980   *Indian Rock Art of the Southwest.* University of New Mexico Press, Albuquerque.

Schaefer, Stacy B.
1989   The Loom and Time in the Huichol World. *Journal of Latin American Lore* 15:179–194.
1993   The Loom as a Sacred Power Object in Huichol Culture. In *Art in Small-Scale Societies: Contemporary Readings*, edited by Richard L. Anderson and Karen Field, pp. 118–130. Prentice-Hall, Englewood Cliffs, N.J.

Schaub, R. Thomas, and Walter E. Rast
1984   Preliminary Report of the 1981 Expedition to the Dead Sea Plain, Jordan. *Bulletin of the American Schools of Oriental Research* 254:35–60.

Scheid, John, and Jesper Svenbro
1996   *The Craft of Zeus.* Translated from the French by Carol Volk. Harvard University Press, Cambridge, Mass.

Schevill, Margot Blum
1993   *Maya Textiles of Guatemala.* University of Texas Press, Austin.

Schlegel, Alice
1977   Male and Female in Hopi Thought and Action. In *Sexual Stratification: A Cross-Cultural View*, edited by Alice Schlegel, pp. 245–269. Columbia University Press, New York.

Schmandt-Besserat, Denise
1993   Images of Enship. In *Between the Rivers and Over the Mountains: Archaeologica Anatolica et Mesopotamica Alba Palmieri Dedicata*, edited by Marcella Frangipane, Harald Hauptmann, Mario Liverani, Paolo Matthiae, and Machteld Mellink, pp. 201–219. Università di Roma "La Sapienza," Rome, Italy.

Schoenholz, Deborah
1996   A Multimedia Scale for Locating Gender Bias in Archaeology. Paper presented at the Fourth Gender and Archaeology Conference, Michigan State University, East Lansing, Mich.

Scott, Joan
1986   Gender: A Useful Category of Historical Analysis. *American Historical Review* 91 (5):1053–1075.
1996   *Feminism and History.* Oxford University Press, New York.

Scully, Vincent
1989   *Pueblo: Mountain, Village, Dance.* University of Chicago Press, Chicago.

Seltman, Charles
1956   *Women in Antiquity.* Thames and Hudson, New York.

Shafer, Harry J.
1982   Classic Mimbres Phase Households and Room Use Patterns. *The Kiva*, 48 (1–2):17–37.

Shafer, Harry J., and Robbie L. Brewington
1995   Microstylistic Changes in Mimbres Black-on-White Pottery: Examples from the NAN Ruin, Grant County, New Mexico. *The Kiva* 61:5–29.

Shaffer, Brian S., and Karen M. Gardner
1995a   The Rabbit Drive Through Time: Analysis of the North American Ethnographic and Prehistoric Evidence. *Utah Archaeology* 8:13–25.
1995b   The Fish-Carrying Pole of the Mimbres: A Perishable Technology Preserved on Pottery. *The Artifact* 33 (2):1–7.

Shaffer, Brian S., Karen M. Gardner, and Barry W. Baker
1996   Prehistoric Small Game Snare Trap Technology, Deployment Strategy, and Trapper Gender Depicted in Mimbres Pottery. *Journal of Ethnobiology* 16 (2):145–155.

Shaffer, Brian S., Karen M. Gardner, and Harry J. Shafer
1997   An Unusual Birth Depicted in Mimbres Pottery: Not Cracked Up to What It Is Supposed to Be. *American Antiquity* 62 (4):727–732.

Shaffer, Brian S., Holly A. Nicholson, and Karen M. Gardner
1995   Possible Mimbres Documentation of Pueblo Snake Ceremonies in the Eleventh Century. *North American Archaeologist* 16 (1):17–32.

Shanks, Michael, and Christopher Tilley
1982   Ideology, Symbolic Power and Ritual Communication: A Reinterpretation of Neolithic Mortuary Practices, In *The Archaeology of Contextual Meaning*, edited by Ian Hodder, pp. 129–154. Cambridge University Press, Cambridge, U.K.

Shennan, Stephen
1990   *Quantifying Archaeology*. Academic Press, New York.

Sherratt, Andrew
1981   Plough and Pastoralism. In *Patterns of the Past*, edited by Ian Hodder, Glynn Isaac, and Norman Hammond, pp. 261–306. Cambridge University Press, Cambridge, U.K.

Shore, Bradd
1981   Sexuality and Gender in Samoa: Conceptions and Missed Conceptions. In *Sexual Meanings: The Cultural Construction of Gender and Sexuality*, edited by Sherry B. Ortner and Harriet Whitehead, pp. 192–215. Cambridge University Press, Cambridge, U.K.

Silverblatt, Irene
1988   Women in States. *Annual Review of Anthropology* 17:427–460.

Simpson, William K., ed.
1974   *The Literature of Ancient Egypt*. Yale University Press, New Haven.

Sjoo, Monica
1975   *The Great Cosmic Mother: Rediscovering the Religion of the Earth*. Harper and Row, San Francisco.

Smith, G. Hubert
1936   Jean Baptiste Trudeau's Remarks on the Indians of the Upper Missouri, 1794–1795. *American Anthropologist* 38:565–568.

Smith, Patricia
1989   The Skeletal Biology and Paleopathology of Early Bronze Age Populations in the Levant. In *L'urbanisation de la Palestine à l'âge du bronze ancien*, edited by P. de Miroschedji, pp. 297–313. BAR International Series 527 (2), Oxford, U.K.

Smith, Patricia, Ronald A. Bloom, and Judith Berkowitz
1984   Diachronic Trends in Humeral Cortical Thickness of Near East Populations. *Journal of Human Evolution* 13:603–611.

Smith, Patricia, and L. K. Horwitz
1984   Radiographic Evidence for Changing Patterns of Animal Exploitation in the Southern Levant. *Journal of Archaeological Science* 11: 467–475.

Smith, Phillip E. L.
1976   *Food Production and Its Consequences*. Cummings, Menlo Park, Calif.

Snodgrass, O. T.
1977   *Realistic Art and Times of the Mimbres Indians.* Privately printed, O. T.
            Snodgrass, El Paso, Tex.

Soffer, Olga
1987   Upper Paleolithic Connubia, Refugia, and the Archaeological
            Record from Eastern Europe. In *The Pleistocene Old World: Regional
            Perspectives*, edited by Olga Soffer, pp. 333–348. Plenum Press, New
            York.

Sokal, Robert R., and F. James Rohlf
1981   *Biometry.* 2nd ed. W. H. Freeman, New York.

Sourvinou-Inwood, Christiane
1973   The Young Abductor of the Locrian Pinakes. *Bulletin of the Institute
            of Classical Studies, University of London* 20:12–20.

1987a   A Series of Erotic Pursuits: Images and Meanings. *Journal of Hellenic
            Studies* 108:131–153.

1987b   Menace and Pursuit: Differentiation and the Creation of Meaning.
            In *Images et Societé en Grèce Ancienne*, edited by Claude Bérard, Chris-
            tiane Bron, and A. Pomari, pp. 41–58. Université de Lausanne,
            Lausanne, Switzerland.

Spector, Janet D.
1982   Male/Female Task Differentiation Among the Hidatsa: Toward
            the Development of an Archaeological Approach to the Study of
            Gender. In *The Hidden Half*, edited by Beatrice Medicine and Pa-
            tricia Albers, pp. 77–99. University Press of America, Washington,
            D.C.

Sperlich, Norbert, and Elizabeth Katz Sperlich
1980   *Guatemalan Backstrap Weaving.* University of Oklahoma Press,
            Norman.

Spier, Leslie
1928   Havasupai Ethnography. *Anthropological Papers of the American Mu-
            seum of Natural History* 29:83–392.

Stager, Lawrence E.
1992   The Periodization of Palestine from Neolithic Through Early
            Bronze Times. In *Chronologies in Old World Archaeology*, edited by
            R. W. Ehrich, pp. 22–41. University of Chicago Press, Chicago.

Stark, Barbara L.
1986   Origins of Food Production in the New World. In *American Archae-
            ology, Past and Future*, edited by David J. Meltzer, Donald D. Fowler,
            and Jeremy A. Sabloff, pp. 277–321. Smithsonian Institution Press,
            Washington, D.C.

Stearn, Ester W., and Allen E. Stearn
1945   *The Effect of Smallpox on the Destiny of the American Indian.* B. Hum-
            phries, Boston.

Stefansson, Vilhjalmur
1926   *My Life with the Eskimo.* Macmillan, New York.

Stehle, Eva
1990   Sappho's Gaze: Fantasies of a Goddess and a Young Man. *differences*
            2 (1):88–125.

Stephen, Alexander
1936   *Hopi Journal.* Edited by Elsie Clewes Parsons. Columbia University
            Press, New York.

Stevenson, Mathilda Coxe
1904   The Zuni Indians: Their Mythology, Esoteric Fraternities, and Cer-
            emonies. *Twenty-third Annual Report of the Bureau of American Ethnol-
            ogy*, pp. 3–634. Smithsonian Institution Press, Washington, D.C.
Stewart, Andrew
1995a   Rape? In *Pandora*, edited by Ellen Reeder, pp. 74–90. Princeton
            University Press, Princeton, N.J.
1995b   Imag(in)ing the Other: Amazons and Ethnicity in Fifth-Century
            Athens. *Poetics Today* 16:571–597.
Stirland, Ann
1991   Diagnosis of Occupationally Related Paleopathology: Can it Be
            Done? In *Human PaleoPathology*, edited by Donald J. Ortner and
            A. C. Aufderheide, pp. 40–47. Smithsonian Institution Press,
            Washington, D.C.
1993   Asymmetry and Activity-Related Change in the Male Humerus.
            International Journal of Osteoarchaeology 3:105–113.
Stirling, Matthew
1942   *Origin Myth of Acoma and Other Records.* Bureau of American Ethnol-
            ogy Bulletin 135. Smithsonian Institution, Washington, D.C.
Stone, Andrea
1990   The Two Faces of Eve: The Grandmother and the Unfaithful Wife
            as a Paradigm in Maya Art. Paper presented at the Eighty-ninth
            Annual Meeting of the American Anthropological Association,
            New Orleans.
Stone-Ferrier, Linda
1989   Spun Virtue, the Lacework of Folly, and the World Wound Upside-
            Down. In *Cloth and the Human Experience*, edited by Annette Weiner
            and Jane Schneider, pp. 215–242. Smithsonian Institution Press,
            Washington, D.C.
Storm, Penny
1987   *Functions of Dress: Tool of Culture and the Individual.* Prentice-Hall,
            Englewood Cliffs, N.J.
Strathern, Andrew
1996   *Body Thoughts.* University of Michigan Press, Ann Arbor.
Strommenger, Eva
1980   *Habuba Kabira: Eine Stadt vor 5000 Jahren.* Philipp von Zabern,
            Mainz, Germany.
Strong, Donald E., and John B. Ward-Perkins
1962   The Temple of Castor in the Forum Romanum. *Papers of the British
            School at Rome* 30 n.s. 17:1–30.
Sudhoff, Karl
1926   *Geschichte der Zahnheilkunde.* 2nd ed. Johann Ambrosius Barth,
            Leipzig, Germany.
Sullivan, Thelma D.
1982   Tlaxolteotl-Ixcuina: The Great Spinner and Weaver. In *The Art and
            Iconography of Late Post-Classic Central Mexico*, edited by Elizabeth
            Hill Boone, pp. 7–35. Dumbarton Oaks, Washington, D.C.
Sunder, John E.
1965   *The Fur Trade on the Upper Missouri, 1840–1865.* University of Okla-
            homa Press, Norman.

Tabanelli, Mario N.
1963   *La Medicina nel Mondo degli Etruschi.* L. S. Olschki, Firenze, Italy.
Tabeau, Pierre-Antoine
1939   *Tabeau's Narrative of Loisel's Expedition to the Upper Missouri,* edited by Annie H. Abel. University of Oklahoma Press, Norman.
Tainter, Joseph
1973   The Social Correlates of Mortuary Patterning at Kaloko, North Kono, Hawaii. *Archaeology and Physical Anthropology in Oceania* 8:1–11.
1978   Mortuary Practices and the Study of Prehistoric Social Systems. *Advances in Archaeological Method and Theory* 4:106–136. Academic Press, New York.
1980   Behavior and Status in a Middle Woodland Mortuary Population from the Illinois Valley. *American Antiquity* 45:308–313.
Talalay, Lauren E.
In press a   Visual Metaphors: Half-body Images from Neolithic Greece. In *Materials for a History of the Human Body in the Ancient Near East,* edited by Terry G. Wilfong and Charles E. Jones, Styx Publications, Groningen, Netherlands.
In press b   Archaeological Ms. Conceptions: The Iconography of Power in Mediterranean Prehistory. In *Gender and Material Culture: Representations of Gender from Prehistory to Present,* vol. 2, edited by Moira Donald and Linda M. Hurcombe. Macmillan, London.
1994   A Feminist Boomerang: The Great Goddess of Greek Prehistory. *Gender and History* 6:165–183.
1996   Women, Gender and Aegean Prehistory: A View From The Front Line. Paper presented at the Fourth Gender and Archaeology Conference, Michigan State University, East Lansing.
Tapper, Nancy
1978   The Women's Subsociety Among the Shahseven Nomads of Iran. In *Women in the Muslim World,* edited by Lois Beck and N. Keddie, pp. 374–398. Harvard University Press, Cambridge, Mass.
Tavakalian, B.
1984   Women and Socio-Economic Change among Sheikhanzai Nomads of Western Afghanistan. *Middle East Journal* 38:433–453.
Taylor, Joseph H.
1897   *Sketches of Frontier and Indian Life.* Historical Society of North Dakota, Bismarck.
Thomas, Julian
1993   The Hermeneutics of Megalithic Space. In *Interpretive Archaeology,* edited by Christopher Tilley, pp. 73–97. Berg, Oxford, U.K.
Tobey, Jennifer
1996   Beyond the Walls: Integrating the House into Deg hit'an Society. Paper presented at the Fourth Gender and Archaeology Conference, Michigan State University, East Lansing, Mich.
Torbrugge, Walter
1968   *Prehistoric European Art.* Harry N. Abrams, New York.
Treggiari, Susan M.
1978   Rome: Urban Labour. In *Seventh International Economic History Conference, Edinburgh 1978* [no editor noted], pp. 162–165. Lewis Reprints, Tonbridge, U.K.

1979   Lower Class Women in the Roman Economy. *Florilegium* I:65–86.

1980   Urban Labour in Rome: Mercennarii and Tabernarii. In *Non-Slave Labour in the Graeco-Roman World*, Supplementary vol. 6, edited by Peter Garnsey, pp. 48–64. Cambridge Philological Society, Cambridge, U.K.

Trigger, Bruce G.

1983   The Rise of Egyptian Civilization. In *Ancient Egypt: A Social History*, contributions by Bruce G. Trigger, Barry J. Kemp, David O'Connor, and Alan B. Lloyd, pp. 1–70. Cambridge University Press, Cambridge, U.K.

1993   *Early Civilizations: Ancient Egypt in Context*. American University in Cairo Press, Cairo, Egypt.

Trimble, Michael K.

1979   An Ethnohistorical Interpretation of the Spread of Smallpox in the Northern Plains Utilizing Concepts of Disease Ecology. National Park Service, Midwest Archaeological Center, Lincoln, Neb.

1987   Infectious Disease and the Northern Plains Horticulturalists: A Human Behavioral Model. *Plains Anthropologist Memoir* 23:115–125.

Trobriand, Phillipe Regis Denis de Keredern de

1941   *Army Life in Dakota: Selections from the Journal of Philippe Regis Denis de Keredern de Trobriand*. Lakeside Press, Chicago.

Troy, Lana

1986   *Patterns of Queenship in Ancient Egyptian Myth and History*. Almquist and Wiksell, Stockholm, Sweden.

Turner, Bryan S.

1996   *The Body and Society*. Sage, London.

Tuross, Noreen, and Marilyn L. Fogel

1994   Stable Isotope Analysis and Subsistence Patterns at the Sully Site. In *Skeletal Biology in the Great Plains: Migration Warfare, Health, and Subsistence*, edited by Douglas W. Owsley and Richard L. Jantz, pp. 283–289. Smithsonian Institution Press, Washington, D.C.

Ubelaker, Douglas H.

1989   *Human Skeletal Remains: Excavation, Analysis, Interpretation*. Taraxacum, Washington, D.C.

Ubelaker, Douglas H., and Pat Willey

1978   Complexity in Arikara Mortuary Practice. *Plains Anthropologist* 23:69–74.

Underhill, Ruth

1991   *Life in the Pueblos*. Ancient City Press, Santa Fe, N.M.

Urla, J., and A. Swedlund

1995   The Anthropometry of Barbie: Unsettling Ideas of the Feminine Body in Popular Culture. In *Deviant Bodies: Critical Perspectives on Difference in Science and Popular Culture*, edited by J. Terry and J. Urla. Indiana University Press, Bloomington.

Vandier, Jacques

1962   *Le Papyrus Jumilhac*. Centre National de la Recherche Scientifique, Paris, France.

Van Walsem, Ren

1978   The *Ps-kf*: An Investigation of an Ancient Egyptian Funerary Instrument. *OMRO* 59:193–249.

Verlinden, Colette
1984   *Les statuettes anthropomorphes crétoises en bronze et en plomb, du IIIe millénaire au VIIe siècle av. J.-C.* Collège Erasme, Louvain-la-Neuve, France.
Vicary, Grace
1988   The Signs of Clothing. *Cross-Cultural Perspectives in Nonverbal Communication*, edited by F. Poyatos, pp. 291–314. Hogrefe, Toronto, Ontario, Canada.
Voth, H. R.
1905   The Traditions of the Hopi. Field Museum Publication 96. Anthropological Series, vol. 8, Chicago.
Waarsenburg, Demetrius
1994   *The Northwest Necropolis of Satricum: An Iron Age Cemetery in Latium Vetus.* Ph.D. dissertation, Faculty of Letters, University of Amsterdam, Netherlands.
Waetzoldt, Hartmut
1972   *Untersuchungen zur Neusumerischen Textilindustrie.* Centro per le Antichità e la Storia dell'Arte del Vicino Oriente, Rome, Italy.
Walde, Dale, and Noreen D. Willows, eds.
1991   *The Archaeology of Gender: Proceedings of the Twenty-second Annual Conference of the Archaeological Association of the University of Calgary.* The Archaeological Association of the University of Calgary, Alberta, Canada.
Walker, Phillip L.
1986   Porotic Hyperostosis in a Marine-Dependent California Indian Population. *American Journal of Physical Anthropology* 69:345–354.
Walker, Phillip L., and Sandra E. Hollimon
1989   Changes in Osteoarthritis Associated with the Development of a Maritime Economy Among Southern California Indians. *International Journal of Anthropology* 4 (3):171–183.
Walker, Phillip L., and Patricia Lambert
1989   Skeletal Evidence for Stress During a Period of Cultural Change in Prehistoric California. In *Advances in Paleopathology*, Journal of Paleopathology Monographic Publication 1, edited by Luigi Capasso, pp. 207–212. Mario Solfanelli, Chieti, Italy.
Wall, Diana diZerega
1994   *The Archaeology of Gender: Separating the Spheres in Urban America.* Plenum Press, New York.
Watanabe, Hitoshi
1968   Subsistence and Ecology of Northern Food Gatherers with Special Reference to the Ainu. In *Man the Hunter*, edited by Richard B. Lee and I. Devore, pp. 69–77. Aldine Publishing Company, Chicago.
Watson, Patty Jo
1978   Architectural Differentiation in Some Near Eastern Communities, Prehistoric and Contemporary. In *Social Archaeology: Beyond Subsistence and Dating*, edited by Charles L. Redman, pp. 131–158. Academic Press, New York.
1979a   *Archaeological Ethnography in Western Iran.* Viking Fund Publications in Anthropology 57, Wenner-Gren Foundation, New York.
1979b   The Idea of Ethnoarchaeology: Notes and Comments. In *Ethno-*

archaeology, edited by Carol Kramer, pp. 277–287. Columbia University Press, New York.

Watterson, Barbara
1991   *Women in Ancient Egypt*. St. Martin's Press, New York.

Weglian, Emily J.
1996   Gender Stereotypes in Temperate European Prehistoric Cemetery Analyses. Paper presented at the Fourth Gender and Archaeology Conference, Michigan State University, East Lansing, Mich.

Weineck, J.
1986   *Functional Anatomy in Sports*. Year Book Medical Publishers, Chicago.

Weingarten, J.
1983   The Zakros Master and His Place in Prehistory. *Studies in Mediterranean Archaeology*, Pocket-book 26, Göteborg, Sweden.
1986   The Sealing Structures of Minoan Crete: MMII Phaistos to the Destruction of the Palace of Knossos, part I. *Oxford Journal of Art* 5:279–296.
1988   The Sealing Structures of Minoan Crete: MMII Phaistos to the Destruction of the Palace of Knossos, part II. *Oxford Journal of Art* 7:1–25.
1992   The Multiple Sealing System of Minoan Crete and its Possible Antecedents in Anatolia. *Oxford Journal of Art* 11:25–37.

Weist, Katherine M.
1983   Beasts of Burden and Menial Slaves: Nineteenth-Century Observations of Northern Plains Indian Women. In *The Hidden Half: Studies of Plains Indian Women*, edited by Patricia Albers and Beatrice Medicine, pp. 29–52. University Press of America, Lanham, Md.

Westendorf, W.
1967   Bemerkungen Zur "Kammer der Wiedergeburt" Im Tutanchamungrab. *ZäS* 94:139–150.

Westenholz, Joan Goodnick
1990   Towards a New Conceptualization of the Female Role in Mesopotamian Society. *Journal of the American Oriental Society* 110:510–521.

Weyer, Edward M., Jr.
1932   *The Eskimos: Their Environment and Folkways*. Yale University Press, New Haven.

Whelan, Mary K.
1991   Gender and Archaeology: Mortuary Studies and the Search for the Origins of Gender Differentiation. In *The Archaeology of Gender: Proceedings of the Twenty-second Annual Conference of the Archaeological Association of the University of Calgary*, edited by Dale Walde and Noreen D. Willows, pp. 366–374. Archaeological Association of the University of Calgary, Alberta, Canada.

White, E. H.
1978   Legal Reforms as Indicators of Women's Status in Muslim Nations. In *Women in the Muslim World*, edited by Lois Beck and N. Keddie, pp. 52–68. Harvard University Press, Cambridge, Mass.

White, Leslie, A.
1962   *The Pueblo of Sia, New Mexico*. Bureau of American Ethnology, Bulletin 184, Washington, D.C.

White, Randall
 1996   Comment. *Current Anthropology* 37 (2):264–267.
Wilfong, Terry G., and Charles E. Jones, eds.
 In press   *Materials for a History of the Human Body in the Ancient Near East.* Styx
             Publications, Gröningen, Netherlands.
Wilkinson, Richard
 1992   *Reading Egyptian Art.* Thames and Hudson, New York.
Will, George F., and George E. Hyde
 1964   *Corn Among the Indians of the Upper Missouri.* University of Nebraska
             Press, Lincoln.
Willey, Pat
 1982   Osteology of the Crow Creek Massacre. Ph.D. dissertation, Univer-
             sity of Tennessee, Knoxville. University Microfilms, Ann Arbor,
             Mich.
 1990   *Prehistoric Warfare on the Great Plains.* Garland Press, New York.
Winter, Irene
 1985   After the Battle Is Over: The *Stele of the Vultures* and the Beginning
             of Historical Narrative in the Art of the Ancient Near East. In
             Pictorial Narrative in Antiquity and the Middle Ages, edited by H. Kess-
             ler and M. Simpson, pp. 11–32. National Gallery of Art, Wash-
             ington, D.C.
 1987   Women in Public: The Disk of Enheduanna, the Beginning of the
             Office of En-Priestess, and the Weight of Visual Evidence. In *La
             femme dans le proche-orient antique,* edited by Jean-Marie Durand, pp.
             189–201. Éditions Recherche sur les Civilisations, Paris, France.
 1996   Sex, Rhetoric and the Public Monument: The Alluring Body of
             Naram-sin of Agade. In *Sexuality in Ancient Art: Near East, Egypt,
             Greece and Italy,* edited by N. Kampen, pp. 11–26. Cambridge Uni-
             versity Press, Cambridge, U.K.
Wirhed, R.
 1984   *Athletic Ability and the Anatomy of Motion.* Wolfe Medical Publishers,
             London.
Wobst, H. Martin
 1977   Stylistic Behavior and Information Exchange. In *For the Director:
             Research Essays in Honor of James B. Griffin.* Anthropological Papers
             61, edited by Charles L. Cleland, pp. 317–342. Museum of Anthro-
             pology, University of Michigan, Ann Arbor, Mich.
Wood, W. Raymond
 1980   Plains Trade in Prehistoric and Protohistoric Intertribal Relations.
             In *Anthropology of the Great Plains,* edited by W. Raymond Wood and
             Margo Liberty, pp. 98–109. University of Nebraska Press, Lincoln.
Wright, Rita P.
 1991   Women's Labor and Pottery Production in Prehistory. In *Engender-
             ing Archaeology: Women and Prehistory,* edited by Joan M. Gero and
             Margaret W. Conkey, pp. 194–223. Basil Blackwell, Oxford, U.K.
 1996   Introduction: Gendered Ways of Knowing in Archaeology. In *Gen-
             der and Archaeology,* edited by Rita P. Wright, pp. 1–19. University of
             Pennsylvania Press, Philadelphia.
Wylie, Alison
 1991a   Gender Theory and the Archaeological Record: Why Is There
             No Archaeology of Gender? In *Engendering Archaeology,* edited by

Joan M. Gero and Margaret W. Conkey, pp. 31–54. Basil Blackwell, Oxford, U.K.
1991b   Feminist Critiques and Archaeological Challenges. In *The Archaeology of Gender: Proceedings of the Twenty-second Annual Conference of the Archaeological Association of the University of Calgary*, edited by Dale Walde and Noreen D. Willows, pp. 17–23. Archaeological Association of the University of Calgary, Alberta, Canada.

Xenophon
1979   *Memorabilia and Oeconomicus.* Translated by E. C. Marchant. Harvard University Press, Cambridge, Mass.

Yates, Timothy
1993   Frameworks for an Archaeology of the Body. In *Interpretive Archaeology*, edited by Christopher Tilley, pp. 31–72. Berg, Oxford, U.K.

Young, M. Jane
1987   Women, Reproduction, and Religion in Western Puebloan Society. *Journal of American Folklore* 100:436–445.
1988   *Signs from the Ancestors: Zuni Cultural Symbolism and Perceptions of Rock Art.* University of New Mexico Press, Albuquerque.

Younger, John G.
1992   Representations of Minoan-Mycenaean Jewelry. In *Eikon: Aegean Bronze Age Iconography: Shaping a Methodology, Proceedings of the Fourth International Aegean Conference*, edited by Robert Laffineur and Janice L. Crowley, pp. 257–293. Universite de Liege, Liege, Belgium.
1997   Gender and Sexuality in the Parthenon Frieze. In *Naked Truths: Women, Sexuality, and Gender in Classical Art and Archaeology*, edited by Ann Olga Koloski-Ostrow and Claire L. Lyons, pp. 120–153. Routledge, New York.

Yoyotte, J.
1962   Les os et la sémence masculine: Propos d'une théorie physiologique égyptienne. *Bulletin d'Institut Français d'Archéologie Orientale* 61:139–146.

Zagarell, Allen
1986   Trade, Women, Class, and Society in Ancient Western Asia. *Current Anthropology* 27:415–430.

Zandee, Jan
1960   *Death as an Enemy According to Ancient Egyptian Conceptions.* E. J. Brill, Leiden, Netherlands.

Zeitlin, Froma
1984   The Dynamics of Misogyny: Myth and Mythmaking in the Oresteia. In *Women in the Ancient World: The Arethusa Papers*, edited by John Peradotto and J. P. Sullivan, pp. 159–194. State University of New York Press, Albany.
1986   Configurations of Rape in Greek Myth. In *Rape*, edited by Sylvana Tomaselli and Roy Porter, pp. 122–151. Basil Blackwell, Oxford, U.K.

Zimmerman, Larry J.
1985   *Peoples of Prehistoric South Dakota.* University of Nebraska Press, Lincoln.

Contributors

Margaret Beck, Department of Anthropology, University of Arizona.

Marshall Joseph Becker, Department of Anthropology and Sociology, West Chester University.

Reinhard Bernbeck, Department of Anthropology, State University of New York, Binghamton.

Barbara A. Crass, Department of Anthropology, University of Wisconsin, Madison.

Karen M. Gardner, Zooarchaeology Laboratory, Department of Anthropology, University of North Texas.

Senta C. German, Department of Art and Art History, Hope College.

Kelley Hays-Gilpin, Department of Anthropology, Northern Arizona University.

Sandra E. Hollimon, Department of Anthropology, Sonoma State University.

Alice B. Kehoe, Department of Social and Cultural Sciences, Marquette University.

Mireille M. Lee, Department of Archaeology, Bryn Mawr College.

Timothy J. McNiven, Department of History of Art and Classics, Ohio State University, Marion.

Lynn M. Meskell, Department of Anthropology, Columbia University.

Jane D. Peterson, Department of Social and Behavioral Science, Marquette University.

Susan Pollock, Department of Anthropology, State University of New York, Binghamton.

Joseph F. Powell, Zooarchaeology Laboratory, Department of Anthropology, University of North Texas.

Alison E. Rautman, Department of Anthropology, Michigan State University.

Ann Macy Roth, Department of Classics, Howard University.
Stephen H. Savage, Department of Anthropology, Arizona State University.
Brian S. Shaffer, Zooarchaeology Laboratory, Department of Anthropology, University of North Texas.
Lauren E. Talalay, Kelsey Museum and Department of Classical Studies, University of Michigan.

Index

abduction scenes, 126, 127, 128, 129, 130; ritual, 127. *See also* violence
Abri de Megarnie site, 212
Abri Pataud site, 203, 206
abuse, 64. *See also* violence
Acoma pueblo, 167, 183
activities, 2, 4, 5, 7, 9, 10, 20, 40, 41, 42, 44, 45, 56, 64, 66, 68, 77, 116, 119, 140, 142, 153, 155, 159, 170, 185; ceremonial, 148; cult, 105; economic, 68, 69, 70, 76, 118, 137; female, 4, 134, 135, 145–149; gendered, 159, 160; male, 104, 143, 144, 149; physical, 119; repetitive, 161; ritual, 171; sexual, 107
activity levels, females, 45, 46, 51
activity reconstructions, 46–48, 51–54
adornment, 83, 109, 168. *See also* dress, jewelry, hair
Adveevo site, 205
Aegean, 6, 8, 95ff; Aegean Bronze Age, 103, 109
Aegean ideas (construction) of gender and sexuality, 104, 107, 119
Aegina, 128
afterlife, 19, 74, 75, 193, 199
age/sex determinations, 29, 48. *See also* sex identification
agriculture/agricultural, 27, 38, 39, 46, 48, 49, 52, 77, 78, 79, 89, 91, 138, 142, 148, 159, 168, 195. *See also* horticulture, plants
agriculture, origins of, 38
agro-pastoralism, 39, 48. *See also* transhumance
Akhenaton's Hymn to the Aton, 189
Akrotiri, 121

alliances, 63, 90
alternative gender categories, persons, 25; burials, 32. *See also* gender categories; genderless figures
Amazon, 128
Amememhet (TT82), 18
American Southwest, 133, 139ff., 165ff.
Amratian/Nagada I periods, 80
Amun, 191
Amymone, 128
anandreia, 129
anatomical traits, 141. *See also* sex identification; sex characteristics
Andernach site, 212
andreia, 124, 129
androcentric, 15, 206, 208
androgynous gods, 191, 197, 199
androgyny, 6, 191, 164, 195, 196, 200, 203
animal(s), 70, 76, 85, 98, 101, 102, 104, 105, 106, 109, 130, 135, 142, 153, 155, 159, 160, 161, 162, 168, 170, 183; domestic, 49, 157, 161; game, 148, 183, 184; wild, 157, 162; animal domestication, 49; fertility, 185, 190, 191, 194; husbandry, 98; sacrifice, 86; sexuality, 184
Antaios, 126
Antiope, 129
Apollo, 124, 188
Arachne, 136
Archaic period in the American Southwest, 168–169, 186; in Egypt, 89, 90, 91
architecture (depiction of), 98, 101, 102, 105
Arikara, 25; diet, 34; gender system, 25; oral traditions, 27